797,885 Books
are available to read at

Forgotten Books

www.ForgottenBooks.com

Forgotten Books' App
Available for mobile, tablet & eReader

ISBN 978-1-331-41756-9
PIBN 10187283

This book is a reproduction of an important historical work. Forgotten Books uses state-of-the-art technology to digitally reconstruct the work, preserving the original format whilst repairing imperfections present in the aged copy. In rare cases, an imperfection in the original, such as a blemish or missing page, may be replicated in our edition. We do, however, repair the vast majority of imperfections successfully; any imperfections that remain are intentionally left to preserve the state of such historical works.

Forgotten Books is a registered trademark of FB &c Ltd.
Copyright © 2017 FB &c Ltd.
FB &c Ltd, Dalton House, 60 Windsor Avenue, London, SW19 2RR.
Company number 08720141. Registered in England and Wales.

For support please visit www.forgottenbooks.com

1 MONTH OF FREE READING

at
www.ForgottenBooks.com

By purchasing this book you are eligible for one month membership to ForgottenBooks.com, giving you unlimited access to our entire collection of over 700,000 titles via our web site and mobile apps.

To claim your free month visit: www.forgottenbooks.com/free187283

* Offer is valid for 45 days from date of purchase. Terms and conditions apply.

English
Français
Deutsche
Italiano
Español
Português

www.forgottenbooks.com

Mythology Photography **Fiction**
Fishing Christianity **Art** Cooking
Essays Buddhism Freemasonry
Medicine **Biology** Music **Ancient Egypt** Evolution Carpentry Physics
Dance Geology **Mathematics** Fitness
Shakespeare **Folklore** Yoga Marketing
Confidence Immortality Biographies
Poetry **Psychology** Witchcraft
Electronics Chemistry History **Law**
Accounting **Philosophy** Anthropology
Alchemy Drama Quantum Mechanics
Atheism Sexual Health **Ancient History**
Entrepreneurship Languages Sport
Paleontology Needlework Islam
Metaphysics Investment Archaeology
Parenting Statistics Criminology
Motivational

SCHOOL OF EDUCATION
LIBRARY

NO. CENTRAL ASSOCIATION

COLLEGES & SECONDARY SCHS.

Proc. 13th An. Meeting
Chicago, 1908

STANFORD UNIVERSITY
LIBRARIES

SCHOOL OF EDUCATION LIBRARY

EDUCATION
BOOK PURCHASE
FUND

STANFORD UNIVERSITY
LIBRARIES

PROCEEDINGS

OF THE

THIRTEENTH ANNUAL MEETING

OF THE

NORTH CENTRAL ASSOCIATION

OF

COLLEGES AND SECONDARY SCHOOLS

HELD AT

CHICAGO, ILLINOIS, MARCH 27 AND 28, 1908

GENERAL INDEX OF PROCEEDINGS FROM ORGANIZATION
OF ASSOCIATION IN 1895

AND

REPORT OF COMMISSION ON ACCREDITED SCHOOLS
AND COLLEGES FOR 1908-9

EDITED BY

THOMAS ARKLE CLARK

SECRETARY OF THE ASSOCIATION

CHICAGO
PUBLISHED BY THE ASSOCIATION
MCMVIII

Copies of the Proceedings of the North Central Association of Colleges and Secondary Schools may be obtained by addressing the Treasurer of the Association, Mr. J. E. Armstrong, Englewood High School, Chicago. The price of single copies is twenty-five cents. The price of the complete set as far as published (fourteen numbers, including the report of the Preliminary Meeting for Organization) is $3.25.

The next meeting of the Association will be held in Chicago, Friday and Saturday, March 26 and 27, 1909.

The North Central Association

of

Colleges and Secondary Schools

Thirteenth Annual Meeting, Chicago, March 27 and 28, 1908

The thirteenth annual meeting of the North Central Association of Colleges and Secondary Schools was held in Chicago, Friday and Saturday, March 27 and 28, 1908.

FIRST SESSION FRIDAY, MARCH 27, 1908.

The Association was called to order at 10 o'clock a. m. in the Banqueting Hall of the Auditorium Hotel by the President, Edmund Janes James of the University of Illinois, Urbana, Illinois. President James delivered the annual address as follows:

CLASSIFICATION OF OUR HIGHER INSTITUTIONS OF LEARNING.

DR. EDMUND JANES JAMES, PRESIDENT OF THE UNIVERSITY OF ILLINOIS, URBANA, ILLINOIS.

In the last few years there has been much discussion as to the possibility of classifying our American schools, colleges and universities in accordance with some definite plan, which should enable us to improve our instruction, and if not raise the quantity, at least improve the quality of our requirements, for graduation from the high school, for admission to college, and for graduation from college and the university. The greatly mixed conditions of our American system of education, if we can speak of such a thing as system in this connection, makes it perhaps desirable to attempt some such classification. It certainly makes it difficult.

The fact that it is difficult, however, is evidently not deterring various people and various agencies from attempting such a classification, and in fact the necessity of such a classification for certain purposes is becoming every day more marked.

State boards of health, for example, are in an ever larger number of states receiving authority to determine the conditions upon which a license to practice medicine shall be granted. One of the common conditions is that the candidate shall have graduated from a reputable medical school. As soon as such a public regulation is adopted it becomes necessary to determine what a reputable medical school is. Hence arise not merely the questions as to the length of course, quality of instruction, character of equipment, etc., but also as to the requisites for admission to said medical school. More and more of our boards of health are requiring that the candidates for admission to the medical school shall have completed the curriculum of a standardized public high school. Hence arises the question immediately, what is a standardized public high school? And the medical boards in the northern states are more commonly requiring graduation from the high school with a four-year curriculum, following the ordinary eight grades of the elementary school. It will thus be seen that in this process of determining the qualifications of the candidates who desire to practice medicine, nearly all the important questions of standardization are raised.

The same thing is true in the case of admission to the bar. An increasing number of states is requiring as a condition of admitting a candidate to the state bar examination, the completion of a public high school with a four-year curriculum; and as a further preliminary condition, attendance at a reputable law school for a period of at least three years. The requirements for admission to practice dentistry, pharmacy, public accountancy, the architect's profession, etc., etc., all involve these fundamental questions of standardization.

The universities on their own account, independent of public examining boards, have also found it necessary, in determining requisites for admission, to define what a high school is. In determining the requisites for admission to their professional and graduate schools they must determine what a college is. As a consequence there has been a strong attempt made of late years to secure some kind of commonly accepted public standard for the work of these various schools.

Our own Association has done important work in the direction of standardizing the high schools, and in co-operation with similar associations in the East and South we are gradually arriving at some rough consensus of opinion.

The Carnegie Foundation for the Advancement of Teaching, having as one of its functions the granting of pensions to men who have served as professors in institutions of a certain grade, has found it necessary to define these institutions in order to classify those which applied for the privilege of being placed on the list of favored institutions. The Rockefeller Board as it expands and enlarges its work will undoubtedly find it necessary to classify in a similar way. The Association of American Universities, which was reputed to have based its condition of admission upon the existence of a strong graduate school in the universities which were to be included in its membership, found it necessary, in passing upon proposed members, to define graduate schools and determine, in a rough way at any rate, the limits between graduate schools and undergraduate schools. The National Association of State Universities has appointed a committee upon the subject of standardization. It looks in fact as if we were inevitably, whether we would or no, advancing rapidly to a time when our American educational institutions will be standardized, i. e., when we shall come to a more or less rough agreement as to definitions, then, as to the actual classification of existing institutions on the basis of those definitions.

We are still a long way from the time when our federal government would or could undertake such definition, though it is probably not impossible that the United States Commissioner of Education may be interested in this common work toward which we are all turning our attention and that he may be of material assistance in working out any practical scheme.

It will be still a long time before all our states will undertake in any direct, immediate and comprehensive way, this work of classification and standardization, though the state of New York has set the example in its state department of education, which other states, I am convinced, will at least tend to follow, though probably at a long interval and at a slow pace. Other states have already begun the work of standardizing institutions within their confines. Those states, which distribute aid to public high schools, must, of course, define in some way or other what a high school is, for purposes of receiving this aid. Other states than New York have begun to define the kind of high school whose certificates of graduation may be accepted as satisfactory evidence of the possession of the preliminary education necessary for the study of the professions; notably the legislature of Illinois at its last session determined that only graduates of public high schools with a four-year curriculum or persons having a similar equivalent training could be admitted to the study of medicine in medical schools which desired the recognition of the state board of health.

All this work of standardization has its disadvantages as well as its advantages. When we once accept definitions we bind ourselves in important respects. Our institutions begin to crystallize and harden. Progress becomes difficult; changes are hard to make, and to some extent, one may say, signs of old age begin to appear in the hardening of the arteries, if in nothing else. A definition once set up will undoubtedly exclude many institutions which for all practical purposes are doing just as good work as accepted institutions. The work of individual teachers is excluded or placed at a disadvantage on formal grounds. We begin to put a stamp upon certain subjects of study, upon certain methods of study, upon a certain order of studies, which as they meet the approval of the standardized authorities may be supposed to be better than those similar features which do not receive similar recognition.

Once the standardization is carried through, it becomes extremely difficult to make changes to adapt the system to necessary improvements. The result oftentimes is that changes are made slowly,—so slowly that revolution is the result with sudden, violent and far-reaching changes. I do not know any better example of this than the remarkable changes made in the requirements for admission to the German universities in the year 1900. The struggle between the old classical gymnasia and the modern real schools, which were different from the gymnasium only in the omission of Greek and the substitution of other languages, had been carried on for a generation with varying fortunes, its advantages being sometimes with one side and sometimes with the other. No later than 1892 the contest seemed to be settled in the direction of a final and complete victory in certain directions of the old classical school. Within eight years we find the government of Prussia proceeding to the extent of recognizing not simply the non-Greek college but the non-Greek and Latin college as on a full parity with the old classical college in the matter of admission to the university, so that now Germany is in this respect more radical than England in its older universities, or France or even the United States, in the case, at any rate, of many of the leading private institutions.

It is not by any means sure that our present system of dividing up the time from the seventh year of the student's life to the twenty-second or twenty-third, is at all the ideal scheme. Many people believe, though I do not share their views, that our American college of the old-fashioned type is destined to disappear, ground to powder beneath the ever-encroaching claims of secondary education as expressed in the high school and the still more voracious claims of the university as standing for professional training in all the different lines in which a society may require such advanced work. Let us once standardize this system as it exists and we have made it with every step of standardization increasingly difficult to adapt it to our needs or to shape it according to our ever-changing conditions.

But after all, I take it, that this classification and standardization is at hand. That we shall accept its disadvantages along with its advantages and the problem before us, probably, is to increase as far as possible the advantages, diminishing, as we may be able, the disadvantages of such a scheme.

One element in this process of standardization ought not to be overlooked, and that is the effect of foreign institutions and foreign systems on our own policy. It has been a custom for nearly a hundred years for the more progressive and enlightened of our American students to seek to complete their home education by study at foreign centers, in England, France and in Germany, and of late in Rome and Athens. Where students desire to receive some recognition from foreign institutions for work done under their auspices, one of the first questions to be raised would naturally be as to whether said students had pursued preliminary courses of study which would justify foreign institutions in conferring upon them their academic degrees. The unwillingness of English universities to depart in any degree whatever from their own stereotyped rules and principles of granting degrees, combined with the lack of opportunity for advanced study in all but a very few lines has always kept the number of American students in England down to very small limits. Something of the same condition of things has prevailed in France. In Germany the liberality of the universities combined with the unquestioned leadership of German science has attracted large numbers of American students who in the last seventy-five years, particularly in the last quarter of the last century, resorted in an ever-swelling tide to German centers. The principle adopted by the German universities has been in general to insist on the same standard for the foreign students as for their own. But as this standard itself was a very liberal one, requiring few formalities, nothing in fact except the completion of a preliminary course of study corresponding to their classical gymnasia and of late to their Latin real schools, three years of residence in a German university or residence in a university, which for this purpose would be assimilated to the German university, and the final examination and presentation for the degree,—all these things could be easily met. But as there was no standard adopted in this country by which German institutions could decide whether a given American institution calling itself a university was really a university or merely a high school or even less than that, there were objections both on the part of the German institutions and American institutions to the liberality with which German universities administered this system. Finally the Association of American Universities sent a formal protest to German universities against their accepting the work of American students which had been done in any other than institutions of first rank. The reply to this was the action taken by the faculty of the University of Berlin, and which has since been imitated by other institutions, limiting the acceptance of credentials from American universities to those particular institutions which were enrolled as members of the Association of American Universities.

That this action is as much too narrow, as the former action of some German universities was perhaps too liberal, no one who knows the circumstances will at all deny. Under this ruling, work which no one with any knowledge of the facts would think of classing below true university work, is quietly ignored because, forsooth, it was not done in one of these particular institutions. Action similar to this was taken by the Dutch government, and somewhat similar action taken by one or two American states in regard to teacher's diplomas.

What practical questions are involved here in this discussion which some people might consider purely theoretical may be seen from the following circumstances, which I presume have been duplicated again and again. A man who had taken his master of arts degree at the University of Illinois in chemistry, presented this degree at the university of Halle as in part fulfilling the requirements of the three years' term of residence at a university for the German Ph.D. The answer of the authorities there was that his master of arts would admit him to the university, but inasmuch as the University of Illinois was not a member of the Association of American Universities, residence at the University of Illinois could not be accepted as residence at a German university, or its equivalent.

Upon further showing as to the quality of this work the university senate asked the minister of education to make a dispensation in favor of this man, and his master of arts was accepted as the equivalent of one year's residence, which was all he had asked for in the premises.

Now the fact of it is that work for the master of arts in chemistry is offered in many American institutions not members of the Association of American Universities, which is quite the equal of chemistry work offered in any German university for the first year or two of university work, and to refuse to recognize this work on the ground that the particular institution is not a member of the Association of American Universities is certainly unsatisfactory, to use no stronger word. Such a rule cannot be justified on any ground except the simple one that the foreign institution or foreign country cannot be expected to go into the question of determining the relative standards of different institutions when the country from which the students come will not take that trouble itself. It is no reflection, therefore, to my mind, upon the German universities that they have grasped at this simple and easy, though very unfair, means of determining a difficult question. We should determine this question not only for them but for ourselves.

There is still another aspect of this whole question which ought not to be lost sight of in such a discussion as this. Many foreign students are resorting to this country for the purpose of special or advanced study, and they desire that the certificates issued by our institutions shall be such as will be accepted in their own country to enable them to practice the professions which they expect to pursue. This is notably true of the profession of dentistry. There is no question that the best American dental schools are far superior, taken all in all, as places of training in theory and practice, to the schools of any other country as a group. There is no doubt that in some of these schools a standard of liberal and technical training is set up which is quite the equal of that required by any other country.

It is difficult, however, to make it apparent to the authorities of any other country exactly what value the certificates of these different institutions may have. As a result, some countries, like Germany, have absolutely forbidden the holders of certain American degrees to state that fact or advertise it in any way and have fined persons who have paraded the degrees they held from such American institutions.

This is a perfectly natural and proper proceeding, and until we in the United States are willing to offer some kind of guarantee which foreign countries may take in regard to these matters, we ought not to be surprised if they discriminate against studying in the United States, no matter how great and valuable may be the opportunities here offered.

This whole question of standardizing has thus the most intimate relation to many important questions connected with public administration in this and other countries, as well as with what may be called educational problems alone.

I propose in this paper to outline what seems to me to be the proper organization or standardization of our American education under existing conditions, and then to examine how far this—I will not call it ideal, but appropriate scheme of standardization and classification may be applied to our schools and colleges and universities as they actually exist, and how far all reputable institutions of any sort may be fitted into such a scheme of classification.

It seems to me that any scheme of standardization for the present, at any rate, and probably for many years to come, ought to have a large element of elasticity. In fact, the necessity of elasticity in any scheme of classification can scarcely be questioned. The only point of difference of opinion, I presume, would be as to the desirable degree of elasticity.

Such a scheme ought, in the first place, it seems to me, to take account of and provide due recognition for, all the work of a given quality, no matter where it may be done, by whom it may be done or under what conditions. In other words, such a plan ought not to proceed to snuff out work of a university or college or high school quality, or grade, simply because it is not done in an institution which itself, on the whole, may deserve the name of university, college or high school.

In the next place, such a scheme of standardization should rest on the one hand upon a psychological basis and on the other upon a social and historic basis, i. e., upon the needs of our present community and of our community as it is likely to be in the near future. Such a scheme, moreover, should be evidently in the line of present development, clearly in harmony with the forces at work in the present evolution of our society, acting at all points to assist the elements that are at work for its uplift, discouraging, as far as may be, the elements which would tend to clog, hamper, embarrass or prevent the development of our society.

Furthermore, in the process of standardization, if we find that, after all, in the essence and in the large, our development is along the lines of development in other nations under the domination of European civilization; that on the whole our wants and needs are essentially the same as those of England, France and Germany, then we should not, merely for the sake of having a different scheme, depart too widely, except for very good reasons, from the course of development which is evidently common to us all.

With these preliminary considerations, then, let us undertake briefly an attempt at classification and standardization of our American college and university system, utilizing as far as possible all the work which has been done up to the present, taking from any and every source any and every valuable suggestion to help us formulate in a clear and definite way the lines of educational classification.

For historic reasons, I think it will be easier to begin with the idea of the university, meaning by that the institution which in a group of professional schools prepares the youth of a country for undertaking the practice of the so-called learned professions, under which we should to-day certainly include theology, medicine, law, teaching in colleges and universities, engineering, and perhaps others as well.

I should classify institutions by whether they are doing a certain kind and quality of work, and to lay the basis for this classification we should find some definition for this work. I should define university work as follows: University work is that kind of work which is directed toward the requisite mastery of a body of knowledge which is necessary or desirable to the adequate practice of a learned profession, carried on by men of suitable age for such work, who have had a proper preliminary training to qualify them to do this work, under the leadership and supervision of men qualified by scholarship and training to give the necessary instruction, and in centers where the equipment in apparatus and libraries is sufficient to make such work profitable.

You will see that the essential elements of university

work as I conceive it, are first the character or quality of the work itself, being directed to the mastery of a sufficiently comprehensive body of knowledge to serve as the basis of a calling or profession. That this work shall be undertaken only by people of suitable age and suitable preliminary training; that it shall be done under the direction of scholars and leaders in their respective fields, assisted by all the apparatus and library material which can be made useful in the imparting of such instruction.

Now if we accept this definition I think we shall be rather surprised to find on looking into the different civilized countries of modern Europe and the United States how generally this definition has already been accepted or is gradually being accepted for university work. And we shall be, moreover, rather surprised to find what general agreement there is, after all is said and done and with all variety in detail as to what is desirable under each of these heads, namely, suitable age of the student entering upon this study, suitable preliminary training, character of instruction and material equipment.

We shall find, for example, that in Germany, the average age of the men who are admitted to such study as this, is about nineteen to twenty. The same thing is true of France, of Italy, of Austria, of Russia and of England, and generally speaking of the United States. The tendency is clearly to require as a condition of entering upon all such study in all these countries, that degree of preliminary education and training which the youth may properly acquire by the time he is twenty years of age; whether we call the school gymnasium or lycee, or public school or athenaeum or high school. The tendency in all these countries alike is very patently voicing itself in the conviction as expressed in the concrete institutions or in the theoretical formulation that the beginning of professional study of this sort should not be delayed beyond the twentieth year. And furthermore, that we may secure by a proper development of our institutions of secondary education all the general or liberal training which is necessary to take up the study of these professions by the time a man has attained that age, and that in the interest of the professions themselves and of the adequate development of the subjects themselves the beginning of such study should not be postponed, speaking in the large, to a later date.

We shall find that the time required for the university part of professional training varies somewhat in different countries, and yet even in this there is, everything considered, an astonishing agreement. For example, the period of three years is the period required for the university part of study in preparation for admission to the bar in Germany and in France, in England and in the United States. The period of four years and five years is quite as generally accepted for the medical profession; three years for the clergy, in those countries in which there is an established church, and three years for those who are preparing for the teaching profession. Underlying the vast variety and multiplicity of details controlling admission to the learned professions in these different countries is this remarkable agreement as to the real essence of things.

If we accept this definition, then, for university work, and this outline of the period of university study, namely, that it shall begin by the twentieth year and extend over three, four or five years, according to the department, we shall see that the first part corresponds in this country, roughly speaking, to the close of the sophomore year in our standard American college. That the university work, therefore, would begin with the junior year and run through the two years of the college, and according to circumstances to the three years of the graduate school. Now some of our institutions have undertaken to set the close of the senior year as the period of beginning university work, and have set out to insist upon graduation from the standard American college as the condition of admission to so-called university or graduate work looking toward the profession of college or university teacher, or university work looking toward the career of law or medicine or theology or engineering. Notably is this true of Harvard, of Columbia and to some extent, though in a little different form, of Johns Hopkins.

I cannot help thinking, myself, that while some temporary service may be done to American education by this step on the part of Harvard and Columbia, on the whole, it represents rather a damage than a service; that historically and pedagogically speaking it is unsound; that even if it would be accepted by our American society as the proper standard, we should thereby be doing our society a positive injury. A man may be injured just as much by keeping him too long at his books as by letting him out too early, and a scheme under which a man shall spend after his eighteenth year four years in college, then five years in the medical school and four years, or three years even, in law, and four years in engineering, represents an amount of time which the average man ought not to spend upon specifically school work as a preparation for the practice of a profession. On the contrary, I think the time indicated by the history of the other nations is in this respect far truer and far more in accordance with our own needs and wants than that which would be indicated by the policy of Harvard or Columbia.

Now that there is a certain reaching out toward this period of two years as marking the maximum time which our American community ought to require that the young man should spend in his preliminary work, is evident by the very striking phenomenon in connection with the advancement of our standards in our American professions. The Council of the American Medical Society after long threshing out of this whole question has come around to the view that two years of the college in addition to the four years in the typical high school, all underlaid by the eight years of the elementary school, represents not only all that can be required under our American conditions, but all that ought to be required, judged by historic and psychological standards.

The young man who has been in school from the age of six years until twenty, if our system is properly organized, ought to be amply ready to take up professional work and carry it on in a professional spirit with a professional end in view. If our schools cannot prepare a man properly by that time for this sort of work, then we ought to alter our schools, change our curriculum, modify our methods of instruction so that he can be properly trained by that time, and not attempt to improve deficient elementary training by simply adding another two years of diletanté, generally scattered, oftentimes purposeless, work of the last two years in college.

I am speaking here of what our requirement ought to be for the study of the learned professions, not of the time which the exceptional man here and there might profitably spend in further study and preparation. That, it seems to me, is an entirely different proposition.

Now it will be noted that in the discussion thus far of university work, I have not spoken of or incorporated in the idea of university work the notion of advanced work at all. In fact the beginning of university work will in very many cases be elementary work at the same time, and cannot but be that, and ought to be that. Thus a student who comes up to the study of the law, say after the close of the sophomore year in college, begins the study of the law. Now the work that he is doing, if done from the point of view indicated, with the purpose in mind and under the conditions described, is university work pure and simple, though it is also elementary work. In other words, university work is not in any sense to be considered as opposed to or set over against elementary or advanced work. The same thing is true of the work in medicine, in physiology, in anatomy, in chemistry. The same is true of theology. The same is certainly true of Hebrew, Assyriology, Egyptology, etc., etc. In other words, those subjects which are proper topics of university study but which either are not proper subjects of elementary or secondary study, must certainly be begun in the university, that is, in their particular cases university work must be of an elementary character. But it will be elementary work done by persons of suitable age and suitable training and under suitable instructors and in suitable conditions as to equipment, etc., to make it truly university work in the sense which we have described. Now owing to the fact that certain subjects have for many generations formed the backbone of the elementary instruction, Latin, Greek, mathematics, and that other subjects have been added to this same curriculum, such as natural science, modern languages, history, etc., it has come about that students who enter upon the study of these subjects in the university may very properly be supposed to have made themselves acquainted with the elements of these subjects before entering the university, and consequently university work in these subjects may begin at an advanced stage of acquirement which could not be insisted upon in the case of the legal, medical or theological studies which I have named.

As a result of this fact and this development we have come to expect in the case of university study in certain of these subjects a more advanced stage of preparation than we should call for in other lines. Thus if the student who has had the preliminary work of a classical college desires to take up the university study of Spanish, which is not a subject included in the curriculum of the school whose course he has completed, he may perhaps fairly enough be called upon to show an acquaintance with the elements of the subject, such as could be acquired in that secondary school which does offer this particular subject.

Now as to the question whether this preliminary work which we divide up at present among the elementary school, the high school and the first two years of the college, should continue to be so divided or whether it should all be put into one school with an introductory period like the German gymnasium and the German real school, or whether it should be divided up among three years in college and three years in the high school and eight years in the elementary school; or three years in the college and four years in the high school and seven years in the elementary school; or two years in college, or one year in college and five years in the high school and eight years in the elementary school or any other particular sub-division of this work— I say this is a matter of detail, an important matter in itself but one which does not vitally concern the university or its work. All that the university need be concerned about is that this suitable preliminary training be secured by, say, the twentieth year.

You will note that I have defined university work by its quality, and its characteristics. Any institution which is doing this work is doing university work. I don't care whether you call it a university, a college, or a high school. I should reserve the name university, however, in such a classification as is here proposed for any institution which is doing university work in a sufficiently large number of subjects, over a sufficiently large field, to be an institution of marked importance for the life of the community whose interests it is serving. I am aware that this is rather an indefinite formulation and yet I think for all practical purposes it is definite enough. For example, we should agree, if you accept my definition, that an institution which is preparing persons for the practice of the traditional learned professions and for teaching in colleges and universities in chemistry, physiology, geology, botany, zoology, history, Latin, Greek, English and other modern languages, economics, sociology, engineering, agriculture—I say an institution which was offering to young men an opportunity to do university work in such a large group of these subjects would certainly be called a university.

I am also aware that if we should insist upon applying the name university only to institutions which were doing such work as I have described we should find that we have very few universities in the United States to-day, though we have many institutions which almost reach this standard and could easily reach it in the course of a few years if we could all agree that this is desirable. And so I should class, for purposes of comparison, the universities as universities of the first class namely; universities which in all their departments were doing university work of the character thus described. Universities of the second class, institutions which are doing university work in most of the departments of instruction which they maintain. Universities of the third class, institutions which are doing less than half of the work which they support of this particular grade. And universities of the fourth class, institutions which are carrying on professional work, without reference to such requirements as are here indicated.

Keeping in mind this definition of university work, we have then to classify a large number of institutions from this point of view, which under our general definition could not be classed as universities at all, and are as a matter of fact ordinarily called colleges. I should take, for instance, all the first class American colleges of the traditional type and standard, such as Amherst, Williams, Beloit, Knox, Oberlin, etc., etc. If these institutions chose to do in the last two years of their curriculum university work as tried and tested by our definition, and many of them could do it if they cared to, I should give to them the title of university colleges, and recognize all the work which they did which could be classed as of university grade, to be of that quality, and give to their students a standing in the universities in the professional schools corresponding to the showing which they would be able to make from this point of view. So far as they were not willing or were unable to adapt their work to this new standard and this new quality, I should continue to label them as colleges. The general literary training which they give to their own students would undoubtedly advance the latter from the standpoint of general culture, but it might not be included as a part of university work.

This plan would necessitate the organization of the university courses at the beginning of the junior year, and if the institutions were large enough and equipped sufficiently, these university courses might run side by side with the present college courses through these two years. By university courses in this sense I mean simply courses that from the very beginning are calculated to introduce the student into the mastery of the subject which he is taking up. They would call for more time, generally speaking, than the ordinary college courses. They would call for a different method oftentimes, and in any case would call for more concentrated energy on the part of the student.

Now those of you who are familiar with our educational

history will recognize that this is a development of the plan which years ago was adopted at the University of Michigan. It has always seemed to me that it was a very wise and statesmanlike scheme. I thought at the time it was born somewhat prematurely, and I have always been sorry to find my prognostication verified. But it was no farther ahead of the times than Dr. Wayland's elective system at Brown university was ahead of the times when it could be tried to the fullest extent at Harvard; and I believe the time has come when if our institutions would be bold, and seize the strategic moment and organize around this idea, we should advance within a comparatively brief time to a position where the entire world would recognize twenty-five or thirty and perhaps forty or fifty of our American institutions as universities in the full and proper sense of that term, and where we should be doing the largest possible service to the country, and where we should have set up the highest possible standards which we can attain to in our day and generation.

To sum up briefly the form which our educational system would take under this scheme.

I. The completion of the sophomore year in college or an equivalent course would be required by all our institutions wishing to be ranked as universities as a condition of admission to the Law School, Medical School, Engineering School, Dental School, and the University Schools in Languages, Mathematics, Chemistry, Physics, Zoology, Botany, History, Economics, Commerce, Business, etc., etc.

II. University work in all these subjects could be organized at the beginning of the junior year. By university work would be meant, courses planned and taught for those who desired to make them the basis of a truly special or professional career.

III. The professional course would extend for three,

four or five years from the beginning of the junior year, three years for law, for teaching in high schools, or for practical courses, like chemistry, three or four years for engineering, four or five years for medicine, etc., etc.

IV. The existing degrees could be retained for the present: Doctor for Medicine, Bachelor for Law; Bachelor for Engineering; Master for Teaching, etc., etc., with the possibility that the Doctor's degree would be ultimately given for all the university courses.

V. General Courses in Arts and Science could be given, for the present, during the Junior and Senior years by the taking of which students could, as at present, take the bachelor's degree in the Arts and Science at the end of the fourth year after entering college or these degrees could be given for the completion of a sufficient number of the university courses to represent two years' work.

VI. Our present independent colleges could continue their present work, their students largely increased during the first two years, at any rate by the fact that no student would be admitted to university work who had not completed such a course; and in all probability during the last two years also because of the fact that an increasing number of students would be inclined to finish the course before leaving the college.

VII. An increasing number of independent colleges could be enabled by the increase of their income to offer university courses in the last two years of the college, thus acquiring the rank of university colleges and serving the needs of their constituency for a year or two at any rate.

Among the alvantages of such a plan would be the following:

1. It presents a perfectly feasible and practical plan of passing gradually over, out of our present chaos, assign-

ing in the meantime to every institution a definite function in this great system of education.

2. It is a plan which involves the minimum of change in our present scheme of organization. It calls for no violent transitions. It leaves things largely as they are, but directs at every point the dynamic forces in operation to a higher level. It upsets no system of degrees but in its organization will doubtless work toward a desirable uniformity.

3. It sets as the desirable degree of preliminary education what is perfectly attainable with our present system of educational institutions. It places admission to the law school, medical school and other university schools upon a psychological and historic basis. It admits the student to the study of the law when by previous training and lapse of years he has attained to the point when he can pursue such study with profit; and it agrees in essence with the requirements fixed for similar work in the great civilized nations.

4. Such a plan if accepted by the educational authorities as a wise one, will command in a short time the assent of the professions and then of the people. It is in this sense also feasible, i. e., a plan which within a reasonable time—say a generation—can be fully carried through.

5. It represents a distinct advance over present standards—as great an advance as our day and generation will accept—and I believe as great an advance as any day and generation will or ought to accept for purely university work, as universities are now organized.

6. It will in a short time raise the standard of preliminary and professional work so that we shall have no lawyers or physicians or teachers who shall not be liberally educated as well as professionally trained men.

7. It would not be long until our Boards of Education

would insist that every high school teacher should have the special professional training for his vocation involved in a university study of the subjects he wished to teach, and our whole system of secondary education would be raised to a new level.

8. It represents a plan of progress in which the great majority of our higher institutions can join without feeling that their interests are being sacrificed to build up the prosperity of a score of great and overgrown complexes of professional schools.

Before closing I will reply to one or two questions which may be asked in regard to the relation of such a plan as this to existing forms or organization.

What will become of the Graduate School under such a scheme?

It may remain what it is in fact, though I should expect to see some change in form.

The American Graduate School is a peculiar institution, of very recent growth. It represents the German Faculty of Philosophy at certain points; and the Honor Schools of Oxford and Cambridge in others.

The formal requirements for the Doctor's degree in our American Graduate Schools are considerably higher than those in the German University, or for the newly created doctorate in France and England.

In fact, the requirements are such that few people think of complying with them unless they are looking forward to teaching in colleges and universities.

Considering the importance of a high standard of training for such advanced positions, our requirements are perhaps not too high; and if we leave the doctor's degree where it is, viz: five years from the beginning of the junior year, or the beginning of university study, as we have defined it, the present plan would call for no change either in form or organization.

On the other hand, it might be desirable to make the Master of Arts a more purely university degree than it is at present. It could be easily adjusted, however, by letting it remain as now, three years in time from the beginning of the junior year, but require university work as defined above, instead of college work for the three years preceding its acquisition. It might then become the usual degree for men expecting to teach in high schools, and thus represent the present German Doctorate, while our present doctorate would indicate what the German doctor is supposed to have attained to by the time he locates himself as Privat-docent in a German university.

Such a scheme of standardizing would enable us to classify every institution we now have which is doing work worthy of recognition.

Accepting the system already worked out in general for classification of high schools and extending it to cover the first two years in college, we might work out in a similar way a classification of colleges and institutions claiming to be universities, by which every student who had actually done the university work could receive credit for it; no matter where he had done it. Such a system, besides securing substantially equal recognition for substantially equivalent work, and thus serving the ends of justice, would be an ever-present force in raising and maintaining proper standards; and would render easy that mutual recognition of academic degrees among modern civilized nations which would be a no mean agency in promoting mutual respect in the world of education and science.

As to the machinery by which such a system should be put in force, there may well be wide difference of opinion. My own opinion would be that the National Association of

State Universities might well undertake the task; for if its members could come to some common agreement, considering the wide divergence in character of institutions represented in that organization, we might well hope for some plan to be submitted which would bear important fruit within the lifetime even of some of us older members, provided we live out our three-score years and twenty or thirty!

The report of the Treasurer, Principal J. E. Armstrong, Englewood High School, Chicago, was presented as follows:

REPORT OF THE TREASURER OF THE ASSOCIATION FOR THE YEAR ENDING MARCH 27, 1908.

RECEIPTS.

Cash on hand at date of last report	$246.56
Sale of reports and blanks	10.25
From one hundred and ten $3 memberships	330.00
From twenty $10 memberships	200.00
From twenty-two $5 memberships	110.00
Total	$896.81

DISBURSEMENTS.

Printing	$376.85	
Expenses of Committees	172.15	
Postage	19.17	
Clerk and Stenographer	27.50	
Express and notary fees	1.94	
Total	$597.61	
Cash on hand	299.20	$896.81

The report of the Medical Committee was presented by the chairman of the committee, Dean E. A. Birge, of the University of Wisconsin, as follows:

REPORT OF MEDICAL COMMITTEE.

1. Medical schools now require for admission at least a diploma from a four-year high school and for graduation attendance on a medical school for four years of at least seven months each. State boards of medical examiners make the same minimum requirements.

2. Since more than 60% of the medical schools still admit students on the completion of the high school course, their first year's work is necessarily adjusted to the needs and capacities of such students and includes subjects more fully and better taught in colleges.

In New York medical schools in 1907, the first year's work included 221 hours of general physics and chemistry (24% of the year's work), 214 hours (23%) of histology and embryology, 173 hours (nearly 20%) of physiology; the remainder being given to anatomy (practically all human anatomy) and materia medica. About 25% of the work of the second year was given to physiological chemistry and toxicology and to bacteriology. All of these subjects are or may be taught in colleges.

3. For a good many years medical schools gave credit for work done in literary colleges and universities (hereafter referred to in this report as "colleges") which was parallel to their required studies. This credit was given either to certain subjects or a time credit was granted for the completion of a number of courses; the time credit not exceeding one year.

Certain schools also gave a flat credit of one year to college graduates, on the theory—which your committee believe was fully justified by results—that the college graduate who had had the basal sciences in his course could accomplish in three years the work done by a high school graduate in four.

4. In 1898 a statute was passed in Minnesota, requir-

ing that every applicant for a license to practice medicine in that state should have had four annual sessions of study in a medical school. This rule was at first applied by the State Board of Medical Examiners to individuals only; but in 1904 the board voted to refuse license to all graduates of a medical school which granted a time credit on any terms to a graduate or student of a college.

The boards of Iowa, Kentucky, Michigan, Wisconsin, and perhaps other states, have made similar rulings. Thus no medical school in the region covered by our Association can give a time credit to any college graduate without having all of its graduates debarred from practice in several states where they might naturally go. Under such conditions credit is not given and the college graduate is placed on the same time basis as the high school graduate.

5. It is thus impossible for a student to pursue a combined college and medical course in less than eight years, except in the few institutions which have arranged such a course for the benefit of their own students. Since an eight year course is more than many students can afford, the result of this ruling is rather to decrease than to increase the number of college graduates in medical schools.

6. In the judgment of your committee this ruling of the Minnesota board, from which have come the difficulties between colleges and medical schools, was not necessary or wise. There are several considerations, however, which make it doubtful whether it is advisable for this Association to press for a reconsideration of the ruling, and especially doubtful whether we should attempt to secure again the flat credit of one year for college graduates.

There are about 160 medical schools in the United States. Of these, two require a bachelor's degree for admission; at least 50 others require either one or two years of college work or will do so by 1910, and by that date the number of such schools will probably be as great as 60. About half of these will require two years. This Association has very little interest in the question of time credit in these schools; since few colleges, except those which are specifically organized for that purpose, will give enough medical work to gain a year's credit in them. The general courses in physics, chemistry, and biology are required for entrance to such schools.

While a time credit might fairly be claimed from schools which still admit on the basis of high school graduation, your committee do not believe that such a credit is of importance; since these schools are the weaker and cheaper proprietary schools, and are of a type to be avoided by college graduates.

Thirty-four medical schools in the region covered by this Association are in the list of those demanding one or two years of college work for entrance. The number includes most if not all of the stronger schools—those to which we should send our graduates. The number is sufficiently great to afford ample opportunity for choice.

7. Your committee believe that the influence of this Association should be exerted to secure from all medical schools a requirement of two years of college study for admission; such a course to include at least one foreign language, English, and the basal sciences.

They believe that the interests of both colleges and medical schools will be served by such a requirement; and they believe that some influence such as that of this Association, will be needed to secure and enforce it. The American Medical Association has recommended a one-year course preparatory to medicine. This course includes physics, chemistry, biology and a foreign language. In our judgment these studies represent a minimum admission requirement. We believe also that it is impossible to give adequate courses in these subjects in one year. There are very few high school graduates who can successfully carry two sciences in freshman year and three sciences ought not to be taken simultaneously by a freshman on any terms. It follows that medical schools cannot stand long on the requirement of one year of college work for admission. They will be forced to advance to two years, or to include part of the basal sciences in their own course, in which case they are likely to fall back to the high school basis for admission.

Or the difficulty might be met by the weaker medical schools in a manner which would rather evade than enforce the requirement of one year's college work. They might add a year of so-called college work to their own courses, extending them to five years. These schools have no proper equipment, endowment or provision for adequate salaries for instruction in science; and a year of real college study cannot be given by them. This preliminary work should be required in a regular college or it will be of little value.

8. There remains a question as to the relations to medical schools of those colleges which are willing to organize and maintain departments which fully represent one or two years of medical work, either on the basis of the higher or the lower requirements for admission. At present a college can gain such credit only by organizing a medical school, giving one or two years of the four-year course.

The medical course naturally separates into two parts of two years each; the first including the basal medical sciences, the second the clinical studies. Your committee believe that the sciences are better taught in college than in medical school. Medical authorities are therefore in error in not recognizing this principle and they ought to encourage rather than prevent the teaching of anatomy, bacteriology, histology, physiology, and similar subjects in colleges. Medical schools and state boards should devise with the colleges such methods of inspection and co-operation as will facilitate giving credit for these subjects. The colleges should recognize that if credit is to be given for anatomy and similar subjects, they must be taught in a way which will serve the needs of the future practitioners as well as the ends of science; and that to secure this result there must be co-operation between the medical schools and the colleges.

9. The State Board of Medical Examiners for New York is an earnest advocate for co-operation between medical schools and colleges and for credit for properly conducted college work. They have found great difficulty in preparing a working plan and so far as your committee can learn have not yet submitted a final report on the subject. It is probable that their scheme, when perfected, will afford a fair basis for co-operation within our territory.

The discussion was continued by Professor George E. McLean, State University of Iowa; Professor John F. Downey, of Minnesota; President Charles E. Shelton, of Simpson College, Indianola, Iowa, and Dean E. A. Birge, University of Wisconsin.

PRESIDENT MACLEAN:

For the information of Dean Birge I may state, that two years ago Dr. Zapffe gave a paper before this Association on the subject of the justification of State Boards of Medical Examiners in excluding from examination students of medical colleges that allowed advance credit for work done in a college of liberal arts. A committee was appointed to investigate the matter and to report at the next meeting of the Association. The committee consisted of President King of Oberlin, Dr. Zapffe, and Dean Birge, but the committee did not report last year.

The rationality of the State Board of Medical Examiners in Minnesota has been questioned. As a representative of a college and university that opposed their ruling as long as it could be done, I will not be considered as partial in saying that the board had, as I discovered later, some reason on their side. There is no ground for the suspicion that has prevailed in some quarters that there was collusion between the University of Minnesota and the board. I have no less authority for this than that of President Northrop. The board thought they had at least two strong reasons for their procedure. They believed in this manner they could best exterminate fake and commercial colleges which readily receive diploma mill degrees, and those of little worth, and give shortened medical courses on the basis of these degrees. It was, then, a genuine attempt to raise the standards of medical instruction. They also felt that the smaller colleges were not equipped with men and laboratories to teach the biological sciences as they need to be taught, or their application to medicine, and certain subjects necessary to be taught from their nature, like genito-urinary diseases, would not be offered.

This question which has agitated the colleges of letters will disappear in 1910, when the requirement of two years in a liberal arts college for admission to a college of medicine is enforced.

The following report was presented by Professor Fred N. Scott, of the University of Michigan, delegate to the Conference on Uniform Entrance Requirements in English:

REPORT OF CONFERENCE ON UNIFORM ENTRANCE REQUIREMENTS IN ENGLISH.

The Conference met at Teachers' College, Columbia University, New York City, on Friday, February 21, at 2:00 p. m., and organized by the election of Professor Francis H. Stoddard as Chairman, and Mr. Wilson Farrand as Secretary.

Delegates were present from the Conference of New England Colleges on Entrance Requirements in English, the New England Association of Teachers of English, and the College Entrance Examination Board. The delegates from the Conference of New England Colleges and the College Entrance Examination Board were accepted as members of the Conference, and the question of future representation was left for subsequent settlement. The delegates from the New England Association of Teachers of English were invited to participate in the deliberations of the Conference. The full membership of the Conference was as follows:

New England Association of Colleges and Preparatory Schools:

Professor Mary A. Jordan, Smith College, Northampton, Mass.

Principal H. G. Buehler, Hotchkiss School, Lakeville, Conn.

Principal William T. Peck, Classical High School, Providence, R. I.

Association of Colleges and Preparatory Schools of the Middle States and Maryland:

Professor Francis Hovey Stoddard, New York University, New York City.

Principal Wilson Farrand, Newark Academy, Newark, N. J.

Professor Franklin T. Baker, Teachers' College, New York City.

North Central Association of Colleges and Secondary Schools:

Professor Fred N. Scott, University of Michigan, Ann Arbor, Mich.

Professor F. G. Hubbard, University of Wisconsin, Madison, Wis.

Superintendent H. E. Giles, High School, Hinsdale, Ill.

Southern Association of Colleges and Preparatory Schools:

Professor J. B. Henneman, University of the South, Sewanee, Tenn.

Conference of New England Colleges on Entrance Requirements in English:

Dean Byron S. Hurlbut, Harvard University, Cambridge, Mass.

Professor Caleb T. Winchester, Wesleyan University, Middletown, Conn.

Professor Wilbur L. Cross, Yale University, New Haven, Conn.

College Entrance Examination Board:

Professor George R. Carpenter, Columbia University, New York City.

Participating, but not Voting.

New England Association of Teachers of English:

Professor Henry G. Pearson, Massachusetts Institute of Technology, Boston, Mass.

Mr. W. M. Cole, South High School, Worcester, Mass.

After an informal discussion on the general question of the English requirement and of the work of the Conference, it was

RESOLVED, That in the judgment of the Conference

changes to be made in the requirement should be in the direction of increasing the emphasis to be placed on composition.

After the appointment of subcommittees to formulate the work to be done on the next day the Conference adjourned at 10:15 p. m.

At the session on Saturday the following changes in the requirement were made for the year 1912:

1. Tennyson's *Gareth and Lynette, Lancelot and Elaine,* and *The Passing of Arthur* were inserted in the list of Books for Study as an alternative to Milton's poems.

2. *Lycidas* was dropped from the list of Milton's poems.

3. In Group VI of the Reading List, Tennyson's *Princess* was substituted for the *Idylls* transferred to the Study List.

4. In Group V, Carlyle's *Heroes and Hero Worship* was changed to Carlyle's *The Hero as Poet, The Hero as Man of Letters,* and *The Hero as King.*

5. The number of books to be selected in Group V was changed from two to one.

6. In Group III, (Book I) was substituted for (Selections) after *Faerie Queene.*

7. In the preliminary statement of the requirement for Reading and Practice, nine was substituted for ten as the number of books to be offered for examination.

The following motions were lost:

To strike out Bacon's Essays from Group II; to strike out Group III; to substitute three for two in Group VI; and to substitute the wording suggested by the Conference of New England Colleges for the preliminary statement in the requirement for Study and Practice.

On motion it was resolved that when the Conference adjourned it should be to meet one year from that date.

A committee of five, consisting of Professors Cross, Henneman and Baker, and Messrs. Giles and Farrand, was appointed to investigate thoroughly the whole question of the English entrance requirement, to secure information and advice from universities, colleges and schools, and report to the individual members of the Conference as early as possible before the adjourned meeting. The committee was further instructed to consider a plan for the permanent organization of the Conference. After luncheon, tendered by the local delegates, there was an informal discussion of a plan for a modified requirement suggested by Professor Scott, and the Conference adjourned at about 4 o'clock.

The discussion was continued by Professor Fred N. Scott, of the University of Michigan, Ann Arbor, Michigan; Dean E. A. Birge, University of Wisconsin, Madison, Wisconsin; Dean C. M. Woodward, Washington University, St. Louis, Missouri; Principal Coy, Hughes High School, Cincinnati, Ohio; Professor C. A. Waldo, Purdue University, Lafayette, Indiana, and Mr. F. M. Giles, Hinsdale High School, Hinsdale, Illinois.

The report of the delegate to the College Entrance Examination Board was presented by Mr. Edward L. Harris, of Central High School, Cleveland, Ohio:

REPORT OF DELEGATE TO COLLEGE ENTRANCE EXAMINATION BOARD.

The annual spring meeting of the College Entrance Examination Board was held at Columbia University, New York, May 11, 1907. Your representative was in attendance. The regular arrangements for the examinations and the examiners for 1908 were made. The question of co-operation with the New York State Examination Board again came before the body. It was decided not to enter into such an arrangement. The Board of Review, the appointment of which was reported to you one year ago, made the following report:

1. That a commission be established, in accordance with the recommendations of the Committee of Five, to consider the revision of the definition of the requirement in Physics.

2. That the Modern Language Association be requested to revise the list of books recommended in French and German, and to consider the question of the number of pages recommended to be read.

3. That a commission be established, in accordance with the recommendations of the Committee of Five, to consider the definition of the requirement in History.

The following amendment was also passed:

The Chairman shall, with the approval of the Executive Committee, appoint annually a Committee of Review, to consist of seven members, three of whom shall be representatives of secondary schools. This committee shall consider all criticisms and suggestions that may be made to the Board in regard to its requirements, and shall make definite recommendations in regard to any modification of these requirements that may from time to time seem desirable. The committee may co-operate with committees of other bodies appointed to formulate entrance requirements, or may, with the approval of the Board, arrange for the appointment of such committees.

The last meeting of the College Entrance Examination Board was held at Columbia University, November 9, 1907. Your representative was unable to be in attendance at that meeting. In addition to a slight amendment to the constitution, the following were the essential matters of business that were transacted:

1. An earlier date of the examinations of 1909, namely, June 14-19.

2. A report of the Committee of Review, especially as to the revision of the definition of History, the entire question having been referred to the American Historical Association, instead of establishing a separate commission as formerly reported.

3. The recommendation, and adoption of the recommendation, that the present list of musical composition for the examination in Musical Appreciation should remain unchanged for the years of 1909-1911.

4. The same Committee of Review was appointed for another year.

This committee met in New York, January 29, 1908. A Commission in Physics, the same plan as recommended last year at the North Central meeting by your President, was established. This commission is composed of five specialists, and two from the four associations: the New England, the Middle States and Maryland, the Southern, and the North Central. This is a very important commission, and it will have great influence on the entire country in this subject.

Within two weeks, two other meetings of the secondary school men of the Board were called to meet in New York, but your delegate felt that he could not attend in justice to his other duties.

The next annual meeting of the Board will be held in New York, at Columbia University, on April 11th, and your representative expects to be present.

The report of the delegate to the National Conference Committee of the Association of Colleges and Preparatory Schools was presented by President George E. MacLean, of the University of Iowa, as follows:

REPORT OF DELEGATE TO THE NATIONAL CONFERENCE COMMITTEE OF THE ASSOCIATION OF COLLEGES AND PREPARATORY SCHOOLS, ASSEMBLED AT WILLIAMSTOWN, JUNE 28 AND 29, 1907.

MEMBERSHIP OF THE COMMITTEE.

The following delegates were duly appointed by their respective associations for this Conference:

President George E. MacLean, the University of Iowa, from the National Association of State Universities.

Professor Herman V. Ames, the University of Pennsylvania, from the Association of Colleges and Preparatory Schools of the Middle States and Maryland.

Dr. William C. Collar, Roxbury, Massachusetts, from the New England Association of Colleges and Preparatory Schools.

Professor Allen S. Whitney, the University of Michigan, from the North Central Association of Colleges and Secondary Schools.

Chancellor James H. Kirkland, Vanderbilt University,

from the Association of Colleges and Preparatory Schools of the Southern States.

Head Master Wilson Farrand, Newark Academy, Newark, New Jersey, from the College Entrance Examination Board.

Professor John K. Lord, Dartmouth College, from the New England College Entrance Certificate Board.

THE CALL.

A preliminary notice of a conference to be held in Williamstown, Mass., or New York City, on June 28 and 29, was sent to all the delegates June 17 from Iowa City by President George E. MacLean, President of the Conference of August 3 and 4, 1906. Replies signifying their ability to attend such conference in Williamstown were received from all the delegates except Chancellor Kirkland, who reported that it would be impossible for him to be present at either place. The final notice of the meeting was issued from Williamstown by President MacLean.

THE CONFERENCE.

Williamstown, Mass., June 28, 1907.

In accordance with this call there met in informal session at 3 p. m. on June 28 in Griffin Hall, Williams College, President George E. MacLean and Professor John K. Lord. Dean Frederick C. Ferry and Professor Asa H. Morton, of Williams College, were invited by the two delegates present to sit with them in informal session and Dean Ferry was requested by President MacLean to act as Recording Secretary of the conference.

President MacLean reported that he had within a few days received information that Professor Ames, Dr. Collar and Professor Whitney would be unable to attend the conference; that Professor Ames had asked Head Master Wilson Farrand to represent the Middle States Association in his stead and that Dr. Collar would send a substitute.

President MacLean reported further that all the Associations who appointed delegates for the conference of August 3 and 4, 1906, had adopted in full the resolutions voted by that conference, with the exception of the Association of Colleges and Preparatory Schools of the Southern States; and that this Association had adopted the second and third resolutions as printed in the minutes to the extent of the appointment of a delegate to attend any conference that may be held.

A general discussion in regard to the subjects to be considered by the conference followed.

At 5:45 p. m. the informal session of the conference was adjourned.

The committee assembled in formal session at the home of Professor Morton at 8:30 p. m., President MacLean, Professor Lord, Mr. Farrand (representing both the College Entrance Examination Board and the Association of Colleges and Preparatory Schools of the Middle States and Maryland), Dean Ferry, and Professor Morton being present. By unanimous vote President MacLean was elected President of the conference; Dean Ferry was requested to act as a member of the conference as a substitute for the delegate of the New England Association of Colleges and Preparatory Schools, subject to the approval of that Association, and was appointed Recording Secretary pro tem; and Professor Morton was requested to attend the sessions of this conference as a corresponding member.

On motion it was unanimously voted that subject to revision at the next session of this conference, the name of this committee be "The National Conference Committee of the Associations of Colleges and Preparatory Schools."

President MacLean presented a letter announcing the

election by the Presbyterian College Union of the Middle West of a delegate to this conference and asking that the delegate be received. On motion it was voted that the request be laid on the table until a later session of the conference.

Mr. Farrand reported that the Association of Colleges and Preparatory Schools of the Middle West and Maryland had appointed a committee to consider the advisability of the organization of a college entrance certificate board or a commission for accrediting schools, as recommended in the resolution on that subject adopted at the Williamstown conference of August 3 and 4, 1906.

Professor Lord then proposed the following resolution:

Resolved, That this committee accepts with much gratification the report of this action of the Middle States Association as given by Mr. Farrand.

The resolution was unanimously adopted.

The conference was adjourned at 11:00 p. m.

June 29, 1907.

The committee re-assembled at 9:30 a. m. in Griffin Hall, the attendance being the same as at the previous formal session.

On motion it was unanimously voted that the name of this committee stand as proposed in the last session of the conference, namely, "The National Conference Committee of the Associations of Colleges and Preparatory Schools."

Professor Lord moved the adoption of the following resolution:

Resolved, That the purpose of this committee shall be to consider requirements for admission, matters of mutual interest to universities, colleges, and preparatory schools, and such other questions as may be referred to it by the Associations.

The resolution was unanimously adopted.

President MacLean reported that a letter had been received from an organization of teachers of Physics asking that action be taken by this committee concerning the admission requirement in that subject. After discussion, Mr. Farrand presented a resolution as follows:

Resolved, That this committee commends the action of the College Entrance Examination Board in calling upon the Associations of Colleges and Preparatory Schools to co-operate in the formation of a new entrance requirement in Physics, and urges those Associations to accept the invitation.

The resolution was unanimously adopted.

Professor Lord moved the adoption of the following resolution:

Resolved, That this committee recommends that both the inspection of the preparatory schools and the record made in college during the first term or semester of the freshman year by the pupils from such schools be the basis for granting the accrediting or the certificate privilege.

The resolution was unanimously adopted.

Dean Ferry presented a resolution as follows:

Resolved, That this committee recommends that, in the transfer of collegiate students, the following points be considered in determining the standing of the college or universities concerned:

(1) the requirements for admission;

(2) the grade and amount of work required, the length of the course, the character of the curriculum, and the degrees conferred;

(3) the number and qualifications of the instructors and the proportion of instructors to students;

(4) the separation of the Collegiate Faculty from the

government and the instruction of a preparatory department;

(5) the acceptance of the graduates by the graduate schools;

(6 equipment; and

(7) endowment.

The resolution was unanimously adopted.

On motion it was voted that the petition of the **Presbyterian College Union of the Middle West** be taken from the table and that President MacLean be requested to reply to the same with explanation of the facts.

On motion it was voted that President MacLean, Mr. Farrand and Professor Ames be appointed a committee to submit for adoption at the next conference a constitution for the government of the National Conference Committee.

On motion it was voted that Mr. Farrand and Dean Ferry, together with such associates as they may see fit to select, be appointed a committee to report at the next conference concerning a scale of values for the interpretation of admission requirements.

A vote of thanks was extended to Williams College for the courtesy of a room for its meetings, and to Professor Morton for the hospitality extended to the committee in his home.

The minutes were read and approved, subject to verbal changes.

The committee adjourned sine die at 12:25 p. m.

It was voted that Mr. F. L. Bliss, of Detroit University School, be appointed as a standing delegate to this commission for this Association.

The President then announced the following committees:

To Audit the Treasurer's Report: Professor C. A. Waldo, Purdue University, Lafayette, Indiana; Superintendent F. L. Smart, Davenport, Iowa; Principal Frank Hamsher, Smith Academy, St. Louis, Missouri.

To Recommend the Time and Place of the Next Annual Meeting: Principal F. L. Bliss, University School, Detroit, Michigan; Professor F. W. Ballou, University of Cincinnati, Cincinnati, Ohio; Professor John F. Downey, University of Minnesota, Minneapolis, Minnesota.

To Nominate Officers for the Ensuing Year: Director George N. Carman, Lewis Institute, Chicago, Illinois; Dean C. M. Woodward, Washington University, St. Louis, Missouri; Principal Edward L. Harris, Central High School, Cleveland, Ohio; President James H. Baker, University of Colorado, Boulder, Colorado; Professor A. S. Whitney, State Inspector of Schools, Ann Arbor, Michigan.

SECOND SESSION, FRIDAY AFTERNOON.

The following paper was read by Dean Thomas Arkle Clark, University of Illinois, Urbana, Illinois:

THE TREATMENT OF INCOMING FRESHMEN.

It is not truer that "The boy is father to the man" than it is that the freshman during his first few weeks in college, in the large majority of cases, settles his entire future career as a student. His friends, his amusements, his habits of study, his morals, his attitude toward everything connected with his new life are pretty definitely fixed before Thanksgiving. Mr. George Ade's transformation, in "The College Widow," of Bud Hicks who, struck town in September as an unsophisticated country "rube," and who went home at Thanksgiving a real college sport, is of course exaggerated for stage effect, but it suggests truthfully the real situation. The transformation of the freshman is so rapid and so complete that college authorities may well give it their careful consideration; for it is out of freshmen that we make seniors, and graduate students, and—some of us hope—men.

As I understood the assignment which was given to me by the Executive Committee of this Association, it was intended that I should make some investigation among the representative colleges and universities of the country with regard to what is being done to advise and direct freshmen students as well as to supervise their work and conduct. It was hoped that from the material and suggestions which it was thought would come to my hand, helpful ideas for us all might be evolved. It was generally agreed that the subject is an important one, which all colleges have no doubt given thoughtful attention to.

I accordingly sent to the president, to the dean, or to a prominent professor of about sixty representative institutions the following letter, with an explanation of my purpose in making the inquiry.

"I should be glad if you would tell me in detail what methods, if any, are employed in your institution for supervising either the work or the conduct of fresmen students. I should like to know whether such supervision is done through advisers, class officers, or other college officials.

"What methods are employed to discover whether or not a student is delinquent in his work, and what is done with him when such facts are discovered?

"At what point in the student's career is disciplinary action taken on account of delinquency in studies or conduct?

"To what extent is an effort made to know what individual students are doing at the beginning of their college course?

"I should consider it a favor if you would send me any printed matter, blanks, or other helps which you utilize in securing information about students."

I received replies of some sort or another to this letter from thirty-seven institutions, representing what is being done from Massachusetts to California, and from Minnesota to Texas. The careful perusal of the returns leads me to the conclusion that something is being done in practically every institution in the country to get into touch and to keep in touch with the work of students, that little difference is made in the treatment of the work of freshmen and that of other students, and that much that is being done is somewhat mechanical and machine-like, with little attention paid to the needs or habits of the individual student.

The action serves to give a virtuous feeling to the college management and it is usually harmless to the student, who goes on his way—sometimes a brief one—undisturbed. There seems to be a willingness on the part of most college officials that something be done, a recognition of the fact that something ought to be done—but other things are often thought more important, and something must be omitted. As one man puts it,

"I regret to say that no organized effort is made to ascertain what individual students are doing at the beginning of their college course. I appreciate that this is a critical time in the career of all students, and that this is one great element of weakness in institutions of this sort. As matters are now organized, however, no one seems to have the time to give to this matter, important though it is." And yet there are but two hundred students in the college referred to.

In advocating the supervision of the work of freshmen, as I have said in a previous paper before the Association, I do not forget the value of freedom, of independent action, of responsibility and initiative on the part of the new student. Much of the value of a college training comes from the fact that the student is away from the fostering care of the home, and at liberty to spend his own money, decide upon the employment of his own time, choose his own friends and come and go within sane limits as he pleases. The boy who is so unfortunate as to be compelled to live at home while he is going to college is losing half of the training to which he is entitled in a college course. But being thrown upon his own responsibility should not mean that no one knows where he is going, or that no one is to be at hand to give the word of caution or advice in times of danger or of trouble. It is conceded that the young people composing the freshman classes of our colleges are not to be treated as children; no more should they be left entirely to their own devices or be taught according to graduate school methods.

Whatever is done to advise, or help or look after the fresman must be done soon. College is a new experience to the freshman and he gets at it early. Nothing will ever take the place of a good start in his work. Half the men to whom I talk concerning their failures lay it to a bad start. "You can lose more time in a week than you can make up in a month," a freshman said to me lately. The average freshman is a pretty reasonable being, I have found, and if he fails it is through carelessness or ignorance rather than through vicious going astray.

Very few high school students have learned what hard, consistent study means. They misjudge what is expected of them in college, and often before they are aware they are so far behind that to catch up seems impossible. Not only do they misjudge the amount to be done, but the right methods of study also are unknown to them. They have not yet learned the application and the concentration necessary to get on easily under the new conditions and with the new work. "I supposed it would be the same as it was in the high school," is the stereotyped excuse for the freshman's downfall. The freedom of college life deceives them for a time, and they frequently awaken too late to recognize the fact that freedom for them means only added responsibility.

Many also appreciate too late the fact that their preparation has not been all that it should have been, and that if they are to make good it must be by the hardest and most consistent sort of toil. New temptations—social, financial and moral—come to them from which they have heretofore been shielded, and they come so suddenly and so unexpectedly that it is a wonder so few are carried away by them. The world is new and the freshman is curious to know all about it, good or bad. There are always those to say "Come;" there should also be someone to utter the word of warning.

Many of these difficulties might be forestalled if at the very outset the freshman could be given a little warning, a little friendly advice, a heart-to-heart talk, on the new situation and the responsibilities which the new conditions have imposed. In institutions where daily chapel exercises are held there is ample chance for such talks by whatever college official seems best fitted to give them. In institutions where there are no regular exercises which bring the college community together there should be pretty frequent and familiar talks by some college officer with the members of the freshman class. I am of the opinion that if the freshman could listen to four or five twenty-minute talks during the first six or eight weeks of the semester on "Methods of study, the spending of money, the employment of time, the value of self-control, college honor," and such timely subjects, the percentage of failures at the end of the semester would be largely cut down.

In the supervision of the freshmen class there is much to be gained by a centralization of the work. The college community is usually a circumscribed one and often a congested one. Everyone knows about everyone else; and no-one is hard to get at. Besides, tradition carries a reputation over from one year to the next and is a great help in suggesting who is able and willing to give intelligent advice. If the responsibility is broken up, uncertainty of action on the part of the student results; he is in doubt as to whom to go to if in need of help. Tradition should make this certain. Otherwise the effectiveness of the organization is impaired. Whatever may be the organization or disposition of the work it should in the end be under the general supervision of one man. The lives of students, even in a large institution, are too intimately interwoven, too closely allied the one with the other for the general supervision to be divided. It is sometimes a good deal better to talk to the freshman's roommate than to the freshman if one wishes to accomplish his purposes and to bring about reform. The supervising officer should know both and have control over both. One general method should prevail throughout the whole institution or the success of the work will fall short of what is possible. No better illustration of the success of centralization in a large institution is needed than that which is seen in the wonderful work of Dean Briggs and later of Dean Hurlbut at Harvard University.

In a small institution the president is, of course, the proper officer to look after such work or, where his duties make it impossible, the dean or some general officer who may give the time and thought necessary to the work.

There are a good many devices, such as monthly or weekly reports by instructors, on the work of students, the requiring of excuses for absence from class exercises, and the relation which exists between the student and a class officer or adviser, all of which are used to get information concerning the student's work.

Most institutions, I discover, require reports to a designated officer (the president, the dean, or some other official), of *delinquent* students only, and at a time so late in the semester, or at such wide intervals as, it seems to me, to be of little value. I am of the opinion that the reports to be of any value should be required upon the work of all students of a class, and should be made early enough in the year for the student to find it possible to recover lost ground if he is behind. The first report of work should come in at the end of the second or third week preferably, and certainly not later than at the end of the first month. Any wide-awake teacher can form a pretty definite idea of every member of a class within a month, and if he cannot do so he ought not to be teaching freshmen.

My reason for advocating the system of requiring reports upon the work of *all* students of the freshman class at stated intervals is based upon my knowledge of the irresponsibility and indifference of the average college instructor with regard to such work. Most instructors are much more interested in the subjects they teach than in their students, and can not be counted on to look after the individual. The more degrees they have the more likely is this to be true. Original research, advanced work, and not the making of the men, seems just now the fetish. As a prominent college officer in the largest institution in the Middle-West said to me only a few days ago with regard to the matter of making reports, "The instructor needs prodding at all times, and requires someone to be eternally after him." It is only when the reports are exacted on a definite date upon all freshmen students that the required information is forthcoming.

If reports on scholarship are required frequently, and the information is at all full, the instructor will feel himself abused if the blank to be used is not carefully prepared in order that the greatest amount of information may be given with an expenditure of the least effort. A good deal of skill has been shown in the various institutions where this system is in operation in devising a report card which will furnish full information without great clerical labor. I shall be glad to show, to any one interested, the one used at the University of Illinois for the excellent features of which we are indebted to the thought of several other institutions.

The reporting to a central office of all absences, for whatever cause, in my mind, has a very decided advantage over the method which is employed in many institutions of throwing upon each individual instructor the responsibility of receiving excuses from students and of reporting only such absences as do not seem to be covered by a legitimate excuse. Such a method may develop mental resourcefulness in students who are regularly absent, but it does not encourage truthfulness. A few years ago when it was the custom at my own university for students to offer excuses for absence, an instructor remarked to me that a clever young freshman had within the previous few weeks offered seventeen excuses for absence, all good and all different. The attitude that absence from class is simply a fact to be reckoned with only in relation to its influence upon the student's work, seems to me to be the normal one. Whether he is absent because he has smallpox, or is lazy, or in love, the effect on his work in any case is detrimental and may very well be taken as legitimate cause for his not being allowed to continue with a course.

At the University of Illinois we employ a system similar to that which is used in many other institutions. Reports of all absences are made daily to a central office. Whenever a freshman receives in any course a number of absences equal to one-eighth of the total number of recitations for the semester he is dropped from the course and may not continue without the permission of the instructor in the course and of a special committee before which he must appear. Students are given formal notice from the office when they have received half the limit of cuts or more. The effect has been to relieve the instructor, to cut down the number of absences, and to reduce lying to a minimum.

In addition to these matters of information I have personally found very helpful, also, the keeping of a card index of individaul students. Whenever a student comes in to see me and I see from thirty to seventy-five daily, I make a card for him on which I put down all matters of information concerning him—his course, the place where he lives, the organization to which he belongs, the name of his roommate, his home town, or any details which will help to differentiate him from other students, or which will help me to remember his situation, his character, or his needs. Sometimes if I am afraid that I shall forget him I add some little item of personal description which will fix the matter in my mind. It is surprising to me what a large number of students will in this way, in a very short time, become familiar to me; and it is interesting to see to what extent such a system develops personal interest in the individual.

No matter how complete the mechanical devices may be for keeping track of the work of freshmen, they will be useless unless they are combined with a complete and close personal relationship between the individual freshman and some college officer. Nothing will take the place of this. The freshman is to be left free and independent, but there should always be someone who has time and who is willing to talk on any topic that agitates or interests the mind of the new student. In no institution, no matter how large, should it be possible for a freshman to feel that no one knows what he is doing and no one cares.

In a large number of institutions there is now found a system of class advisers in which one man or several men have an advisory relation with the students of a certain class. I have endeavored to find out, as far as possible, what the duties of such officers are in the various institutions. So far as I can discover the main duty of the class officer concerns itself with the student's schedule. Having decided whether the student might better elect Greek history or farm mechanics, whether he should take rhetoric at eight o'clock or at one, whether he may carry seventeen hours of work or be cut down to twelve, his chief functions have been performed. These matters are important, but they are by no means the chief things which a class officer should do for the freshman.

He should be a man of broad culture who has time enough to talk with the young student, the number of students assigned to him should not be so large as to make it impossible for him to form a personal acquaintance with each one, and he should have a sufficient sympathy for young people and a wide enough knowledge of human nature to make him the friend of those whom he advises. Such men are not impossible to find if college authorities wish to find them, and if we are to develop character as well as scholarship, if we are to save as large a part of our freshmen class as possible, someone should have regard to the character of the teachers and the advisers to whom they are assigned.

I should be the last man certainly to decry high scholarship as a basis for appointment or promotion in college, but I have sometimes wondered if we are not at times inclined as college officials to over-value an instructor's ability to write books or to conduct original investigation, and to give too little weight to the strong sympathetic teacher. In our search for scholars we have often missed good teachers. A friend of mine, who is both a good teacher and a doctor of philosophy, said to me not long ago that the scholar under whom he did his graduate work, a well-known man in one of the oldest and largest institutions of this country, in advising him said, in substance, "Don't pay much attention to your students when you get into college. The good ones will get on alone, and the poor ones might as well be thrown out. The only thing that will win promotion and preferment for you will be original research and publication. Good teaching doesn't count these days."

I am afraid that in too many cases the wisdom of his advice is apparent. Too often we are after the spectacular, or that which can be given space in the papers and which will make a show. But the development of character is still worth while and should never be lost sight of in our college work. The men who are able to do this should be sought as earnestly, promoted as rapidly, and paid as liberally as are those men who have profound scholarship but little knowledge of human nature or interest in those they teach. Many of our freshmen failures may quite as legitimately be laid to the indifference of the teacher as to the fault of the student. Not until we give as careful attention to the choosing of teachers of freshmen as we do to the selection of those who are to have charge of graduate work, will we do for our freshmen students all that we may be expected to do. The character of the freshman teacher has quite as much to do with the result at the end of the semester as has the character of the freshman.

My ideas, then, of the sane treatment of the incoming freshman are these. To furnish for him the best and the most sympathetic teaching possible; to give him whenever it does not seem directly in opposition to his best interests entire liberty to come and go as he pleases; to have within reach all necessary information with regard to his studies, his attendance, his friends, his habits of life, in fact, anything which will individualize him and separate him from the crowd. And to have this information as early as is possible in his college course, and at latest by the end of the fourth week. To give to him during the early part of the first semester specific talks which will acquaint him with college customs, college life, and the new and peculiar temptations and conditions which surround him. To have someone who will show a sympathetic interest in the individual, and who will make it evident to him that some one knows what he is doing, and that someone cares.

Even in our largest institutions I am sure that this is

possible—possible even for one man without much help. With an interested corps of teachers in an institution of moderate size it would be even an easy and a pleasant task. Very few of our institutions are in large cities; and even those that are so located are usually isolated, or in rather circumscribed localities. Student communities in general are congested ones, where he who wishes may soon get the run of things and know what is going on and who is the motive power. I think it will be admitted that I am not ralical; that a general knowledge of what freshmen are doing, a system which aids in the securing of such knowledge, and the sympathetic attitude toward the individual is not undesirable. Insomuch as the members of the freshman class fail, or go astray, we have deprived ourselves of upper classmen and of graduate students. Our only hope is in the entering class; and if we succeed with them we shall have succeeded with the classes that follow. There will be but few scholars if we lose the freshmen.

There is no other chance so opportune for the building of character, for the development of men, as that which is presented by the freshman class of any college, and the man who gives his time and his thought to it is doing as noble an educational work as is the most noted scholar in the land.

The discussion was continued by Dean E. A. Birge, University of Wisconsin, Madison, Wisconsin; Dean Thomas Arkle Clark, University of Illinois, Urbana, Illinois; President W. L. Bryan, Indiana University, Bloomington, Indiana; Superintendent J. W. Carr, Dayton, Ohio; President John W. Cook, Northern Illinois Normal, DeKalb, Illinois; Principal J. E. Armstrong, Englewood High School, Englewood, Illinois; Professor A. W. Rankin, University of Minnesota, Minneapolis, Minnesota; Professor E. J. Babcock, University of North Dakota, Grand

Forks, North Dakota; and Principal Arthur S. Wilde, Evanston Academy of Northwestern University, Evanston, Illinois.

DEAN BIRGE:

I do not think it would be quite proper to let the subject drop without having a word said in discussion. I am entirely in agreement with the general principles laid down in the paper. There is one matter, however, in which my experience would lead me to differ, and that is in respect to the reporting of absences to the central authority and receiving excuses there. We have followed in our university, the University of Wisconsin, in various forms the plan of having absences reported and considered by a central committee and that of leaving the absences in charge of the individual instructors. We have found the latter plan, on the whole, distinctly more advantageous. It was our experience that when we had a rule somewhat similar to that laid down in the paper it became a matter of pride on the part of the student to secure as many cuts as the law would allow him, and that the student who would naturally attend every class was looked upon as somewhat of a weak-kneed individual if he did not cut for the purpose of getting as near to discipline as he could safely go. When we turned over the care of the absences to the individual teachers, telling the students that they were expected to be present at every class, that there was no allowance of cuts at all and that they were expected to account to the individual instructors for every case in which they were absent, we found that the number of absences decidedly decreased. That has been in effect with us for several years, and absences which become noteworthy on the part of students are reported to me as Dean. Under our system of keeping accounts the absences of each student are noted on cards which are turned in with his report at the end of the semester, and we have found no special tendency to increase the number of absences. A few students need to be checked on the number of absences, but I think, in fact, I am very sure, that the total number of absences under the system of leaving it with the instructors has been very decidedly smaller than when it was in the hands of a central committee with a disciplinary limit set on the absences and the warning when the student approached the danger line.

DEAN CLARK:

Perhaps I ought to say that our own experience has been absolutely the opposite. The instructor is usually indifferent as regards the matter of absences and ordinarily would not know. Our rule for twenty-five or thirty years was that students might not have more than three unexcused absences. Any excuse went. We all knew that when I was in college, and I think the students afterwards were no less keen than we. It simply meant stopping at the desk and saying that one felt rather tired or sick or had been out of town or in some other unusual mental condition the day before, and that settled it. I am sure that absences have been cut down one-half since we adopted the other regulation. I should say that there are not a dozen students in 3,000 who feel it an obligation under which they are resting to take all the cuts coming to them.

PRESIDENT BRYAN:

We have been trying two devices with freshmen which seem worth while. An instructor of freshmen in English composition gives two hours of instruction in the week to his section and gives the two hours of time besides for conference with members of the section one by one. In this way it is possible to meet each freshman for a short time several times in the term. In freshman mathematics the instructor meets the class four times in the week in recitation and for one hour in the week he meets these students in groups of four or five for an hour, and in this way each student comes into very close touch with the instructor each week. We are particularly well pleased with this latter device. It would seem that if the student has four recitations a week in freshman mathematics in a section not exceeding twenty-five, if he has besides that an hour's conference each week in a group of four or five, he should be able to tell whether or not he is fit to carry that work.

DEAN BIRGE:

If I may speak a word in following that—we have been following the same plan in mathematics, although with a slight difference in practical details. The present professor of mathematics told me the other day that they were developing a system of chronic paupers, that the students who did not know very much about mathematics were the ones that were there at the conference every time and were getting all the help they could, and that they had had to assure the students that they could not get through the examinations at the end of the semester with what they picked up in conference. Of course that is not true of the majority of students. Most of them get a good deal of benefit from it.

SUPERINTENDENT CARR:

I do not wish to engage in this discussion at any length, but I would like to emphasize and note one or two statements that have been made by Dean Clark. As a public school man and as a father of four children who have gone through the freshman class of college, I feel very deeply the necessity of having as instructors in our colleges men and women who are thoroughly interested in the students, not simply as to whether they are absent or tardy, but as to what they are doing and who are able to direct their course in college; and I think it is a sign of remarkable progress in our college work when college men in a meeting like this will take the interest and time to discuss this question. As a public school man, I want to say to you that we sometimes hesitate whether to advise students to go to college or not, and I want to say to you that it is a problem many times whether they should go or not. When the time comes that the colleges will look after the moral interests and welfare of these young people, it will mean much to the homes of this country and much to the country we love, and I believe much to the colleges themselves; and I do not believe, for one, that the colleges can address themselves to any subject that is of any more vital importance to higher education than this very question of caring for the freshmen. A great many of the troubles we have in secondary schools, that you have not even yet been able to supervise us out of, grow out of certain college practices that must be eradicated or trouble and more trouble is to come in the future.

President Cook:

Mr. President, I wish to add only a word. There seems to my mind a defect in the assignment of this kind of work rather indiscriminately. It may be that the man who has the work in composition or literature or mathematics is fitted for it and it may be that he is not at all fitted for it. It seems to me that there should be a very careful and intelligent examination—as has been done in one of the institutions of the state to which I should more particularly refer if the gentlemen involved were not present—into whether or not the man has a genius for that kind of work, that sympathy of disposition for these young men and a devotion to this work which will see that it is done well, and there can be, I think I need not say, no nobler work. Those of us who are directing young people to the universities feel far more solicitous for the way that work is done than we do with regard to the mathematics or to the philosophy.

PRINCIPAL ARMSTRONG:

Mr. President, it may not be expected that I, as a secondary school man, should have anything to say on this topic, but as a matter of encouragement of what the universities and colleges are doing for freshmen, I would like to say that it is quite different from the attention that was given to first year students when I was in the university. We had what was called student government and we looked after all those things ourselves, until at last it became necessary for the chief justice of the student court to fine the president for not doing his duty, and then the government went under.

There were two or three things that were spoken of by Dean Clark that impressed me as of great importance for the consideration of secondary school men. One was the fact that any school is apt to treat all its pupils as being of the rank of development of its oldest students or pupils. It is the tendency of the high school to treat its first year pupils just the same as its third and fourth year pupils. Now when we come to think of the very rapid change of the pupils in growth, the maturity of the pupil of fourteen and that of eighteen, we can easily see what a mistake we are making in treating our first year pupils in anything like the same way that we do our third and fourth year pupils, and that brings me to think, too, of the fact that the high schools have stood trembling between the criticisms of the community and those of the university above them; that they have not dared, it seems to me, in many cases, to even state their problem and act intelligently upon the things they find, the conclusions they are able to draw themselves, because of the fear of not heeding the demands of the taxpayer below and of the higher institutions above them. So what I would plead for is that we should give more attention to the need of different treatment, of conduct, of everything pertaining to the life of the first year pupil, and that we should be independent enough to work out our own methods of treatment of the pupil. The kindergarten method of making things pleasant for people creeps up through the intermediate school and often into the high school, as if there had been no change in the character and the development or the needs of the pupil.

Professor Rankin:

In Minnesota we have prepared a statement which the superintendent or principal of the high school sends on to the university to which the student may be accredited in such a way that the principal or superintendent has an opportunity of giving us some information as to the personal habits of the student who is sent on. It seems to me that the high school men have information about the student during the four years there which should be of great service to the university authorities, and I believe that we should take advantage of that and that the university should expect from the high school man some information not only as to the scholastic attainments and ability and capacity, but also something as to the personal habits of the student, so that we may have something to start with when the student comes in. It is a new thing, but the superintendents are heartily in favor of it and say they will cooperate with us to that extent. They say (I am not sure that they will, however) that they will make a discrimination between those who are graduated and whom they consider fit for university work and those who are graduated and whom they do not believe fitted to go into university work; they will say, "This person is graduated, but we do not believe he has the capacity or is desirable to go into the university work."

DEAN BIRGE:
We have the same experience. We have the same opportunity and occasionally a word or two reaches us, but those reports are placed on file at the university, they are part of the official reports of the university and every once in a while a student goes to see what his report was and he has seen occasionally that he was not sized up as high as he thought he ought to be and the matter has gone back to the high school principal and made him trouble, and the result is that the high school principals, while occasionally sending us a word that would help us, have on the whole reported the full work of the student and left us to draw our own conclusions on it, and as a whole I think we can tell by the report what he has been doing.

While I am on my feet I would like to tell a story that happened this year. A boy came to the university who was a brother of a student who had been there for some time and was a very good student, but this younger boy would not work and I got after him a number of times—he was in my immediate charge; but finally the situation got so that it was necessary apparently to drop him. I sent for the brother and said, "What is the matter? What is the reason your brother won't, apparently, do any work?" "I will tell you, Professor, just how that is," he said. "I was always a good student and Bill" (to give him a name that doesn't belong to him) "was not, and my father thought I could do well in the university and he sent me here. He thought Bill couldn't stand it in the University of Wisconsin and he sent him to a college where he would be looked after," and he named one of the best colleges in the northwest—not in Wisconsin. I asked him, "Why didn't it work?" He said, "Well, the fact was, Bill found there a whole bunch of boys whose fathers sent them for the same purpose."

PROFESSOR BABCOCK:

I just wish to call attention to one point which was brought out partially in the address, and that is, I believe, the importance which should be attached to giving an inspiration, a setting forth of principles which should guide the freshman on through the rest of his college course, and I believe that the colleges, the universities, are to some extent at fault in not presenting to their freshmen classes, as far as their means will permit, men who are of sufficient age and sufficient skill and who are sufficiently willing to break away from the text book, from the library, to bind the freshman to something higher and to a principle which will guide him all the way through his college course. Now I believe that if it were possible we should assign our experienced men in the university to the freshman class, especially men who will break away and give ideals to be aimed at in the freshman work.

PRINCIPAL WILDE:

It seems to me not necessary that all responsibility should be left to the university. We are trying an experiment in our academy this year which we have found helpful thus far. The principal of the school is meeting members of the fourth class this year and discussing with them college life, indicating some changes in manner of instruction and now and then giving a lecture in college form, the student taking notes and going through the matter as he would in college class. The matters of discussion will be such matters as social life in college, the college fraternity and its relation to it, the student in relation to the work, in relation to his fellow students, and so forth. Thus far I think there has a great deal of interest been manifested in this course. I think one of the advantages in the course is that the principal himself or the instructor enters into closer contact with his graduating class, with mutual advantage.

Preliminary statements of committees on revised definitions were submitted as follows:

COMMERCIAL SUBJECTS.

PROFESSOR E. V. ROBINSON, UNIVERSITY OF MINNESOTA.

Your Committee on the Definition of Units in Commercial Subjects begs leave to submit the following report:

In the first instance, it may perhaps be well to indicate some things which the Committee has not undertaken to do.

It has not undertaken to argue again the old question of formal discipline versus utility. It is assumed that the two are not incompatible; in other words, that a subject does not need to be useless forever after in order to serve as a means of formal discipline.

It has not sought to prove that commercial units should be accepted for college admission because commercial subjects have cultural as well as vocational value. It is assumed that any subject demanding systematic application of the mind, and bearing a vital relation to life, has a cultural value.

It has not argued that vocational education at the public expense is justifiable. That question seems to have been settled some time ago by the establishment of schools of law, medicine, engineering, etc., supported at the public expense.

It has not attempted to establish the proposition that education for business can be taught as effectively as education for law, medicine or engineering. That would seem to be self-evident; and the great increase in the number of schools offering commercial subjects and in the number of students pursuing such subjects during the last ten or fifteen years, would seem to establish this conclusion on the basis of experience.

It has not attempted to make out a course of study for secondary schools, but to define units of work as a guide to such schools as may wish to offer them.

It has not sought to determine what studies are the best as a preparation for college; though if forced to choose between the dictum of the Committee of Ten, that those studies which best prepare for college best prepare for life, and the opposite dictum that those studies which best prepare for life best prepare for college, your Committee would choose the latter.

Finally, the Committee has not presumed to recommend how many units of commercial work should be accepted by colleges for admission. This is a matter with which the individual colleges will have to deal in any case, and some of them will accept more, others less, and others perhaps none at all.

What your Committee has sought to do is, in brief, to define units of work in the various subjects now taught in commercial high schools, such as those of Boston, New

York, Brooklyn, Philadelphia, Washington, and likewise in the commercial courses of the best class of regular high schools, to the end that the schools may know what is expected in the several subjects, and to the end that the colleges may agree on units which they will accept in case they decide to accredit any commercial work for admission.

As a preliminary to the definitions, it may be well to review briefly the official reports and other important papers dealing with the subject.

In 1892 the Conference on History, Civil Government and Political Economy reported to the Committee of Ten as follows: "The subject of Political Economy appears to be taught in only about one-twentieth of the high schools. Here as in Civil Government, we believe that the essential principles are not above the reach of the high school pupils; but that an attempt to master the whole subject will result in the understanding of only a small part. * * * In this difference of opinion, it has seemed to the Conference wise to recommend that there be no formal instruction in Political Economy, but that the general principles be taught in connection, particularly with Economic History, Civil Government and Commercial Geography. The subject would, therefore, appear in its most elementary form in the third year of the Grammar School, and would be revived in the last two years of the high school."

In accordance with this report the Committee of Ten of the National Educational Association (Par. 30) passed the following resolution: "Resolved, That no formal instruction in Political Economy be given in the secondary school, but that in connection particularly with United States History, Civil Government and Commercial Geography, instruction be given in those economical topics, a knowledge of which is essential to the understanding of our economic life and development."

From the foregoing, it would seem at first glance that Commercial Geography was recognized as a proper high school subject, even though Political Economy was deemed inappropriate; but the concluding sentence of the quotation from the report of the Conference seems to indicate that by Commercial Geography they meant grammar school Geography. At that time, therefore, commercial subjects received no recognition in connection with college preparation.

In July, 1899, the Committee of Thirteen of the National Educational Association on College Entrance Requirements, reported as follows (Page 19): "The Committee recommends that our colleges and universities should accept as one unit for admission, a year's work in Economics, including under this head a course in Elementary Political Economy, supplemented by adequate instruction in Commercial Geography and Industrial History."

At the meeting of the National Educational Association in Detroit, July 12, 1901, a resolution was moved in the Department of Business Education to appoint a Committee of Nine with reference to Business Education. This committee undertook investigations, and at the Minneapolis meeting of the National Educational Association in July, 1902, held open meetings for discussion and the receipt of suggestions from all quarters. A preliminary report was presented at that meeting. A second report embodying an outline of a four-year commercial high school course was presented at the Boston meeting of the National Educational Association in July, 1903, and a supplementary or final report accompanied by various appendices was issued under date of September 1, 1903. These several reports and documents are published as Bulletin 213 of the College Department, University of the State of New York, with the subtitle, Commercial Education in High Schools.

In addition to the foregoing, the University of the State of New York issues a syllabus on business subjects for secondary schools, which has proven of considerable value in preparation of the definitions.

Other discussions of the subject which have been consulted somewhat at length are the following:

James: Education of Business Men.

Herrick—Commercial Education (Supplement to Fifth Year Book, National Herbart Society).

Herrick—Meaning and Practice of Commercial Education (MacMillan).

Proceedings of the Convention on Higher Commercial Education (Michigan Political Science Association, June, 1903)

Proceedings of the Conference on Commercial Education (University of Illinois, 1906).

Brown and others—The Place of Vocational Subjects in the High School Curriculum (IV Year Book, Nat. Soc. for the Scientific Study of Education).

Herrick and others—Vocational Studies for College Entrance (Sixth Year Book, Nat. Soc. for Sci. Study of Education, 1907).

Person—Industrial Education, A System of Training for Men Entering upon Trade and Commerce (H. M., 1907).

An examination of the courses of study offered in the classes of schools above named shows that a considerable portion, perhaps 50 to 60 per cent of the work, is similar to that offered in other courses and in other high schools. The remaining portion, which may be properly called commercial, includes the following distinct types of subjects: first, those treating the technique of business, including (1) applied mathematics in the form of business arithmetic and bookkeeping, (2) business language in the form of stenography and typewriting, commercial correspondence, (3) business law; secondly, courses of a historical, descriptive or theoretical nature, dealing with commerce from the social point of view and including the history of commerce, economic history of England, economic history of the United States, the materials of commerce, commercial geography and elementary economics.

PHYSICS.

PROFESSOR C. R. MANN, UNIVERSITY OF CHICAGO.

During the year 1907-8 this committee has co-operated with the similar committees of the fifteen other associations in studying the situation in regard to physics. These joint committees have issued one circular and four circular letters. The circular contains a revised statement of the proposed new definition of the unit. This was sent to two thousand principals and physics teachers, and all the suggestions that were submitted have been incorporated in it in the form in which it is presented below.

Having now discussed the matter very thoroughly, not only within the committee itself, but also with the other committees of the fifteen associations from all parts of the country, and having received suggestions and criticisms from over five hundred teachers and principals, your committee feels justified in offering herewith a new definition of the unit. Your committee is aware that this association is co-operating with other associations in appointing a committee to define the unit in physics for the use of the whole country. Because of our careful investigations in this matter we believe that the requirement which this committee will adopt cannot differ materially from the one which we herewith recommend; we therefore urge that these requirements be put into practice as soon as is practicable, in order that the way may be opened for the immediate amelioration of the conditions of physics teaching.

GERMAN.

PROFESSOR LAWRENCE FOSSLER, UNIVERSITY OF NEBRASKA.

I. The Chairman, in endeavoring to reach the consensus of opinions and judgments touching this subject, directed a communication to each member of his committee, said communication containing (1) a statement of the requirements as formulated at present (really the Report of the Committee of Twelve; (2) a request to examine and criticise said requirements in the light of experience and to suggest such changes and improvements as seemed to be called for; (3) a request for a statement, printed or otherwise, of such modifications or formulations of the requirements, as have been in actual force in the respective states of our territory and under the immediate supervision of each member of the Committee. The responses to the above-mentioned circular are the basis of this Report.

II. (1) We find, generally speaking, that the desire for standardizing the requirements or courses is practically unanimous. Well-nigh all parts of our section of the country are making efforts to reach substantial uniformity and the standard which that implies. Naturally enough, this uniformity can and does extend only to essentials. Conditions vary in different sections, vary some even in communities and schools of the same section. Now, while differences are bound to exist, there is, nevertheless, a well-defined and growing tendency to raise the study of modern languages to a more satisfactory plane. We are convinced that the setting-up of a standard course of study, or formulation of the amount, character and scope of work, which can fairly be asked of students of high school age and advancement, has been and is productive of great good. We believe that the co-operation of the universities or colleges and the secondary schools have materially assisted in raising modern language study to its proper level. We recognize thoroughly that the work done in the secondary schools must primarily be, in kind and amount, such as is adapted to the needs and circumstances of the school in which it is done, and of intrinsic value to the youth, who may never enter college halls. Preparation for college is only one, a secondary, although an exceedingly important element in high school instruction.

(2) From the information available it appears that the great majority of secondary schools in the North Central region maintain only a two years' German course, though there is a fair sprinkling of schools in which three, occasionally even four, years are given. But, for the present, collegiate work should accommodate itself to this condition. Experience has shown that strong and well-trained high school students, bringing four semesters of German to college, may be permitted to undertake the *fourth* semester's work in college.

(3) The Committee subscribe unhesitatingly to the view that *quality* and not *quantity* should be the aim of instruction and measure of success, that "To work intensively rather than extensively, to stress quality rather than quantity is the salvation of our modern language work." To this end your Committee would urge the need of greater insistence on correct and ready pronunciation, on more thorough drill in, and unwearied application of, the fundamentals of grammar, on greater persistence in the teaching of word formation, and the vocabulary of every-day life; in a word, on a more complete mastery of the fundamental "mechanics" of the foreign idiom. All recognize that to drop, or discontinue, the systematic study of grammar when the student has advanced far enough to begin reading, is not only perilous, but fatal. All recognize the absolute necessity of continuing the study of the *formal* side of language study by

way of simple composition exercises, or—perhaps not so successful a method—by close attention to the forms and the study of paradigms found in connection with the reading matter. Your Committee desires especially to insist upon great attention being paid to the mastery of a systematic and formal grammatical apparatus. Moreover, the student should be led to appreciate the essential unity of structure of German and his native tongue. Through the careful study of German the mysteries of English grammar may well be dispelled and cleared up. Witness *e. g.* the English passive voice, the subjunctive mode, the use of modal auxiliaries, etc.

(4) There is well-nigh absolute unanimity in regarding simple narrative prose, by modern authors, the most suitable material for students in the elementary courses.* Many teachers (and among them some of the most successful, no doubt) strongly urge the necessity of dealing with the *Realien,* rather than the *"Idealien"* of German life. They urge that our high school youth cannot be expected to appreciate fine literary expression or idealistic art, that to arouse and hold the interest of the young we should put into their hands and heads reading and other matter which is not too far above their mental horizon. This view demands that texts descriptive of German customs and life, or of the character of Germany's great men and their deeds be read, rather than fiction or pure literature, no matter how exquisite *per se.* That there is great force to this view cannot be denied, and yet it would be unsafe and unfair to the average student to deny him all opportunity to taste of the fountain of pure literature. For it must never be forgotten that the vast majority of our school youth will never

---

*Some members of the Committee, however, feel that an exception should be made in favor of *Tell,* particularly in schools which do not maintain longer German courses.

enjoy the benefits which collegiate literary training affords.

(5) In order to realize the best results in reading, the old adage *Eile mit Weile* needs, no doubt, to be observed. Set phrases and the more common idioms should be repeated and digested. Under no circumstances should the teacher tolerate interlinear helps of vocabulary or translation. The constant aim should be to develop *power*, the ability to solve the ever-varying problems arising. Occasional, and even frequent, dictation exercises and the committing of choice bits of poetry may well form a part of every well-regulated secondary school course.

The report of the Committee on Manual Training for Girls was presented by Dean C. M. Woodward, Washington University, St. Louis, Missouri, as follows:

REPORT OF COMMITTEE ON MANUAL TRAINING FOR GIRLS.

Mr. President, I am aware that my presence here to present a report on this subject will cause a smile, as I have not said much about girls during the preaching that I have gone through.

Mr. Chairman, the committee appointed for manual training two years ago made a preliminary report last year, covering only the two subjects of shop work and drawing for boys. The committee did not then assume that its function extended to a consideration of what the girls should do at the same time and during the corresponding years. But last year this Association instructed that committee to include under the domain of manual training that which would be proper for girls and the personnel of the committee remained unchanged.

No ladies were added to the committee, as would have been appropriate. So we have been obliged not only to use all the wits we had ourselves but to consult very freely with those women who knew better than we did what could be done and how and when. Therefore, the committee have availed themselves of the advice and suggestions from the experience of very competent teachers, and I wish especially to acknowledge the assistance that we have received from the teachers of the Teachers' College of New York, from the teachers of the McKinley High School in St. Louis, and from the teachers of Lewis Institute in this city, who have given us their advice and assistance in blocking out the work.

The committee therefore consider that manual training, as now interpreted and acted upon, covers the broad domain of manual arts: on the boys' side covering shop work and drawing, and on the girls' side sewing and cooking and related subjects. What we have prepared is for the two departments of sewing and cooking, using plain language and not going into fine distinctions of words.

We first considered the fact that in nearly all of our large cities and in many of the smaller ones, pupils of the seventh and eighth grades have received the rudiments of sewing and have been taught the rudiments of plain cooking; they are familiar with the apparatus and with the processes, to a certain extent. And yet there are many high schools in which that is not true—or many cities in which that is not true, and I suppose as this report will go out to a very large number of high schools it is fair to assume that a very large proportion of the pupils will come up without any previous training at all, either at home or at school, in these subjects, and the only way, therefore, is to begin *de novo* in each. What they have is of no harm, and it is like drawing; those who have had drawing and those who have not and who appear to be very much differentiated at the start very soon get together again and the difference disappears. So it will be with the girls.

We have followed this plan. We have as a rule declined to state the article upon which the girl should learn needlework, and in cooking we have declined to state the particular thing that she must learn to make. On the other hand, we have done as in a department in physics and in other things—insisted upon the illustration of important principles, and we have put this statement down, which applies equally to both the sewing and the cooking, namely, that every exercise in sewing and in cooking should illustrate an important principle or process or a simple combination of such principles and processes. In sewing hand and machine work must be insisted upon.

FIRST, PLAIN SEWING, SIX HOURS A WEEK FOR A YEAR. ONE UNIT CREDIT.

Various stitches and their special uses; hand sewing; the use and care of machines and their attachments; the nature and uses of cotton, linen and woolen goods; the use of patterns, and making of simple garments. And that is the story of one year.

SECOND, SEWING AND MILLINERY.

Making of shirtwaists; making of wash dresses and similar garments as those ordinarily used by girls and young women. Then millinery: making, covering and altering hat frames; the study of materials for hats and the planning, making and trimming of sensible hats of appropriate materials, and throughout the teacher should insist upon economy and good taste in dress and in every department of dress. That finishes the second year.

Now we come to the third year. There was in my copy a whole page which I have left out, touching upon the relation of cooking to chemistry. I stated, and I think we ought to insist upon the idea, that a high school which teaches chemistry should not neglect its most important application of the arts of preparing food, and it would be fortunate if the class which begins the study of cooking should simultaneously, if not before, take up the study of chemistry, so that the pupils could be familiar with the processes of the chemical laboratory. They will know what a test tube is and they will know what tests can be made in the test tubes, and they will understand something about chemical action, as the pupils in the grammar grades cannot understand it. My idea is that cooking should be a science ending in a fine art, and that chemistry should come into it. Unless we do that we fail to improve our opportunities and we fail to lift chemistry upon the platform of applied science. It is arbitrary otherwise.

Now, remember that we insist here upon the same idea that every exercise in the kitchen or in household economics of any sort illustrates an important principle or an important typical process.

Cooking six hours a week for one year: Plain cooking; foods, classified and tested for food principles (there are simple methods of testing which are not very elaborately or peculiarly chemical); a study of the effects of heat upon foods alone and in combination (that brings up the whole question of different temperatures for producing different results); experiments with leavening agents and their use shown in actual cooking; bread-making; the theory and practice of canning and preserving fruits, vegetables and meats; planning, cooking and serving meals; waiting on table. Six hours a week for one year.

SECOND YEAR.

The cost of food; market prices; the cost of meals; household accounts; formulæ; dietary; the planning, weighing and cooking of apportioned meals; diet for infants, invalids and convalescents. Sanitation: The location of the site for a home, house planning, heating, lighting and ventilating; water supply; disposal of waste of all kinds; furnishing and decorating. Cleansing processes, including laundry work.

The discussion was continued by Principal E. W. Coy, Hughes High School, Cincinnati, Ohio; Dean C. M. Woodward, Washington University, St. Louis, Missouri; Principal W. J. S. Bryan, Central High School, St. Louis, Missouri; and Director G. N. Carman, Lewis Institute, Chicago, Illinois.

PRINCIPAL COY:

I should like to inquire whether that six hours means six literal hours or six periods. It seems to me that it would be very difficult indeed to make a program of six hours, as we have usually five days in the week and our periods would not divide into six hours. I do not quite see now how the program would be made unless we have nothing but domestic sciences.

DR. WOODWARD:

The committee lumped the time which should deserve a unit. They agreed upon this: that 240 hours of what could properly be called laboratory work in either cooking or sewing, 240 hours of sixty minutes each, should constitute a unit, or should be given a unit. Schools can arrange that to suit themselves. How that time is divided, how many periods a week, a day, is a matter of no concern to anybody else. It is left free to the school to put in ten hours if they choose, as they do at Lewis Insitute, or to put in four hours and extend it over a larger period.

PRINCIPAL BRYAN:

I wish it had seemed wise to the committee to state the unit in terms of the ordinary practical unit such as is used in other parts of the reports of committees on units to be given to different subjects. It seems to me that would have two advantages. In the first place, it would fit the programs more conveniently, as has been stated by Mr. Coy, and, in the second place, it would enable us better to apportion the work between manual training in both its forms and the other subjects of the course. It is usually recognized that drawing is essential both to the shop work and the wood work and various form of manual training for boys, and also to that for girls, as would appear especially from the latter part of this report. If the girl is to be acquainted with the decoration of a home, the location of a home, the various arrangements of a home, it is well that she should know what the principles of art are, so that she might apply them. Would it not be possible to say that manual training, with its adjunct drawing, and domestic science with its adjunct drawing, should be given two periods a day throughout the year, and that those together, if need be, should constitute a unit. That would give us in the four years, of course, four units for manual training either for girls or boys. I should like to suggest the advantage of that arrangement and trust the committee will consider it.

DIRECTOR CARMAN:

The question is something like the question of physics which includes laboratory work. The committee I think felt that it was unwise, as the chairman stated, to indicate precisely how the work should be done, and though I do not wish to cut off discussion, in view of the important matters that are on hand for the afternoon, I am inclined to urge that any discussion of these reports be referred back, if necessary, to the Commission, so that we may take up these matters we have on hand for this afternoon. I move that there be no further discussion of the details of the units presented to the Association, and that they simply be accepted and referred to the Commission.

The motion was carried.

Report of Commission on Accredited Schools and Colleges:

The first section of the report of the Commission on Accredited Schools and Colleges, consisting of the list of accredited schools for the year 1908-9 and the standards of admission, was presented by Professor A. S. Whitney of the University of Michigan, Chairman of the Board of Inspectors. For report containing list of schools and standards of admission see Appendix.

Professor Whitney reported that the Board of Inspectors, fifteen in number, had met according to their custom two or three days before the meeting of the Commission and had gone carefully over the reports from the various schools, working fearlessly, honestly and untiringly.

The report of the Board of Inspectors was adopted by the Association.

The second section of the report of the Commission was presented by the Secretary, Director G. N. Carman, of the Lewis Institute, who announced that the Commission had adopted new definitions in German, physics, manual training, and commercial subjects, (See Appendix) and had revised the definition of a unit course of study in general, as published in 1902, which read as follows: "A unit course of study is defined as a course covering a school year of not less than thirty-five weeks, with four or five periods of at least forty-five minutes each per week," so as to read: "A unit course of study is defined as a course covering a school year of not less than thirty-six weeks with five periods of at least forty-five minutes each per week."

It was moved and seconded that the report of the Commission on definitions of units be adopted.

In discussing the question Miss Ellen C. Sabin (Milwaukee Downer College), objected to requiring five periods a week for every subject of study, in that it leaves a school no opportunity for freedom and initiative. Objection was also made to the forty-five minute period, as thirty minutes of intense interest is all that children from fourteen to eighteen should be subjected to.

Superintendent W. H. Elson (Cleveland, Ohio), asked for a statement from the Commission which would indicate its particular reasons for proposing this distinct change of enlarging the standard school year.

President James H. Baker (University of Colorado), said that one of the great standardizing boards of this country had felt obliged, when there was an alternative of four or five periods per week, to make their reckoning upon the smaller requirement, and this reduced fifteen units on the four-period basis to twelve units on the five-period basis. Moreover, the American Medical Association defines a point, or half unit, as five periods a week for eighteen weeks.

Professor H. A. Hollister (University of Illinois), called attention to the fact that the Board of Inspectors accepts schools in which the recitation period is forty minutes in the clear, additional time being allowed for change of classes.

Principal E. W. Coy (Cincinnati), entered a protest against adding to the work the secondary school has to do to-day. He was convinced that better work could be done if less were required.

Professor C. A Waldo (Purdue University), urged that a thirty-minute period for a class of twelve or fifteen may be more satisfactory than a forty-five minute period for a class of thirty

Superintendent J. W. Carr (Dayton, Ohio), asked if the change of definition proposed was made to meet the requirements of the Carnegie Foundation, in order that college professors may be eligible to the pension fund.

Professor A. S. Whitney (University of Michigan), said that the Board of Inspectors recognizes thirty as the maximum number of students per teacher and that many schools have been rejected because they exceeded that number. He also reminded the Association of the fact that the majority of our schools run ten months and that the definition adopted by the Commission calls for an equivalent of five forty-five minute periods a week for thirty-six weeks, which is not in excess of what most schools are now offering.

President J. R. Kirk (State Normal School, Missouri), believed that outside of the large cities and a few favored localities, the high schools were trying to conform to college and university requirements and were dissipating their energy over a large number of subjects, when, if they were left alone they would teach a smaller number of subjects much better, and their graduates would go to the colleges with not quite so many units but with a good deal more scholarship and ability to think for themselves. He moved that the definition of a unit be amended to restore the four or five recitations instead of five as originally read and the number of minutes to forty minutes in the clear. The motion was seconded.

The question was discussed further by President Samuel Plantz (Lawrence University, Appleton, Wisconsin), Professor H. A. Hollister, Director G. N. Carman, and State Superintendent C. P. Cary, of Wisconsin.

Dean E. A. Birge, of the University of Wisconsin, moved that the question be referred to a committee of ten appointed by the President, consisting of representatives of the colleges and secondary schools here present to consider the matter and report to the Association to-morrow morning, the committee to consist of five from the Commission and five additional.

The motion was seconded and carried.

President James appointed as the committee of ten to consider the definition of the unit: Director Carman (Chairman), President MacLean, President Baker, Inspector Whitney, Inspector Hollister, President Kirk, Superintendent Carr, Superintendent Cary, Principal Coy, and Superintendent Nightingale.

The third section of the report of the Commission was presented by the Chairman, President George E. MacLean, of Iowa State University. Attention was first called to the preliminary report of the Committee for Inspecting and Accrediting Colleges, which reads as follows:

By action of the Association, March 23, 1906, the name of the Commission on Accredited Schools was changed to the Commission on Accredited Schools and Colleges. (Proceedings of 1906, page 130.) The Commission at the same time was instructed to report at the next annual meeting of the Association on the advisability of adopting a plan for the inspection of colleges and universities and the standardizing of their work. The Commission accordingly appointed a committee consisting of the Chairman, Vice-Chairman, and Secretary, to prepare and present to the Commission a plan for inspecting and accrediting colleges. No report was made last year, and the members of the Committee are not now ready to recommend the adoption of the report in the present form. It is submitted in a shape designed to lead to the discussion of the main features involved in the inspection of colleges.

REPORT.

I. That the Commission undertake the work of inspecting and accrediting colleges and universities through the Board of Inspectors, such changes being made in the constitution of the Board as may seem advisable in view of the proposed extension of its work.

II. That the following constitute the standards of admission to the accredited list of the North Central Association of Colleges and Secondary Schools.

A. For Colleges and Schools. (Schools, as used in this section, includes colleges and universities).

1. That the minimum scholastic attainment of all instructors shall be equivalent to graduation from a college belonging to the North Central Association of Colleges and Secondary Schools, including special training in the subjects they teach, although such requirements shall not be construed as retroactive.

2. The laboratory and library facilities shall be adequate to the needs of instruction in the subjects taught as outlined by the Association.

3. The location and construction of buildings, the lighting, heating, and ventilation of the rooms, the nature of the lavatories, corridors, closets, school furniture, apparatus, and methods of cleaning shall be such as to insure hygienic conditions for both pupils and teachers.

4. The efficiency of instruction, the acquired habits of

thought and study, the general intellectual and moral tone of a school are paramount factors, and therefore only schools which rank well in these particulars, as evidenced by rigid, thorough-going, sympathetic inspection, shall be considered eligible for the list.

5. Wherever there is reasonable doubt concerning the efficiency of a school, the Association will accept that doubt as ground sufficient to justify rejection.

6. No school shall be considered unless the regular annual blank furnished for the purpose shall have been filled out and placed on file with the inspector.

7. All schools whose records show an abnormal number of pupils per teacher, as based on average number belonging, even though they may technically meet all requirements, are rejected. The Association recognizes thirty as a maximum.

8. The time for which schools are accredited shall be limited to one year, dating from the time of the adoption of the list by the Association.

9. The organ of communication between accredited schools and the Secretary of the Commission for the purpose of distributing, collecting, and filing the annual reports of such schools and for such other purpose as the Association may direct, is as follows:

a. In states having such an official, the Inspector of Schools appointed by the state university.

b. In other states the Inspector of Schools appointed by the state authority, or, if there is no such official, such person or persons as the Secretary of the Commission may select.

B. For Colleges and Universities.

The Association will decline to consider any college or university:

1. Which has an income, exclusive of tuition, of less than ten thousand dollars a year.

2. Which has fewer than seven distinct departments, organized with separate heads.

3. Which requires for admission less than fifteen secondary school units as defined by the Association.

4. Which requires less than twelve college units, or sixty year-hours, for graduation.

C. For Secondary Schools.

The Association will decline to consider any secondary school:

1. Which has fewer than four teachers, exclusive of the Superintendent.

2. Which requires of any one teacher more than five periods of class-room instruction, each to extend over at least forty minutes in the clear.

3. Which requires for graduation less than fifteen units of secondary school work as defined by the Association.

III. That amendments be made as follows:

1. To the act establishing the Commission on Accredited Schools Sec. (2). That the clause "to define and describe unit courses of study in the various subjects of the high school program" be changed to read "to define and describe unit courses of study in the various subjects of the high school and college program," and the clause "to prepare a list of high schools within the territory of this Association which are entitled to the accredited relationship" be changed to read "to prepare a list of high schools colleges and universities within the territory of this Association that are entitled to membership in the Association."

2. To the Constitution of the Association.

Article III. Change Section 7 to Section 8 and insert as Section 7:

No college or university shall be eligible to membership

which has fewer than seven professors giving their entire time to college and university work, and which requires for graduation less than twelve units or 60 year-hours of college work as defined by the Commission on Accredited Schools and Colleges.

A technical school to be eligible must have entrance and graduation requirements equivalent to those of the college, and must offer courses in pure and applied science of equivalent grade.

To be ranked as a college an institution must have a productive endowment of not less than two hundred thousand dollars.

IV. That the following be adopted as an annual report blank for colleges and universities:

ANNUAL REPORT FOR COLLEGES AND UNIVERSITIES.

Date....................

Name of Institution ....
Address ....
Control (religious or non-sectarian) ....
Educational organization of institution into schools or departments ....
What proportion of work, if any, belongs to secondary school? ....

COLLEGE OR UNIVERSITY STATISTICS.

Number of teachers in each grade of instructing staff—
Professors ....——Men——Women
Associate or acting professors ......——Men——Women
Assistant professors ....——Men——Women
Instructors ....——Men——Women
Assistants ....——Men——Women

Number of students in each collegiate department—
Undergraduate ....——Men——Women
Graduate ....——Men——Women
Professional ....——Men——Women

Value of Plant Used for Instruction—
Grounds .... $———
Buildings .... $———
Equipment .... $———

Number and kind of degrees conferred at last commencement ....
Value of Dormitories and Residences .... $———
Amount of Outstanding Debt, if any.......... $———
Amount of Productive Endowment and Income therefrom ....$———
Amount of Appropriation from State or Denomination ....$———
Annual Income from Tuition .... $———
Amount of Total Annual Income Devoted to Paying Salaries of Teaching Force....... $———
What are Principal Items of Annual Expense, besides pay of Teachers and Assistants....$———

President MacLean also submitted the following:

PROPOSED AMENDMENTS TO THE COMMITTEE'S REPORT FOR INSPECTING AND ACCREDITING COLLEGES.

In I. Strike out "through the Board of Inspectors, etc.," and substitute:

"There shall be two visitors in each State through whom the inspection of Colleges shall be done. One of the inspectors shall be the High School inspector from the state and the other a president or dean of an institution in this Association from outside the state to be appointed by the Commission. The inspector shall be the organ of communication between the college and the commission."

In II. A. amend to read:

For secondary schools. Strike out "schools as used in this section, etc."

In II. A. 9. Add after inspector, "Unless the standard of the School shall warrant the omission of the report for any given year."

In II. A. 11. Add after Association "except as provided in 9."

For II. B. and C. read: B For Colleges and Universities.

1. The minimum scholastic requirement of all instructors shall be equivalent to graduation from a college belonging to this Association, and graduate work equal at least to that required for a Master's degree, it being understood that a Ph. D. is the ideal and that a fair proportion of the instructors have the latter degree.

2. The number of class hours for the professors shall not average to exceed fifteen hours a week, and the same average shall apply to students, with rare exceptions.

3. The proportion of instructors to students shall be taken into account.

4. The average salary of the heads of departments, exclusive of the salary of the President, shall be at least $1,400.

5. The College shall maintain at least ten separate departments or chairs. The heads of these departments shall be devoted to College work.

6. The College shall require for admission not less than fifteen secondary units, as defined by this Association.

7. The College shall require not less than 12 College units, or sixty year-hours for graduation, or 120 semester units.

8. The College must be able to prepare its graduates to enter without conditions as candidates for advanced degrees reputable graduate colleges.

9. The character of the curriculum, the efficiency of instruction, the scientific spirit, the standard for regular degrees, the conservatism in granting honorary degrees, the tone of the institution shall be chief factors in determining its eligibility.

10. The College shall have a permanent endowment of not less than $350,000, or a fixed assured income, exclusive of tuition equivalent to the interest derived from at least $350,000 at 5 per cent.

11. The library shall consist of at least 10,000 volumes selected with reference to College subjects and exclusive of public documents.

12. The laboratory equipment shall be worth not less than $5,000 and so distributed as to establish at least an efficient chemical, physical, botanical, and zoological laboratory.

13. No institution shall be considered for membership or retain membership, unless a regular blank has been filed with the Commission, and is filed triennially unless the inspectors have waived the presentation of the triennial blank.

14. The local inspector shall be the organ of communication between the College and the Commission.

President MacLean then spoke as follows:

President James's address this morning was providential, a magnificent pathfinder for this report, and makes unnecessary certain explanations by way of introduction to the report. The President's address makes clear that the standardizing of colleges is going on apace and that if we educators do not immediately undertake our share of the work we shall have little or no share in it. The work has already come to issue even in the statutes of certain states, and the work is carried on by professional associations not as well equipped pedagogically or educationally for doing it as are associations like this. The President's report further made clear that this Association has been a path-finder in the matter of standardizing. The movement that this report presents to-day is five years old in this Association. It goes back to reports gathered by a committee of which President Thwing was chairman, concerning the standards for an A. B. degree. If you will look into the proceedings of this Association for 1905 you will find all the elements that are essential in this report of to-day. Data were there gathered, and two years ago the Association, in view of the data that had been gathered and in view of a paper presented by Mr. Carman and a paper presented by Mr. Coffeen of Iowa, a secondary school man, instructed this Commission to present a plan for inspecting and accrediting colleges. Your Commission has been so cautious that we have been two years in turning over this subject, and to-day I wish you please to notice that we come before you in a tentative and cautious spirit, as this preface shows.

The members of the committee are not now ready to recommend the adoption of the report in the present form. It is submitted in a shape designed to lead to the discussion of the main features involved in the inspection of colleges.

In taking up the report please remember that it proceeds from the Commission and that the Commission represents equally secondary school men and college men; that the Commission represents not state university or private college but every institution simply on the democratic basis of membership in this Association. Therefore it comes without suspicion of representing either this or that element, secondary school or college, private or public institution, and it comes, in candor, pushed upon us by great national educational movements.

Let us then take up the report and observe, first, "the Commission shall undertake the work of inspecting and accrediting colleges and universities." That has been determined by previous action and of course our report expects that to stand. Then second, in paragraph I. we proceed to say "through the Board of Inspectors, such changes being made in the constitution of the board as may seem advisable in view of the proposed extension of its work." Here is problem number one. I think we will all agree that it should be done through the machinery that has operated so well, but with a readjustment of the machinery to take up the problem of accrediting a different kind of institution. Various suggestions have been made as to how the machinery shall be readjusted. First, it has been suggested that it be the Board of Inspectors, just as it is. These inspectors have experience. They know the feeling. They have the sympathy of the secondary school men and are often talked of as secondary school men from their close companionship with them. They know the trials of the secondary school men, and are their representatives. But the college men at first thought would say, We want college men. It may be replied that the present inspectors are to a man college-bred men; they are in a high sense college men. Secondly, the genius of this Association is to knit together colleges and secondary schools, and therefore these men would have particular significance if they inspect both classes of institutions. They would promote unity, and so there is a group who would have the present Board of Inspectors, just as they are, proceed with this business. There are, however, two sides to the question. The inspectors we happen to know do not seek this job. On the contrary, they are prepared, I fancy, except as you may lay hands on them and put it as a duty to them, to refuse the task.

A second possibility was suggested by one, not a state university man, that the inspection should be by three—appointed by the Commission, namely—the local or state inspector of schools, the State Superintendent of Public Instruction and the President of the State University.

Another suggestion has been made that the inspection should be undertaken by those non-resident in a given state, in order to escape the influences and embarrassments of locality, as judges sometimes change their circuits.

The first amendment proposed on the printed slip is an alternative or something more definite than what is proposed in the report:

"There shall be two visitors in each state through whom the inspection of colleges shall be made. One of the inspectors shall be the high school inspector from the state and the other a president or dean of an institution in this Association from outside the state, to be appointed by the Commission."

There is an economic law that demands that the inspectors shall be as few as possible. The local inspector's expenses are borne. If some one is to come in from outside the state it would be quite sufficient as a financial burden to bear the actual expenses of one man. It is proposed that the one man who comes from outside the state shall be, if you please, more than a professor, more than a mere college graduate; he shall be a man of executive experience, and so a president or dean of any institution in this body named by the Commission. Of course it is clear that your Commission, before proceeding in this delicate matter, would confer with the parties concerned, and there would be an adjustment with reference to both expense and persons that would give efficiency and agreeableness.

Then I may say that if you can agree, first, that what was once proposed by the Association stands and goes forward, that there shall be without delay the inspecting and accrediting of colleges and universities, and, secondly, that your present machinery, with this slight readjustment to meet the conditions, shall do it, you have to-day made it possible for us to proceed. So much the committee trusts you will see your way clear in some form to agree upon.

We come now to what would be the pointers, the general principles, the directions, the criteria, the objective standards, whatever you want to call them, that we are to make use of. It is possible to have more or less of these things set out in greater or less detail. These things can be worked out as you go forward, but there are two sets of pointers before you. On the original preliminary report under A on the first page the present requirements of this Association for accrediting are simply reprinted and extended to apply to the colleges. There is nothing new under A, practically, but the extension to the colleges and universities. And then, inasmuch as the different character of the colleges and universities requires something special, on the top of the second page, under B, there are supplementary points for colleges and universities, four of them. That was the most conservative possible way to indicate the character of criteria with which we would begin this work and let it grow upon our hands. You see the natural objections. Immediately some will say, "There are such essential differences between secondary schools and colleges and universities that it is unwise to adopt by the wholesale these directions that we had for accrediting secondary schools." And some of the directions, as you see, would be somewhat wide of the mark. Therefore the alternative is presented upon your printed slips. Look at B. I am passing over a couple of insignificant amendments to your present regulations that are purely incidental and not of any importance in our report to-day. We go at once, then, to

B, and you will please take B on the slip, with the fourteen points, as a substitute for all that is under A on the original report, leaving what is under A just as it is to apply to the schools, and a substitute also for the four points under B on the second page. These fourteen points would follow the spirit of the points, as far as they are cognate, that you have for schools.

"1. The minimum scholastic requirement of all instructors shall be equivalent to graduation from a college belonging to this Association, and graduate work equal at least to that required for a Master's degree, it being understood that a Ph. D. is the ideal and that a fair proportion of the instructors have the latter degree."

Briefly to analyze, we begin with the teachers. The word instructor is used generically, including professors of all grades and full instructors; it does not include the assistant instructors or the many assistants that are in a college. Otherwise you perceive at once that a small college would be hugely embarrassed, taking, as they often do, some one who has recently graduated or sometimes some one who is experienced as a teacher from the senior students.

A MEMBER: Are we, then, to read professor instead of instructor?

PRESIDENT MACLEAN: It has been suggested by some of the college men that it would greatly relieve the situation if it were amended to read "The minimum scholastic requirement of all professors shall be, etc." They would not consider it too idealistic with the word professor substituted for instructor. But please make it clear that we did not mean by instructor to include all kinds of assistants, but to use it technically from instructor up through professor.

Then, secondly, it would be well to notice that a Master's degree is not required. Some of us are certainly young enough with the spirit of freedom and some of us are old enough with the spirit of experience not to come here with Procrustean technical or paper things, and we use the word equivalent here. We are not putting as much weight on a sheepskin as a casual objector might at first think—"graduate work equal at least to that required for a Master's degree." Then the third point is that we are not Ph. D. fiends. We hold it up as an ideal that a fair proportion of the instructors have the degree; and of course it is understood that this is not retroactive. We did not put that on, because the law and gospel both teach that. So I hope that if you have a first impression that there is undue stiffness or idealization here, you will see that we have made it just as reasonable and progressive as possible.

"2. The number of class hours for the professors shall not average to exceed fifteen hours a week, and the same average shall apply to students, with rare exception."

I think that needs no explanation.

"3. The proportion of instructors to students shall be taken into account."

"Some will ask with a cynical smile, "Does that mean anything? Why not state the proportion?" Because we are growing here, because this Association has done so much by pointing in a certain direction and then going forward and later becoming specific. But we put out the principle, and we will soon find as our inspectors get to work that the colleges have approximated what is a practicable, reasonable proportion; but not to enunciate the principle since there are schools in our region who have not thought of these things would be to stultify ourselves.

"4. The average salary of the heads of departments, exclusive of the salary of the president, shall be at least $1,400."

Please remark that we have had in mind, or attempted to have in mind, the smallest, tenderest, true college. Those we are here to nourish. But quackery colleges, commercial diploma mills, in fact, we must discredit. So this says "average salary of the heads of departments," every word a limitation. We may have in a small college a given professor at $1,000, we may have another at $1,700, another at $1,800. The application is only to the heads of departments. You strike thus an average of $1,400. Secondary school men say, "Well, this is degrading. We average more than $1,400." We thank the Lord you do; but in the colleges, where there has been so much of the spirit of consecration, it is true that the average is low. We submit all these pecuniary statements with great modesty and are quite ready to hear argument.

THE CHAIR: Mr. President, we will have to hasten a little on this. Our time is getting on.

PRESIDENT MACLEAN: I will not read the rest. I think you can all read. I will answer any questions on the rest of the report.

DEAN BIRGE: May I ask one question, Mr. President? Is this system of inspecting and accrediting intended to apply primarily to the colleges that are now members of the Association or is it intended to apply to those who are not members and may apply for membership, or to those who are outside and do not apply for membership, or to all?

PRESIDENT MACLEAN: First, it applies only to colleges that seek the inspection, just as in high schools the inspection is had by invitation. It may apply, therefore, within or without where the inspection is invited. Institutions are members of this body that do not bear an accredited relation at this time and may continue so.

SUPERINTENDENT CARY: Mr. Chairman, may I ask a question? Is there anything this committee can do on the side to determine who can teach and who cannot, in addition to determining whether he has the degree of A. M. or Ph. D.?

PRESIDENT MACLEAN: The question is most timely, and we had that in mind, as you will observe by looking at point 9. "The character of the curriculum, the efficiency of instruction, the scientific spirit," and so forth, and point 9 is more important, as that is a spiritual point, than all your other points put together.

PRESIDENT HILL M. BELL (Drake University): Mr. Chairman, I would like to say No. 3 is pretty good phraseology to apply to both 4 and 10. It seems to me that would come nearer making it possible to recognize those institutions that deserve it and would give more latitude and freedom in the consideration than fixing definite figures.

PRESIDENT MACLEAN: The chairman will say that the suggestion seems to him an admirable one, and it may be explained that the doctrine of proportion was applied in stating figures here. There is, of course, scarcely anything original in these objective standards. We have had before us the objective standards that have been sent out by the State of New York, the State of Pennsylvania, the Carnegie Foundation, the Williamstown conference (that is your own national conference committee), the Iowa State Board of Educational Examiners and the proposed scale of the Collegiate Alumnæ Association. As is well known, $200,000 has been set out, for example, as the endowment fund by the State of Iowa, by the Carnegie Foundation, and if that was to apply to a college of six distinct departments, if you had ten distinct departments $350,000 would be a proportional figure. With reference to salaries the thing is not so clear there, but the college so small that it had but six or seven professors would be likely to have the lowest salaries also and perhaps might have some latitude.

PRESIDENT KIRK: Mr. Chairman, may I ask another question, please? I notice in section 10 of your list you say, "The college shall have a permanent endowment of not less than $350,000." Now I understood the chairman to report in connection with another section of this that this report was not meant to be retroactive. There are several colleges members of this Association now whose interest-bearing endowment is not much above $100,000. Are we to understand that the committee wishes to say that this shall not be retroactive and affect those colleges, but that from now on and for all time, so far as those colleges now in this Association are concerned, even though it may be forty years before they have the $350,000 endowment, they may remain members of this Association?

PRESIDENT MACLEAN: It would be for this Association to say when this should go into effect. It would not be retroactive, that is clear. It might not bear upon those already members of this Association. The chairman would infer it would be put into operation with reference to new accredited colleges, but it would be for the Association to say how to apply this.

PRESIDENT CHARLES E. SHELTON (Simpson College, Iowa): I would like to ask if that is intended to apply to those institutions that do not have any fixed and definite endowment, but depend upon appropriations from legislatures and other bodies entirely for their support?

PRESIDENT MACLEAN: It is so drawn as to take care of either a state or a private institution, "a fixed assured income." So far as I know, every state institution has in fact either a millage tax or a permanent appropriation. There is nothing surer than taxes, except death.

PRESIDENT KIRK: But, Mr. Chairman, there are state institutions that simply receive their support and they have no appropriation for more than two years in advance.

PRESIDENT MACLEAN: The only answer would be that in a fixed legal way you could not say they had an assured income, but as the American people are a moral people and when they have brought forth a child they support it, both history and moral obligation assure this as fixed, better fixed, than statute.

PRESIDENT SHELTON: Are we to take into consideration consecration as well as taxation?

PRESIDENT MACLEAN: We have. If not, we should put in a minimum wage of not less than $2,000.

PRESIDENT SHELTON: For instance, a school that has a denomination of 100,000 in a state, that denomination guaranteeing its support and its care and rising to every emergency, are we justified in saying that the Commission means under such circumstances, as well as the state university, that those people are supposed to be rational in their consecration as well as taxation?

President MacLean: Exactly. That is why it says a fixed, assured income as an equivalent for an endowment.

Professor C. A. Waldo (Purdue University): As I understand the situation, this accrediting committee may act upon colleges and universities that are not already members of this Association and also upon such colleges and also upon such universities as shall invite it to act. Now there undoubtedly is a residuum there, a pretty large one, that will not invite this committee to act. May I ask how you are going to standardize that residuum?

President MacLean: Just as we have done with the high schools. There have been and still are magnificent high schools that have not bowed the knee to this Association. This Association is nothing but a voluntary association, lifting up standards, and those standards are open before the eyes of all men, and those who wish to adhere can get fair judgment and adherence, and those who do not wish to we bless in the name of the Lord.

Professor Walter Libby (Northwestern): I would like to ask the chairman whether there has been any thought of having the secondary school men represented on this examining body? If I understand the minds of some of the high school men whom I have an opportunity of visiting, they would like this visitation to be a sort of mutual thing, not merely that the university men should go out to see them occasionally, but also that they should come to see us. They want to know what will become of their graduates and whether their graduates are going to proper institutions or whether they are going to fake institutions, whether these graduates pass out of the hands of expert men in the high school to go into the hands of inexpert young fledglings, perhaps with Ph. D., who have become attached to the university. Wouldn't it be a feasible thing to have men from our great secondary schools go to these smaller institutions as well as to the larger ones, where they will always be welcome, to see for themselves that they are not marked by charlatanry and quackery, as some of them are inclined to suspect, and whether in all the institutions the same care is exercised over the studies and character of the freshman class as has been set forth in the paper by Dean Clark this afternoon?

PRESIDENT MACLEAN: The remarks seem to me most timely, and our thought was that the secondary school men are on this Commission, as many of them as college men on the Commission. This work is really done by your Commission. Of course you immediately reply, "But you have provided the inspectors." They have been named often secondary school men. They know the spirit of these secondary school men. They live, move and have their being with them, and the thought was that the present inspectors would know what those secondary school men would like to have looked into in the colleges, and that the second man, the president or dean, would placate anybody who might be suspicious from the college point of view. Of course, it would be possible to amend here—there is nothing but the economic law in the way—and have a secondary school man, or you might say president, dean or principal or superintendent, for that man from the outside.

PROFESSOR LIBBY: I admire your ingenuity, Mr. President, and the way you put it.

PRESIDENT MACLEAN: These points we have thought of ourselves.

PROFESSOR LIBBY: I am trying to prove that I am what you claim I am, a secondary school man as well as a university man. I believe some of us have that character, but I do not know but what our extra university experience might very well be supplemented by some co-operation from secondary school men of a high standard.

PRESIDENT MACLEAN: How would it be if this commission of two should use a liberty to invite from the neighborhood a prominent superintendent or principal, high school man, to go with them? The matter of expense is the matter that holds us down, you see, in making a large body.

PROFESSOR LIBBY: The expense of a secondary school man would be no more than that of an imported dean or a president; less, I imagine.

PRESIDENT KIRK: Mr. Chairman of the Committee, I notice in section 2, in the upper part of the report, that one of the inspectors shall be the high school inspector from the state. Some states have several high school inspectors, a high school inspector from each university and a state high school inspector that is not connected at all with any institution. I suppose you mean by this that in a state which has a state high school inspector independent of all institutions he would be the one through whom this business would be done?

PRESIDENT MACLEAN: Unless otherwise designated by the Commission. If you will turn to the organization of the Commission you will find that it is provided that the Commission may designate where there is more than one inspector or where there is no inspector. This is all to run under the law as now established. Of course, that might be made definite in the report.

PRESIDENT KIRK: In your first report, your preliminary report, under 12, you say: "A. In states having such an official, the inspector of schools appointed by the State University, but in other states," that is, in states not having a university inspector, I assume, "the inspector appointed by the state authority"; but in your amendment here you simply say: "One of the inspectors shall be the high school inspector from the state." There are some states who have a high school inspector not provided for by law, no statute providing for him; he is just an appointee of the university, while some of the states have by law provided for a high school inspector and a state elementary school inspector. Then further it is said the inspections of this inspector shall be received at certain state institutions. Your explanation, it seems to me, does not clear that up. And then down here at the bottom you say, "The local inspector shall be the organ of communication between the college and the Commission." I do not understand what individual you mean to designate as the local inspector.

PRESIDENT MACLEAN: The local inspector would be "the" inspector referred to in section 12. The inspector was supposed to be under the spirit of our present statute which you read, point A, which would be the state inspector where there is one, and where there is not, one to be designated by the Commission.

A MEMBER: Then the state inspector would mean the one appointed by the state and not by the university?

PRESIDENT MACLEAN: If that is the relation in that state. It is just your present scheme with reference to inspectors.

PRESIDENT KIRK: I beg your pardon for asking so

many questions, but I am unable to understand whether the chairman is making a report which, in behalf of his committee, he recommends for adoption, or whether he is securing our criticisms with a view eventually to having a report written out.

PRESIDENT MACLEAN: The answer, I think, is in what we have at the beginning: "We are not now ready to recommend the adoption of the report in the present form. It is submitted with an especial design to lead to the discussion of the main features involved in the inspection of colleges."

PRESIDENT C. H. RAMMELKAMP (Illinois College): Since questions and criticisms are apparently what are invited by the chairman of the committee, I should like to make a few suggestions and possibly criticisms.

It seems to me that when one is attempting to mark out the way, as the chairman says, it is somewhat dangerous to be altogether specific and detailed and to bring in points about which there may be considerable doubt. For example, we have here fourteen different requirements. That at once, I think, raises the question whether too many detailed regulations and specifications are not inserted. Usually in attempting to get together on some proposition we lay down three or four or five fundamental questions and try to agree on them. For example, it seems to me to be rather unnecessary to have both requirement 10 as to the amount of endowment and also requirement 4 as to the amount of salary. I think the two will usually go together, and that an institution with a certain amount of endowment will naturally pay a certain average salary. It seems to me from that point of view there might be very well a revision of some of these recommendations of the committee.

I get the impression from the report, the preliminary report that is before us, that these recommendations involve a rather higher standard than that set up by the Carnegie Foundation. The recommendations here involve a larger endowment, as I recall now. The Carnegie Foundation requires $200,000.

PRESIDENT MACLEAN: Two hundred thousand dollars, but you will recall the $200,000 is for six chairs.

PRESIDENT RAMMELKAMP: It is an increase both of endowment and the number of instructors. I think that the trustees of the Carnegie Foundation felt that in setting the standard up they have set up somewhat of an ideal. Now our committee apparently is trying to set up a higher ideal, at least from those two points of view, than that set up by the trustees of the Carnegie Foundation. It would seem to me, therefore, that that would be a point that would have to be pretty carefully considered. Possibly since the Carnegie Foundation had in view Southern institutions, which in general, it is admitted, are not up to the standards of these Northern institutions, the committee is justified in this higher standard, but I should think it would require careful looking into. It is a higher standard that you are maintaining or attempting to recommend here, is it not?

PRESIDENT MACLEAN: It is. The Carnegie Foundation, as everyone knows, on account of their desire to help Southern institutions, set the low standard, which they hope steadily to raise, and this is on the same proportion relatively—ten, $350,000.

Let us get out on to the table, so far as the President will allow us time, anything else that will help this report.

PROFESSOR WALDO: I am not clear with reference to

the interaction of Nos. 1 and 9, as they have been explained; that is, as to what amount of importance the committee attaches to certain kinds of preparation for college work. The chairman of the committee has said that the ideal is that a college instructor shall have a Ph. D. degree, and then he afterwards assented that efficiency of instruction is paramount. Now suppose that two men are under consideration for instructors in a college—I put it instructors, young men coming to take care of certain parts of the lower grade work—and one of them is a Ph. D. and is not a good teacher, the other is not a Ph. D. and is a good teacher, which does the committee recommend?

PRESIDENT MACLEAN: I know what I would recommend as a president. I know what you would recommend. I know what Dean West over there would recommend. We would like some good teachers in the colleges and the secondary school men would like us to have more good teachers in the colleges.

PROFESSOR WALDO: I thought that point had been left somewhat uncertain.

PRESIDENT MACLEAN: These are simply pointers to be inter-related by judicious administration.

DEAN BIRGE: There is one other question I would like to ask. Do you intend to bring technical schools in with the colleges? I notice in the report it seems to intend to bring in the technical schools.

PRESIDENT MACLEAN: We have proposed no amendment to what is under C for secondary schools except verbal amendments to make perfect, and also to add a footnote.

DEAN BIRGE: B, the amendment to article 3, technical schools to be eligible—equal to college, and so on.

PRESIDENT MACLEAN: Yes, that is part of the report.

DEAN BIRGE: I would ask the relation to that of the requirement of students for more than fifteen hours per week, as given in point 3 of your proposed amendments. I think that engineering schools ordinarily require more than fifteen hours a week.

PRESIDENT MACLEAN: It was supposed that the equation that has ordinarily operated, Dean Birge, would prevail. That is a detail that might well be set out, but, as has been remarked, we have gone a good deal into detail to begin with, perhaps too much. But the usual equation in adjusting the relation between colleges of liberal arts and applied science is supposed to work.

A MEMBER: In paragraph 2 of the introduction, did I understand you to say that in the appointment of a man from outside the state to take place on the examining board a conference would be held with the colleges to be examined?

PRESIDENT MACLEAN: Well, perhaps I virtually did say that. I suspect I did say just that thing. What I meant was that this Commission when it begins to function will look over these fields and will study what is just, intelligent and agreeable for the communities.

THE MEMBER: Would it be objectionable to insert some such provision as that?

PRESIDENT MACLEAN: No objection at all, sir, only we are trying not to get too much in the way of detail and to suppose that the same confidence that has prevailed in our Commission heretofore—and I think perhaps they have deserved it—will prevail.

THE MEMBER: One or two other questions of minor importance. Under 2 you say that the instructor shall not average to exceed fifteen hours a week. In the case of the division of a freshman class into sections and a teacher had two or three sections, is that to limit his class work to work with the freshman class is case he taught three sections a day?

PRESIDENT MACLEAN: You notice there is that blessed word "average." It is the sphere of mathematics to take you into the infinite. As you are aware, I don't know much about mathematics; it is always infinite to me. It is not to average to exceed fifteen hours. That might include an instructor at a certain kind of work that would have twenty hours, and here is a professor with nine or ten hours.

MR. RIGG: Let me call attention to another point: Instructors is not the word used, but professors, fifteen hours a week.

A MEMBER: "The college shall maintain at least ten separate departments or chairs." One statement that was made led me to infer that that meant professors; is that right?

PRESIDENT MACLEAN: Yes, if I understand you. Put your question, and then I want to make a remark.

THE MEMBER: That is my question.

PRESIDENT MACLEAN: This is the twentieth century standard, to be honest in educating our boys and girls in a college. Can we, except as there are very peculiar circumstances, honestly educate collegiately a boy or girl today without ten heads of departments or ten chairs? Now let us see: We ought to have a professor of English—we will begin with the mother tongue. 1. We ought to have at least one professor for modern languages, French, German, Spanish are called for now. 2. We ought to have at least one professor for Greek and Latin. 3. We ought to have at least one professor for mathematics. 4. He can have astronomy, too, or something else, if you want to. There will be great liberty here.

THE MEMBER: That is my point exactly.

PRESIDENT MACLEAN: You may make such combinations as you please if you have ten chairs.

THE MEMBER: When a man can teach pure mathematics and astronomy, is that one department or two?

PRESIDENT MACLEAN: That is one department. We have four—

THE MEMBER: My question is answered. Thank you.

PRESIDENT MACLEAN: You would not dare have less than three physical sciences; 3 and 4 make 7. Where is the college that knows any prestige as a college that does not have a chair of philosophy? 8. Where is the college that would dare to have less than one chair in history, all the field of history? 9. Where is the college that would dare have less than one chair in the economic, the political, the social sciences? Would you send your boy to a college where there were less than ten masters of that sort? Now let us be honest with the boys and girls. We are talking about a college.

THE MEMBER: I do not want to be put down as anti this. I am simply asking for information. I believe very cordially in just what you say.

SUPERINTENDENT A. F. NIGHTINGALE: Mr. President, the hour is getting very late, people are passing out. It seems to me we ought to accomplish something along this line, and I would like to move that the report be recommitted with suggestions from this Association, and that we spend the next ten minutes in presenting these suggestions, one after another, to be recorded for the committee.

The motion was seconded.

THE CHAIR: Is this satisfactory to the chairman of the Commission?

PRESIDENT MACLEAN: Entirely so.

The motion was carried.

In accordance with the motion additional suggestions were offered by members of the Association.

THIRD SESSION, SATURDAY MORNING, MARCH 28.

The Association was called to order by the President at 10 o'clock a. m.

The Secretary of the Executive Committee presented his report, as follows:

DEAN THOMAS ARKLE CLARK: There was presented to the Association at its last meeting the following amendments to the constitution, which having been on the table for one year now are before us for final action.

First, that Article 3, section 3, be stricken out. This article reads as follows:

"In the membership of the Association the representation of higher and secondary education shall be as nearly equal as possible." This is before us for action.

THE CHAIR: This amendment that was presented at the last meeting has been before the executive committee for a year, and the Association will now proceed to vote upon it. Striking it out will practically enable the Association to increase the representation of the colleges or the representation of the secondary schools without reference to the other element.

PRINCIPAL J. E. ARMSTRONG (Englewood High): I feel that the amendment to the constitution is a good one, and that there is no particular danger that the high school men will in this way dominate the Association. Of course, when this institution was formed there was the feeling that the membership should be kept equal in order that, everything considered, the two parts of the system should be equally represented, but, as we all know, the high school men are scattered over a large territory; they are not able to get away from their schools in many cases; they in nearly all cases have to bear their own expenses, while the colleges are more accessible to the institution. They are men who perhaps have the more vital interest in the questions which are to be discussed by this Association, but it seems to me that we are simply going to be able to hold the interest of a larger number of secondary schools by admitting them to membership, and the history of the past shows that a very large proportion of the secondary schools hold their interest by paying their dues and by receiving, perhaps reading, the proceedings, and keeping posted as to the requirements for admission to the universities. So I believe the policy is a good one of having a large number of secondary schools interested enough in the Association to hold their membership, and I hope the motion will prevail.

THE CHAIR: I may say that this does not change the method of election to membership in the Association at all. It simply abolishes that one restriction. Any further discussion?

The motion was put and carried.

DEAN CLARK: The second amendment is that the following section be added: "If the dues of any member shall remain unpaid for two years such membership in the Association shall lapse."

On motion, the amendment was adopted.

DEAN CLARK: It was voted by the executive committee to recommend the following also, not as an amendment to the constitution but as an interpretation of the constitution: "Colleges and secondary schools whose membership has lapsed shall become members only by making a new application, which shall be approved by the executive committee of the Association."

THE CHAIR: What shall be done with this recommendation of the executive committee?

On motion, the recommendation was adopted.

DEAN CLARK: The executive committee recommend the following for institutional membership in the Association:

Baker University, Baldwin, Kansas, President, Lemuel H. Murlin;

Purdue University, Lafayette, Indiana, President, W. E. Stone;

Illinois College, Jacksonville, Illinois, President, C. H. Rammelkamp;

Marietta College, Marietta, Ohio, President, A. J. Perry;

Kenyon College, Gambier, Ohio, President, William F. Pierce;

Coe College, Cedar Rapids, Iowa, President, William Wilberforce Smith;

Case School of Applied Science, Cleveland, Ohio, President, Charles S. Howe;

Chicago Teachers' College, Chicago, Illinois, President, Ella F. Young;

Illinois State Normal School, Normal, Illinois, President, David Felmley;

Eastern Illinois State Normal School, Charleston, Illinois, President L. C. Lord;

Western Illinois Normal School, Macomb, Illinois, President, Alfred Bayliss;

Southern Illinois Normal School, Carbondale, Illinois, President, D. B. Parkinson;

Northern Illinois Normal School, De Kalb, Illinois, President, John W. Cook;

Grand Prairie Seminary, Onarga, Illinois, President, H. H. Frost;

Lincoln High School, Lincoln, Nebraska, Principal, F. W. Sanders;

Fargo High School, Fargo, North Dakota, Principal, W. E. Hoover.

On motion, the recommendations were approved.

DEAN CLARK: It was voted also to recommend that the following institutions who were once members of the Association but whose membership has lapsed, be readmitted:

University of Minnesota, Minneapolis, Minnesota;

Wheaton College, Wheaton, Illinois;

On motion, the recommendation was approved.

DEAN CLARK: The following are recommended for individual membership:

Mr. C. P. Carey, State Superintendent of Schools, Madison, Wisconsin;

Superintendent C. C. Schmidt, Jamestown, North Dakota;

Professor Frank E. Thompson, University of Colorado;

President F. B. Gault, Vermillion, South Dakota;

Richard Heyward, Inspector of Schools, Grand Forks, North Dakota;

Professor F. G. Hubbard, University of Wisconsin, Madison, Wisconsin.

The motion and the recommendation of the committee was adopted and the individuals named above were elected to membership.

THE CHAIR: Report of the committee on the audit of the Treasurer's report, Professor Waldo, chairman.

PROFESSOR WALDO: Mr. President, in making out this report one member of the committee, Mr. Smart, was not present, and I could not secure his services at the time that the committee took action. However, it is signed by two members of the committee.

"The auditing committee have compared the items of expense with the vouchers and have added the items in the accounts, and find the Treasurer's report agrees with these in every particular.

"C. A. WALDO,
"FRANK HAMSHER,
"Committee."

On motion, the report was adopted and ordered entered on the minutes.

THE CHAIR: Committee on time and place of meeting, Mr. F. L. Bliss, chairman. Is the committee ready to report?

MR. F. L. BLISS: Mr. President, the committee on time and place of meeting beg to submit the following report:

"The committee begs to recommend that the next annual meeting of the Association be held at the Auditorium Hotel, Chicago, the date to be fixed by the executive committee as near April 1, 1909, as may be practicable.

"F. L. BLISS,
"FRANK W. BALLOU."

I would say also that the third member of this committee we were unable to find to sign the report.

On motion, the report was adopted.

Moved that the members of any of committees, or the chairmen of the same, may incur such expense in carrying on their work to be defrayed by the Association as they may have secured the approval of the executive committee for in advance of incurring the expense.

The motion was put and carried.

THE CHAIR: We have two other reports left over from yesterday that perhaps we will call for now—the report of the committee of ten of which Mr. Carman was chairman, upon this question of units.

DIRECTOR CARMAN: The committee of ten, appointed to consider the definition of a unit course of study in general, after considering the matter in detail, recommend the following definition for the present, with the understanding that the Commission shall be asked to investigate the matter fully and report later: "A unit course of study is defined as a course covering a school year of not less than thirty-six weeks, with four or five periods of at least forty-five minutes per week." The only change made in the original form as printed in our report of 1902 is that thirty-five weeks is changed to thirty-six weeks.

THE CHAIR: You have heard the report of the committee. What shall be done with it?

A MEMBER: Mr. Chairman, I raise the question as to whether or not the statement was made correctly by the secretary in saying that the limit of the period is forty-five minutes. The present status is forty minutes, is it not?

DIRECTOR CARMAN: The original definition as adopted and published in 1902 was forty-five minutes. The Board of Inspectors have interpreted that as forty minutes in the clear. It seemed wise to the committee to leave it forty-five minutes, with the understanding that the time for the change of classes is included; therefore it was left as it was originally made, forty-five minutes. That was the action of the committee. If I am wrong I shall be glad to be corrected by any member of the committee.

On motion, the report of the committee was accepted.

THE CHAIR: President MacLean, of Iowa, chairman of the committee on classification of colleges.

PRESIDENT MACLEAN: Mr. President, the committee unanimously recommends that the report presented yesterday be re-committed to the Commission and that the following be adopted at this time:

1. That the Commission undertake the work of inspecting and accrediting colleges of liberal arts, whether separate or in universities, through a committee of three in each State. The committee shall be constituted as follows: The first member shall be an inspector of schools.

(a) In States having such an official the inspector of schools appointed by the State university.

(b) In other States the inspector of schools appointed by the State authority, or if there is no such official such person as the secretary of the Commission may select.

This is the present rule of this Association with reference to inspectors.

The second member of the committee shall be a president or dean of a college institution in this Association selected by the officers of the Commission.

The third member shall be a superintendent or principal of a secondary school in this Association selected by the officers of the Commission.

The inspector shall be the organ of communication between the college and the Commission.

2. The inspection will be upon invitation.

3. The accrediting shall be by vote of the Association upon the recommendation of the Commission based upon the report of the committee of inspection.

4. The Commission shall report at the next meeting of this Association the standards for accrediting.

5. The officers of the Commission are authorized to make blanks to secure the necessary data for the use of the accrediting committee.

6. In case the Association at its present meeting is ready to set out the standards for accrediting, point 4 above is withdrawn.

THE CHAIR: What is to be done with this report? This practically continues all debated points, I believe, to the Commission for further report.

PRESIDENT MACLEAN: Unless the Association wishes to proceed with reference to standards.

THE CHAIR: In other words, these various points are simply formulizations of what the Association is doing or has done already, the main report being recommitted for further consideration. What is to be done with this report?

It was moved and seconded that the report be adopted.

The motion was adopted.

President William O. Thompson, of Ohio State University, then presented the following paper on "Moral Character in the Recommendation and Certification of Teachers."

MORAL CHARACTER IN THE RECOMMENDATION AND CERTIFICATION OF TEACHERS.

From the very beginning good moral character has been assumed as vital for a teacher. No one has ever advocated that this requirement was a matter of indifference In fact, a good moral character in American experience has been assumed as the background upon which all individual efficiency has been written. Whether written into the statutes or not, there is no place in this country where responsible men and women would be willing to entrust the interests of the community to people of uncertain morals or of known delinquency. This requirement, however, has always been stated in general and somewhat indefinite terms. So long as the external life of the individual did not clash with the accepted customs of the community, the element of moral character was regarded satisfactory. No very definite inquiry upon this subject or careful examination into the effects of the moral character of the teacher upon the pupil has ever been made. A large amount of testimony could easily be gathered which would disclose the fact that hundreds and thousands of teachers, by their moral excellence, have inspired pupils and students to better living and even to better scholarship. This testimony, however, is more or less general but is not to be discredited on that account. On the other hand, no measure has ever been made of the damaging effects that have come from disclosing to the public mind the lapses from high ideals and good morals than have occurred in the experience of teachers. There would be general agreement that in this general and popular sense the moral character and with it the good reputation of the teachers of the country is of the highest importance. Nor could words be too strong in expressing the regret when unfortunate disclosures have shattered the faith of the public in an occasional teacher here or there.

In addition to these general considerations, the topic assigned evidently suggests the desire to be a little more specific and discover, if possible, a direct connection between the moral character of the candidate to teach and the desired results of character building in those who are taught. Doubtless this inquiry has been stimulated by the general awakening of the American conscience and by the deepening conviction that the results of education are to be measured more in the future from the ethical than from the merely intellectual point of view. A hasty review of the educational literature and the discussions at educational gatherings will reveal the fact that moral character looms up large as one of the great aims of all education. There is a growing conviction that we cannot be indifferent to the ethical ideals obtaining in those who have been enjoying the opportunity and discipline of our schools. Manifestly, we cannot expect these results to be better than the agencies used in producing them. On the general theory that "a good tree bringeth forth good fruit," the public is anxious that the moral character of our leaders shall be reliable and trustworthy. The widespread influence of education adds to the importance of this question. Every philanthropic, patriotic, and humanitarian motive puts a new emphasis upon this requisite in a teacher.

As already intimated, the older measures of moral character have been somewhat general and indefinite. It has usually been so indefinite that a person without particular offense to community ideals was regarded as a person of good moral character. This was chiefly a negative view of morals. Because one did no outlandish thing he was assumed to be good. In many instances this assumption was probably justified. In the homogeneous community of somewhat simple life there would naturally be no very severe or exacting tests of a positive sort and the absence of public transgression was about all that was required. It was always easy to testify to the good moral character of young men and young women. Probably in thousands of instances teachers in their teens began under such general approval but this carried no accurate information as to the ideals that ruled in their lives. The desire to teach was probably taken as an evidence of a worthy ambition and therefore of a certain idealism indicating a life of a little higher character than the average. This was doubtless true, but it was entirely consistent with the lack of maturity and strength essential to any accurate definition of character. The fact that a great many of such teachers developed into men and women of high character does not prove that the old tests were adequate; in fact it rather proves that whatever of good came from such methods was accidental rather than intentional.

In consideration of the importance of this requisite in a teacher, one must take into account the fact that a great many foreign ideals have obtained in the minds of newly-made Americans. Of course, America has been largely filled with a foreign population. In the earlier days, however, the man who sought this country sought it for certain definite reasons under the general theory of religious and political freedom and the pursuit of liberty and happiness. These early men had sturdy convictions upon the questions of fundamental religion and morality. They determined the social ideals of character and early American life. It is a matter of common observation that the emigration into this country in later years has been of a different character and that in thousands of instances men come not out of any conviction that America offered an opportunity for civil and religious liberty but from the fact that certain commercial interests in this country were eagerly searching for cheap labor. Many who have come under this motive have been totally lacking in the high ideals current two generations ago. It is also a matter of common observation that the children of these people often become the teachers of American youth and that they are more or less under the sway of the family ideas as to religion, morality, and civic virtue. It is needless to say that these people do not represent the historic spirit in American life. Neither the first nor the second generation has been completely Americanized. The problem of the school in many of our cities and, indeed, in many of our institutions of higher learning, has been to assimilate these elements and to convert them to the American position. No theory of freedom or personal liberty can be justified that looks toward a compromise between Oriental, European, and American ideals. These conditions seem to warrant the statement that the tests of moral character in the teaching force of the present generation need to be more careful, perhaps, more rigid than heretofore, unless we are willing to accept a sort of composite result which shall lack the characteristic features of American ideals.

I am not disposed to affirm that the American ideals have lowered or that we cling with less tenacity to our ideals. Without pessimism, however, one must see that there is a struggle in our country between what may be called the home and the foreign ideals. Unless we are to be defeated in a measure, or unless we are willing to haul down our banner of high ideals, the American school, which should be the doorway to all citizenship, must be directed and controlled by teachers of positive moral conviction, whose beliefs work out in a definite effort to secure the highest results in the moral character of pupils. There is some evidence that our generous freedom has furnished opportunity for all sorts of vagaries to find lodgment in the public mind. The toleration of such things is probably necessary, but we should be awake to the fact that the prevalence of such ideals is a menace to American morals. The school is one of the great agencies to counteract these tendencies.

The spirit of religious freedom and the desire to have our schools free from any sectarian bias meets universal approval. We must recognize, however, that in our eagerness not to impose upon the rights of others there is danger that we fail to carry the message of instruction. Mere theorists have so exaggerated the dangers of religious instruction in education and have so emphasized the importance of non-sectarianism that many teachers have felt relieved of responsibility for the moral character of students and have drifted into a kind of indifference toward moral issues. Such inactivity comes perilously near being moral delinquency in the teacher.

It is worth while to call attention to the fact that increasing population, highly diversified society, and extensive division of labor, all unite to make the moral problems of society more vital and fundamental than is possible in a more primitive condition. Every progressive city must define rights and duties more carefully than a village must do. The older society becomes the more important it is that the relations between people and the effect of every man's conduct upon his neighbor's welfare shall be clearly defined and universally understood. Ethics at the bottom is the science of human relationships. The questions of integrity, of honor, of truthfulness, of obedience to law, and of the binding force of contracts are infinitely more intense in a crowded city than in a partially settled rural district. Without offering any suggestion as to the sanctions of morality, it is manifest that the teacher who proposes to train citizens for such a life must be well trained in, and sympathetic with these vital questions to society. Whether any person should be recommended to teach or legally certified to teach who is not competent to discriminate between the true and the false in these difficult questions and who is not heartily in accord with approved American ideals, is a question of very serious doubt. To employ teachers who fail in these particulars is to endanger the results which we all desire.

We need not disguise the difficulty in applying satisfactory tests of moral character. It is probably true that we cannot always be assured of the individual. All legal requirements will be more or less formal. For that reason they will probably be to some degree inadequate. The state, however, is warranted for its own sake in making a sincere effort to secure an honest assent to the formal requirements of good morals. Whether examination in fundamental and elementary ethics is desirable, is worthy of consideration. All schools preparing teachers should insist upon it. We must always keep in mind that all formal examinations are in a degree failures in the sense that they do not disclose real character. Some most important qualifications cannot be tabulated on paper.

It seems altogether feasible to discover the ideals that dominate the individual. "As a man thinketh in his heart, so is he." It would require some moral courage to reject an applicant to teach who met all intellectual requirements but whose social or moral ideals were out of harmony with what I conceive to be the American spirit. If school officers regarded a certificate as simply a legal document and would carefully inquire into the personal life and character of candidates, it would be possible to eliminate undesirable candidates. I believe this discrimination on the part of superintendents and Boards of Education and of college authorities to be an important duty that ought to be faithfully met.

The discussion of this paper was lead by President John W. Cook, Northern State Normal School, DeKalb, Illinois, as follows:

MORAL CHARACTER IN THE RECOMMENDATION AND CERTIFICATION OF TEACHERS.

Mr. President and members of the Association: Although President Thompson has not arranged his address under the forms of firstly, secondly, thirdly, it seemed as it was revealed to me by study of the paper submitted to cover the ground very thoroughly. Certain additions have been made to the paper since the original draft was sent to me that make it cover the ground still more completely. The problem which we are to discuss, if we are to give it a practical character, seems to me to be an extremely difficult one, difficult because we are endeavoring in this Association to determine things and these things that we are discussing this morning are extraordinarily difficult to determine in any practical way. The subject seemed comparatively simple when I first began to reflect upon it, but as I thought more and more upon it the difficulties increased with great rapidity.

There seem to be two matters involved in the discussion, first, the certification of teachers, and, second, the recommendation of teachers. The first of those we shall have very little trouble over. The second it seems to me we may have a great deal to do with, for our institutions from which persons are selected to engage in teaching work are expected to certify to the character of those persons; and now that many colleges and universities have arranged for committees who are especially to exercise that function, it gives them a control which they have not heretofore had. Of course normal schools are always called upon to speak as to the character of their graduates, and they can usually determine two things, first, whether they are fit to graduate as determined from this point of view, and, in the second place, as to whether they are fit to be employed even if they have not graduated. It is unnecessary to discuss the question of personal morality. Of course every organization requires of those who are members of it a certain set of activities. These requirements may be said, I suppose, to constitute a sort of minimum character that will be looked to and examined in order to see whether the person is qualified to enter that organization. The state, since it has assumed the control of education, prescribes certain requisites in addition to intellectual requirements; it sets up a certain general, very general requirement, to the effect that those who receive certificates shall be persons of good moral character. We rest upon no very definite, clear specification of qualities.

Most of those who have the certification of teachers can not know very much about them, and so they rely upon recommendations, and generally I think the reliance is comparatively safe from one point of view, that is, as to the personal qualities in this matter of morality of the candidate. Yet there are really very different standards. I have visited quite a number of times a certain county in this state in which the pedagogical societies formerly met—I am not sure now as to their meeting—in the leading beer saloon of the city, and nothing was thought of it, because the community sentiment was in harmony with that sort of thing. I think that the pedagogic quality of their doctrine was very good. I can not speak advisedly as to the beer. I was present on more than one occasion when questions were discussed, and the interesting thing about it was that the superintendent of the city (and he was subsequently for two terms the Superintendent of Public Instruction of the State of Illinois), had for his special hobby the formation of moral character in the young, and worked to that end, and he accomplished a very great work. Perhaps it is well to say in passing that the German estimate of the saloon is very different from the American estimate of it, chiefly because the German saloon in German communities, is very different indeed from the American saloon in American communities. The Germans drink beer and the Americans run to a more ardent fluid.

Now I am not sure that we can do anything at all in changing this specification. The county superintendent is the main examiner under our laws in Illinois, and he is obliged to certify that the candidate is of good moral character, which means that he has not seriously affronted public opinion as to the estimate of his conduct.

All that the county superintendent has done by his certification is to constitute a certain group of persons from among whom the teachers may be selected; but the community is entirely at liberty to exercise its opinion as to those persons, and should know about them. I asked the Secretary of the Association what field he thought this discussion should cover, and he said all classes of schools. I suppose those classes of schools would be included under the general category of the elementary school and the secondary school and the college or higher educational schools.

The matter is entirely under the control of the higher institutions, because those persons are not obliged to be certificated. You go where you please to make your selections and you determine as to the qualifications on the side of morality as to these people whom you will employ. With the secondary schools, however, and the elementary schools, the proposition is materially different. The question, then, that has arisen in my mind, and that has given me a great deal of anxiety so far as I have had anxiety with respect to this discussion, was this: What shall we do in the recommendation of teachers beyond the ordinary requirement of common morality? It is not enough that one to be a teacher shall simply be a person of ordinary moral character, of good moral character. There must be on the part of the teacher the further consciousness that his business, his main business, is to see to it that the outcome of his work is a moral product, distinctly and unqualifiedly, an energetic moral product, a product that is conscious of the character of its activity and scrupulously careful with regard to it.

These three types of institutions develop three different sets of teachers. The subject is to be approached from one point of view in the elementary school; it is approached from a different point of view in the secondary school, where these tremendous forces which come in with adolescence are energizing in their extraordinary way, and the attitude is still different in the higher institutions of learning. I think I may say, although I can hardly pose as an expert with regard to this matter, that there is unfortunately in the university and college a certain indifference perhaps, not in thought but in the exercise of influence upon the pupil. The thought I think was well expressed here yesterday by somebody who said that the good ones can take care of themselves and the poor ones mostly drop out any way, because it is poor material and is not worth our effort. The very question we were discussing yesterday of endeavoring to influence the freshmen is along this very line. I find very great difference, for illustration, in the normal school between those persons who are set aside as advisers, in their influence upon those under their charge. It is our plan to divide up our school, placing a group here and a group there under these advisers who are supposed to look after them patiently and faithfully; but I find the greatest difference in the interest which they manifest in regard to it. I think the matter is easily explained, because in the higher institutions of learning the element of knowledge, the intellectual aspect of the situation, is far more prominent. People go to the university and to the college in order especially to enlarge their store of knowledge, and it is perfectly natural, I suppose, that the teachers should be engaged with those conceptions, those employments, rather than with other employments where they feel extreme solicitude for the individual student. They think by that time a person ought to have developed enough personality to look after himself.

If we turn to the secondary and to the elementary school, we find there distinct and definite problems of a moral character. If the schools are disposed to adopt the Socratic proposition that knowledge is virtue, then they are satisfied that if they instruct these people well and they are excellent scholars, we may rest satisfied with their conduct. But we know very well we can not be satisfied with that. We must supplement the Socratic with the Aristotelian view, that is, that the formation of moral habits is the thing upon which we must rely and to which we must turn our attention with the greatest solicitude all through the elementary school and into the life of the adolescents in the secondary school. And, furthermore, if we would make these people those who, in the language of Rosenkrantz, consciously select the good, we must rationalize these habits, and we may advantageously study Aristotle in that connection.

Thus our solicitude with regard to these persons whom we recommend will be determined from two points of view, the first as to their personal character. Are they people who not only meet the standard of the community, but are they, in addition to that, idealists in this matter of character? Do they really give the matter attention, and do they consciously struggle to achieve superiority, because in the attitude of teacher one's moral character should be a conspicuous fact. We know that all through the elementary and secondary schools the principle of imitation is operating with tremendous energy, and the teacher should be such a person as feels consciously the joy of the moral life and the necessities of it. He should have those high ideals, as I said awhile ago. He should be the idealist, who has a pride in, and a hunger and a thirst for, the moral life.

Furthermore, ought we not to expect from them a thorough interest in the moral aspects of instruction so that the outcome of their teaching shall quite inevitably be not only an acquaintance with the general principles of ethics but also a skill in the practical adaptation of the general principles of ethics to the production of a moral life? Ought we not, then, to pick out those who are interested in the moral aspect of education? Can we not in some way through our recommending committees do something to impress these young people who aspire to be teachers with the fact that we are looking after that sort of thing? As a rather low incentive, I have noticed that people who desire to get recommendations usually adapt their lives to what will get that recommendation. That is a little dangerous, I fancy. It ought to come with spontaneity. Nothing is of any value except the purest self-determination, and the situation is so delicate that if we touch the bloom of the flower it is possible the very thing that we are seeking for will fall to ashes in our grasp. That renders it extremely difficult.

Now what can we do? Can we in a way popularize this conception in the schools that we expect this active and energetic attitude toward the production of moral character in pupils? If we can do that and have it generally understood in these institutions where we propose to recommend young men and young women for teachers that they can not hope for any cordial recommendation from those who have that function in charge unless they take the attitude toward it which we hope will eventuate in something like genuine results.

I have not time to discuss the awakening which has come to us from Herbartianism, which has been potent in changing the mental attitude of many of those who are interested in the work. It has done its work and we do not need to talk very much about it, just as the old child study movement has done its work and we do not need to talk very much about it.

I trust, then, that the attitude of those who have the function of recommending teachers will be changed somewhat if we thoroughly discuss this question which has been submitted by the executive committee.

Dean C. M. Woodward then presented the following:

Mr. President, I would like to ask the personal privilege for one minute.

We were all deeply shocked and grieved yesterday to hear of the death of Superintendent F. L. Soldan, of St. Louis. You have known him and I have known him. I have known him for over forty years and have been associated with him in educational work for twelve years. I have been a member of the Board of Education while he has been the superintendent of our schools in St. Louis. I offer this resolution for the Association to adopt:

"Resolved, That the members of the North Central Association of Colleges and Secondary Schools learn with profound sorrow of the sudden death of our associate Superintendent F. L. Soldan, of St. Louis.

"For a third of a century he gave to the cause of education the full value of his tireless energy and his splendid abilities, as a teacher and educational leader. He was perhaps better known and more widely recognized than any other educator of the Central West.

"We gladly place on record this expression of our high esteem for him, and of our deep sympathy for the city and schools of St. Louis, his immediate associates, and the members of his family."

On motion, the resolution was adopted.

It was also voted that the Secretary of the Association be directed to telegraph Mr. Blewett, the Assistant Superintendent of Schools, St. Louis, some sentiment expressive of the feelings of the Association regarding the death of Superintendent Soldan.

Following this, Principal J. S. Brown, of Joliet, Illinois, read the following paper on "Commercial and Industrial High Schools versus Commercial and Industrial Courses in High Schools."

COMMERCIAL AND INDUSTRIAL HIGH SCHOOLS VS. COMMERCIAL AND INDUSTRIAL COURSES IN HIGH SCHOOLS.

Four and a half score years ago, when Chicago with its environs took its place among the states of this union under the name of Illinois, it brought with its entrance, among other things, a heritage from the sacred ordinance of 1787, which read after this manner, *"Religion, morality* and *knowledge* being necessary to the perpetuity of a free government, schools and the means of education shall forever be encouraged."

I wish that statement were cast in deathless bronze and hung up in a conspicuous place in every college and high school, because it places on record the thought of our fathers, the government's founders, and gives to the church, the home and the school their fundamental significance and their respective places in the development of a government by the people.

We do not believe in the worship of ancestors but we do believe in acting upon the assumption that we are indeed the "heir of all the ages in the foremost files of time," and hence all the usable good resulting from experience should be appropriated and embodied in any new educational effort.

Any new educational effort will fall short of accomplishing its purpose if it fails to reckon seriously and continuously with the fact that we are living in a *representative democracy* and that any scheme which tends to weaken that fact is striking at the very foundation on which the public school system *rests*. "It hath been said by men of old time, 'We hold these truths to be self-evident, that all men are created equal, that they are endowed by their creator with certain inalienable rights, that among these are life, liberty and the pursuit of happiness,'" etc. Do we need to interpret once more some of these fundamentals in the light of the twentieth century standards?

Now it is not my purpose to show the plan or function of industrial and commercial work, or any other kind of work, but to show whether it is advisable to establish a special school to do a special work every time the evolution of our educational thoughts suggests the addition of some new phase of education. Of necessity new phases of education will present themselves in the future just as they have in the past and there ought to be determined some basic principle by which we might be judged in the introduction of this new work.

Any scheme which means the separation of the people of secondary school age into groups to be educated in separate schools is a great blow to democracy, because it recognizes *social classes* in schools supported by *public taxation;* because it recognizes no system of school organization, no uniformity of procedure; because it recognizes no central authority and because it stands for dissipation of energy.

We believe in concentration of both effort and energy. We believe in consolidation of courses of study in public high schools. We believe in educating all boys and girls of secondary school age together, and providing different courses to suit their varying needs. We believe that in this adolescent period when naturally there is much of unrest, uncertainty and etherealization there is great need of the balancing and ballasting effect which comes from keeping in close touch the boys who know they are going to be lawyers and those who know they are going to be farmers, mechanics, engineers and business men. The one exercises a wholesome influence on the other in showing and exercising that mutual interest which comes from close contact between young men and young women who have chosen to exert their powers along unrelated lines of work.

Is the man a poorer lawyer because he knows from first hand knowledge the struggles of a fellow student who learned the machinist trade. But suppose we put together in a separate building all the boys who are to become mechanics or blacksmiths, and in another building all the boys who are to become lawyers and doctors, is the bond of common knowledge which comes from intimate association continued as when each worked alongside in the same school? You know the reverse is true. What was sympathy and good fellowship in the first case when both were educated together becomes antipathy and bitter suspicion and jealousy.

Boys and girls in this character-forming age need to learn that a truly American democracy can not be formed like a stratified rock and that the creation of separate schools, instead of broadening the courses of study means sooner or later the arraying of one element of society against another, a condition far too prevalent now in certain quarters, for the good of the state.

Let the prospective domestic, the prospective milliner and the prospective candidate for a foreign title by right of purchase be educated together and it will tend to reduce the number of such entangling alliances and their desire for them. We ought to have one type of high school and that with courses of study enough to meet the demands of the community. When more than one is needed make another of the same type and thereby give to each community the same scholastic opportunity.

Does any kind of sound pedagogy defend the establishment of an English High School, an Industrial High School, a Classical High School, a Commercial High School, a Latin High School, a Mechanic Arts High School, an Agricultural High School, when all the lines of work here represented and any others which our national development may render desirable may be taught in one kind of high school? We have one taxing unit for our public school support. Why set up one type of high school to fight another and to demand according to a temporary change in public sentiment an unreasonable proportion of public funds? Shall we erect a special school for those who are going to college? Another for those who are going to teach? Another for those who will enter upon a business career? Another for those who are going to enter the military or naval service or the diplomatic or consular service?

Where shall the end be? and who shall set the limitations? Is it not clear that such a procedure is a dissipation of effort, a real waste of energy?

I am unalterably opposed to the sorting of pupils after the manner proposed at the Chicago meeting for the promotion of Industrial Education. No man may sort my children in the adolescent stage and say to one, "You are to be a watchmaker"; to another, "You are to be a lawyer"; to another, "You are to be a typewriter". We can't sort folks as we sort potatoes and apples, sheep and cattle. The potter hath power over the clay to make of the same lump one vessel to honor and another to dishonor, but in a great house there are not only vessels of silver and of gold, but of wood and of earth, and some to honor and some to dishonor, and if a man purge himself from these he shall be a vessel unto honor sanctified and meet for the Master's use and prepared unto every good work.

Boys and girls of adolescent age are not clay, nor can they be made this or that at the behest of the schoolmaster; they must, very largely, choose for themselves, and that, too, regardless of financial, scholastic or social ranking by any teacher or set of teachers. The creation of public schools by the public to teach the industries, agriculture, commercial branches, manual arts, etc., means the separation of young people into fixed classes according to their occupations.

Again, in most communities, we find now a good high school sentiment, a good defense in public opinion for their continued maintenance, but every time we make a separate school to teach one small field of work we divide that public sentiment and the logical outcome of such division is the disappearance of public sentiment favoring public high schools of any kind.

Dean Davenport well says in a recent publication, "To segregate any class of people from the common mass and to educate it by itself and solely with reference to its own affairs is to make it narrower and more bigoted generation by generation.

It is to substitute training for education and to breed distrust in the body politic. Knowledge is necessary to a just appreciation of other people and their professions and mode of life. With this only can a man respect his own calling as he ought and love his neighbors as he should. We can not segregate and make an educational cleavage at the line of occupations except to the common peril."

We maintain that separate schools should not be established for each new line of work as presented, but that new courses and new departments should be made setting forth new lines of endeavor as rapidly as our changing conditions render such action necessary, for the following reasons:

1. Such a step can not be defended on economic grounds. Funds available at present are inadequate to meet the real needs of the high school now, and to make a separate school, to teach the work of a department means that we cripple seriously the work we are now doing and do indifferently the new work. Moreover, such a step really means a duplication, in large measure, of library and laboratory facilities and hence a greater cost per pupil. The creation of a new department to do well any new work is easily defended on economic grounds.

2. The "esprit de corps" in any secondary school is one of the most valuable assets of the school. A division of the total pupilage made necessary in the formation of separate schools utterly destroys this school spirit and tends to lower

the plane of the institution to that of an apprentice school or a factory. If such a condition makes for either a more complete life or greater social efficiency we fail to understand how it is done.

3. Almost the only democratic institution remaining in American life to-day is the public school, and we look upon any attempt to sweep this secondary institution of learning from its democratic moorings as nothing less than public calamity. The classification of pupils of adolescent age by placing some in a preparatory school for the professions only and others in separate and different schools to prepare them for the industries, the offices, the machine shop, the farm and the factory must mean a social cleavage which savors too much of difference only in dollars and cents, in kind of clothing and social prestige. To us this looks like an importation upon which the tariff should be made immediately prohibitive. Too well do many in secondary school work know that in all this great middle west and the far west where there is much smaller opportunity to send the boys and girls to expensive fashionable fitting and finishing schools, the public high school has been infested with small, exclusive, barbaric, undemocratic cliques, called frats, and that these organizations have done unmeasured harm to the schools. Let us avoid any step in our educational development which would recognize, foster, give aid or comfort to or in any way encourage such an innovation. "An ounce of prevention is worth a pound of cure."

4. It is bad pedagogy to magnify the training and minify education proper and yet this is precisely what is proposed in the formation of separate schools instead of creating a new department in the same school. The point of view is necessarily confined to the particular field of endeavor in the separate school, but in the separate departments all other departments contribute in the determination of the

point of view. Is not this the broader, the wiser, the saner method of procedure?

5. It is not in the number of our school buildings, nor yet in the narrowness of our curricula, but in the oneness of effort that we are to go on to higher and better things in education. Consolidation of educational effort means greater efficiency at smaller cost.

Concentration of capital makes it possible to pay a higher wage and produce better food, better clothing, better machinery.

In the factory world we no longer look for men who can make an entire shoe, an entire coat, an entire watch, but we have a large number of people especially skilled whose combined effort gives us a better and cheaper shoe, a better and cheaper coat, a better and cheaper watch.

It seems to me there is a justifiable parallelism in our proposition. In the high school development on the departmental plan, with many courses meeting the changing needs of the community, we have teachers who are especially prepared to do their work, but their combined efforts are at the service of all students in the school; while in the separate school, with its narrow field of work and its consequent teaching force, the combined effort can not mean greater efficiency nor more complete life.

Co-operation, consolidation, combination, concentration, unity of effort have their places in educational economy and the sooner the directors of our educational institutions realize this the sooner shall we be able to secure and maintain the highest rank in the educational world.

A second paper was read upon this same subject by Professor W. A. Scott, of the University of Wisconsin, Madison, Wisconsin, as follows:

COMMERCIAL HIGH SCHOOLS VERSUS COMMERCIAL COURSES IN HIGH SCHOOLS.

The subject before us for discussion has practical significance in only a comparatively small number of the localities represented in this conference. Financial considerations alone would probably prevent the establishment of commercial high schools in towns of small size, and even in larger towns which have students enough desirous of pursuing a commercial course to warrant the equipment of a school for them alone, their wide distribution might prove a serious obstacle. However, I assume that the subject we are supposed to discuss is the relative advantages and disadvantages of commercial high schools and commercial courses in high schools in localities where there is an effective choice. If one were able to have either the one or the other which ought he to choose?

As I view the matter, commercial high schools have the advantage over their competitors in the matter of the creation of a business atmosphere and in the shaping of their courses to practical ends. By business atmosphere I do not mean an atmosphere of greed or the kind of an atmosphere created by over-emphasis of the money-making and gain-acquiring spirit. Such an atmosphere ought not to be created anywhere, least of all in a school where young people are training for their life work. The kind of an atmosphere of which I am speaking results from hard work, from the constant application of the test of ability to do specific things and from constant insistence on accuracy, punctuality and the strictest integrity. These are some of the demands made upon young men when they go into business, and it is desirable that during the process of their training they should have had some experience of an environment created by such demands. My point is that such an environment is more easily created in commercial high schools than in commercial courses in high schools. My chief reason for so thinking is the fact that these must be paramount and conscious aims in a commercial high school and the entire machinery of the school can be made to work toward their realization, while in commercial courses serious obstacles may be thrown in the way by the necessity of co-operation with other departments of the school. Take, for example, the matter of hard work. In a commercial course it is impracticable to raise the standard in this particular above that of the school as a whole because students from various departments are certain to be herded together in a large number of the classes and it is necessary to treat all students in the same class in the same way. In a commercial high school it seems to me to be practicable and proper to set a higher standard. It is proper to assume that because of the definiteness of their purposes commercial students will submit to greater pressure and will put forth greater energy under the same pressure, and that both they and their parents can be more easily taught the value of the discipline of hard work.

A higher and more definite standard of attainment seems to me also to be possible in a commercial high school. Here one course follows another in the sense that the student must be able to do certain specific things, such as calculate accurately, write legibly, compose a readable and pointed letter, analyze and properly record the elements of an account, etc., etc., before he can do the work of the next course. His ability to do or not to do specific things is thus constantly put to the test and his right to promotion from one class to another accurately determined. If students who are not put to these subsequent tests are trained in the same classes with the commercial students the standard is certain to be determined by the capacity and willingness to work of the average student rather than ability to do the specific things required.

The ease with which accuracy may be lost sight of in a mixed class was impressed upon me recently while inspecting a recitation in review arithmetic in a high school in Wisconsin. In that particular class commercial students were in the minority and the teacher felt that ability to state the problem clearly and to write down the various steps involved in its solution were the important things to drill upon. The result was that every student made an elaborate statement of his problem and in recitation rattled off the lingo he had been taught in a manner approaching perfection, but not one out of ten secured the correct result. That defect, however, was passed over very lightly, the teacher suggesting that the error may have been due to incorrect multiplication here, to incorrect subtraction there, or to incorrect addition in the other place. In discussing the matter with him after class the teacher made a strong defence for his method of procedure on the ground that if he had insisted on correct results, he would have had little or no time for anything else, and that for the vast majority of the students in the class ability to state the problem and to see the various steps involved were more important than accuracy. The students in that class certainly received the impression that in the computing of interest a correct result was of small importance compared with the method of procedure. I do not believe such a mistake in emphasis could have been made in a commercial high school in which the teacher in accounting would have been obliged to send most of those students back into the arithmetic class. The criticism of the attainments along this line of the small percentage of the arithmetic class I inspected would have made little impression. Their deficiencies would probably have been thought due to their own carelessness, the other members of the class never having been submitted to the test.

Further illustrations are probably unnecessary. In matters of punctuality and integrity the case does not differ essentially from that just described. Because these aims may there be emphasized and the student's progress towards them constantly tested and everybody held up to the same standard, the commercial high school has the advantage.

The peculiarity of courses in commerce is the fact that they should be so constructed and administered as to develop the commercial virtues and the ability to perform commercial processes. This applies quite as much to the general as to the strictly professional or commercial subjects, as they are sometimes called. In a commercial course, for example, instruction in the foreign languages should aim at the acquisition of the ability to use the language for commercial purposes; instruction in English should develop the ability to write an effective business letter; instruction in arithmetic, to perform accurately the mathematical calculations required in everyday commercial processes; instruction in history, to understand the deeper influences which affect commercial life, etc., etc. In a general high school all of these subjects may and should be used for other purposes as well. The difficulty with a commercial course in such schools is likely to be that students from all departments must be taught together in these subjects, and consequently a compromise between various aims reached. Such a compromise necessarily involves some sacrifice by each group of students. A commercial high school is not subjected to such limitations. It has a free field. If its courses do not accomplish the results desired, the blame cannot be laid on the rigidity of the system imposed upon it by the machinery of which it is only a part. It may create its own machinery and modify and adjust to suit its own purposes.

Another obstacle in the way of commercial courses in high schools is the necessity of using teachers not specially trained for commercial work and not specially interested in that phase of their work. Special teachers are rarely employed except for the so-called commercial subjects, and these very often feel that the atmosphere of the school is not congenial. A commercial high school can create an esprit de corps in its instructional force which will encourage the right kind of specialization in its teachers of foundational subjects and strongly back the teachers of the strictly professional subjects. It may be obliged to take raw material, but it stands some chance of shaping it to the proper form in time. There is little chance of this being done if the main work of the teacher is remote from commercial lines and the influences surrounding him but slightly, if at all, sympathetic with that branch of education.

On account of the definiteness of its aims and freedom from distraction due to a multiplicity of demands from different departments, a commercial high school is also apt to have the advantage in the matter of material equipment. Its books and apparatus are apt to be better selected and more abundant and it is apt to devote more attention to equipment for practice than is found possible in a commercial course.

It is obvious that in particular instances a commercial course might be able to overcome most, perhaps all, of these obstacles. In a large school it is not impossible completely to separate commercial from other students and to employ special teachers for them. In this case the difficulty of applying commercial standards and of introducing a business atmosphere would be diminished. The likelihood of such a result, however, depends largely upon the extent to which the school authorities appreciate the other side of this question, the side I wish now to present.

Every person interested in commercial education has encountered the objections of the advocates of what is called liberal education and of the opponents of early specialization. Many people believe that specialization, certainly along vocational lines, ought not to come before the end of the college course; that up to that time the aim should be breadth of view, culture, survey of the widest possible field of knowledge, etc., etc. Many persons who thus believe object to commercial courses anywhere, in high school or college, in special or in mixed institutions. Others, however, admit the necessity of catering to the popular demand for such courses, and some few are broad enough to see that only commercial courses will bring certain classes of young people into our high schools and colleges, and are willing thus to accord them a value as educational attractions. Such persons are sure to object to the commercial high school on the ground that it keeps these promising lads out of reach of other and higher influences. Their hope is that under the influences surrounding them in the high school some may become innoculated with the virus of culture and desert the commercial course for something better. Every young man and woman ought at least to have a chance to learn that there are other objects in life worth working for besides the getting of a living or the making of money. It may be claimed that such chances are more likely to come in his way in a commercial course in a high school.

For this view, there is certainly much to be said. Barring from consideration the extravagant statements and claims often made by both parties to the controversy over liberal education, specialization, vocational courses, and similar topics, everyone must regret the temptations placed before young people to choose their life work before they have laid the proper basis for a choice, and to cut themselves off from the widest possible contact with the learned world. For one, I should be glad if every American young man and woman could have the advantage of the broadest kind of a high school and college course before beginning technical preparation for their life work. If this were possible, how enormously would the problems of technical education and vocational training be simplified and the general level of civilization raised! But this is not now possible and probably never will be. There will always be a great number who are incapable of taking and profiting by that amount of training, and still others who are capable but have no desire for it and cannot be induced to take it. It must not be assumed, however, that every young man who at the beginning of his high school course decides to fit himself directly for business belongs to one of these classes. Many of them may wake up to the other possibilities before the high school course is ended, if the proper kind of stimuli are applied. Is it not well to keep such young men within easy reach of such stimuli, and from this point of view does not the commercial course in a high school have an advantage worth serious consideration?

In attempting to answer this question one must not, of course, lose sight of those who will finish the commercial course and go directly into business. Granted that the commercial training they receive is not so good as they might have had in a commercial high school, have they received any compensating advantages? It is possible, I think, that contact with other students pursuing different lines of work and actuated by different purposes may have a broadening influence on even these students, and that this may properly be regarded as an offset to the sacrifice they have made in the quality of their commercial training. Whether or not it is an adequate offset depends largely on the character and fiber of the student.

The situation I am discussing would not be met by crediting commercial courses for entrance to college. The question does not so much concern the terms on which a commercial student shall be admitted to college as it does the awakening of the desire to go to college. The commercial course in high schools, however, seems to have the advantage along both lines. It is in a better position than its competitor to stimulate students to go to college, and having awakened the desire, to steer their preparation in that direction.

As I view the matter, therefore, a commercial high school, which makes full use of its opportunities, should have to its credit a better business atmosphere, more practical courses, better instructors, and better material equipment than a course established in a high school of the same grade and equally well managed. As offsetting advantages, the commercial course should be credited with superior opportunities for learning of other occupations than business and of other purposes in life than the acquisition of gain, greater ease of transfer to other courses in case of a change in the student's desires or prospects regarding his life work or his training beyond the high school, and a more broadly civilizing influence on those who actually make the high school commercial course the avenue through which to enter business life.

The choice between these alternatives is not easy. The balance of advantages and disadvantages will be differently estimated by different people, and it will actually be different under different conditions. The character and prospects of the young people with whom one has to deal is a primary consideration. If college is clearly out of the question for them and if they are certainly destined for business at the end of the secondary course, and if their capacity to take on polish from contact with others is relatively small, the balance in favor of the commercial high school will be large, and the decision tolerably easy. If, on the other hand, one has to deal with the average group of young Americans to be met with in the villages, small cities, and certain portions of the large cities of this country, the balance may quite as decidedly turn to the side of the commercial course. These young people need to be carefully assorted. They are certain to have decided in favor of a commercial course from very different motives, some of which are wrong. They frequently need to be protected from their own or their parents' bad judgment. The American's birthright of unlimited opportunity to turn in the direction fortune or interest or desire dictates ought to be kept easily and temptingly within his reach at least to the end of his high school course.

I am conscious that it is very easy to exaggerate both the advantages and the disadvantages of the two institutions I have been attempting to compare. There are commercial high schools and commercial high schools, commercial courses and commercial courses. I have read programs of the former which so closely resembled those of ordinary high schools that I wondered why the adjective commercial was used in the title, and I have inspected commercial courses that did not deserve the name course. They consisted of a little type-writing, stenography and book-keeping taken on the side by the best students and as snaps by those who did not want to work and must in some way be kept in the school and ultimately given a diploma. Obviously if one were to make a judicious selection of his institutions for comparison, he could easily support any conclusion desired. I have attempted to hold before my mind's eye high but attainable ideals along both lines, and balance advantages and disadvantages as they would appear under identical conditions.

The Committee on Nominations recommended the names of the following officers for 1908-09.

FOR OFFICERS FOR THE YEAR 1908-1909.

President, Principal E. W. Coy, Hughes High School, Cincinnati, Ohio.
Secretary, Dean T. A. Clark, University of Illinois.
Treasurer, Principal J. E. Armstrong, Englewood High School, Chicago.

VICE-PRESIDENTS.

WISCONSIN.

President Ellen C. Sabin, Milwaukee-Downer College.
Principal Edwin P. Brown, Wayland Academy.

MICHIGAN.

Professor W. W. Beman, University of Michigan.
Superintendent S. O. Hartwell, Kalamazoo.

OHIO.

George M. Jones, Secretary Oberlin College.
W. M. Townsend, Principal Central High School, Columbus.

IOWA.

President Wm. F. King, Cornell College.
Principal Geo. Edward Marshall, Davenport High School.

ILLINOIS.

Dean Marion Talbot, University of Chicago.
Principal Oliver S. Westcott, Waller High School, Chicago.

MISSOURI.

Dean J. C. Jones, University of Missouri.
Principal W. J. S. Bryan, Central High School, St. Louis.

NEBRASKA.

Professor A. A. Reed, University of Nebraska.
Principal F. W. Sanders, Lincoln High School.

INDIANA.

The Rev. Matthew Schumacher, University of Notre Dame.
Principal George H. Benton, Shortridge High School, Indianapolis.

KANSAS.

President Norman Plass, Washburn College.
Principal H. L. Miller, Topeka High School.

MINNESOTA.

President S. H. Bridgman, Hamline University.
V. K. Franda, Central High School, St. Paul.

COLORADO.

President William F. Slocum, Colorado College.
Principal W. H. Smiley, Denver High School.

OKLAHOMA.

President David R. Boyd, State University.
Superintendent L. W. Baxter, Guthrie.

SOUTH DAKOTA.

F. B. Gault, Vermillion.
Superintendent Clyde Stone, Huron.

NORTH DAKOTA.

E. J. Babcock, University of North Dakota.
Richard Heywood, Inspector of Schools.

MEMBERS OF THE EXECUTIVE COMMITTEE.

President W. L. Bryan, University of Indiana.
Professor Fred N. Scott, University of Michigan.
Principal J. Stanley Brown, Joliet High School.
Superintendent W. A. Greeson, Grand Rapids, Michigan.

On motion the report was adopted, and the persons nominated were declared elected.

The President announced the appointment of the following members of the Commission from 1908 to 1911:

President George E. McLean, Iowa; Director George N. Carman, Lewis Institute; President John R. Kirk, Kirksville, Missouri, and Principal Frederick L. Bliss, Detroit, Michigan.

On motion of Professor Mann the following committee

was appointed to urge on the National Education Association the preparation of an adequate report on the subject of industrial education in public schools:

Principal J. Stanley Brown, Joliet, Illinois; Professor Otis W. Caldwell, Chicago, and Professor C. R. Mann, Chicago.

President James then introduced the new president with the following remarks:

I take very great pleasure in introducing my successor as President of the Association for the coming year. I have a deep personal pleasure in introducing Professor Coy. It is thirty-five years ago about this time that he was putting the finishing touches on me in a preparatory school in this state to send me off to college. In those days he was a very cruel and harsh teacher and had thrashed off the class with which I began, of something like fifteen to twenty, to one, the result of which was I had the benefit of his private instruction for over a year, at the very critical time of my preparation for college. I believe I got from that year's work from Professor Coy more solid advantage than I ever got from instruction and intercourse with any other teacher in the high school, college or university, and I am glad to have this opportunity for this little personal word, and to introduce him to the Association.

PRESIDENT COY:

Mr. President, ladies and gentlemen: This is so sudden. I recall to mind that one of our presidents received a nomination in a convention here in Chicago largely because he made a very eloquent speech in behalf of another candidate. I will say I made as eloquent a speech as I could in behalf of a more worthy candidate to some of the members of the nominating committee for this position, not, however, with the expectation that the same result was going to follow. I appreciate very highly the honor you have done me and I shall undertake to do the business of this office, with your assistance, as well as I can.

I want also to thank the outgoing president of this Association for the very kindly words that he has spoken. If my efforts with him for that year were so successful, it was very largely because I had a very excellent pupil.

On motion, the Association adjourned.

THOMAS ARKLE CLARK,
Secretary.

LIST OF MEMBERS.

INSTITUTIONS.
(c. m. means charter member.)

OHIO.

Ohio State University, c. m., Columbus, President W. O. Thompson.
Western Reserve University, c. m., Cleveland, President Charles F. Thwing.
Oberlin College, c. m., Oberlin, President H. C. King.
Ohio Wesleyan University, c. m., Delaware, President Herbert Welsh.
Denison University, '99, Granville, President Emory W. Hunt.
University of Cincinnati, '99, Cincinnati, President C. W. Dabney.
Miami University, '04, Oxford, President Guy P. Benton.
Case School of Applied Science, '08, Cleveland, President Charles S. Howe.
Marietta College, '08, Marietta, Ohio, President A. J. Perry.
Kenyon College, '08, Gambier, Ohio, President William F. Pierce.
Central High School, c. m., Cleveland, Principal Edward L. Harris.
Hughes High School, '96, Cincinnati, Principal E. W. Coy.
Central High School, '96, Toledo, Principal W. B. Guitteau.
Walnut Hills High School, '99, Cincinnati, Principal W. Taylor Harris.
Woodward High School, '99, Cincinnati, Principal Geo. W. Harper.
West High School, '00, Cleveland, Principal Theo. H. Johnston.
East High School, '02, Columbus, Principal F. B. Pearson.
University School, '02, Cleveland, Principal Geo. D. Pettee.
South High School, '02, Cleveland, Principal G. A. Ruetenik.
Lincoln High School, '02, Cleveland, Principal J. W. McLane.
East High School, '02, Cleveland, Principal B. U. Rannels.
Rayen High School, '03, Youngstown, Principal W. L. Griswold.
North High School, '05, Columbus, Principal C. D. Everett.
Glenville High School, '06, Cleveland, Principal H. S. Cully.
Central High School, '06, Columbus, Principal W. M. Townsend.
South High School, '06, Columbus, Principal C. S. Barrett.
Central High School, '96, Toledo, Principal C. F. Ball.

MICHIGAN.

University of Michigan, c. m., Ann Arbor, President Jas. B. Angell.
Central High School, c. m., Grand Rapids, Jesse B. Davis.
Michigan Military Academy, c. m., Orchard Lake, Principal L. C. Hull.
High School, '95, Kalamazoo, Superintendent S. O. Hartwell.
East Side High School, '95, Saginaw, Superintendent E. C. Warriner.
Detroit University School, '00, Detroit, Principal Frederick L. Bliss.
Olivet College, '06, Olivet, President E. G. Lancaster.
Central High School, c. m., Detroit, Principal David Mackenzie.
High School, '06, Charlotte, Superintendent M. R. Parmelee.

INDIANA.

Indiana University, c. m., Bloomington, President W. L. Bryan.
Purdue University, '08, Lafayette, President W. E. Stone.
Wabash College, c. m., Crawfordsville, President George L. Mackintosh.
University of Notre Dame, '06, President John Cavanaugh.
High School, c. m., La Porte, Superintendent John R. Wood.
High School, '96, Fort Wayne, Principal C. F. Lane.
High School, '01, Lafayette, Superintendent E. Ayers.
Howe School, '04, Lima, Rector T. H. McKenzie.
Shortridge High School, c. m., Indianapolis, Principal G. W. Benton.

ILLINOIS.

University of Illinois, c. m., Urbana, President E. J. James.
University of Chicago, c. m., President H. P. Judson.
Northwestern University, c. m., Evanston, President A. W. Harris.
Lake Forest College, c. m., Lake Forest, President John S. Nollen.
Knox College, '96, Galesburg, President Thomas McClelland.
Illinois College, c. m., Jacksonville, President C. H. Rammelkamp.
Chicago Teachers' College, '08, Chicago, President Ella F. Young.
Illinois State Normal School, '08, Normal, President David Felmley.
Eastern Illinois State Normal School, '08, Charleston, President L. C. Lord.
Western Illinois Normal School, '08, Macomb, President Alfred Bayliss.

Southern Illinois Normal School, '08, Carbondale, President D. B. Parkinson.
Northern Illinois Normal School, '08, DeKalb, President John W. Cook.
Wheaton College, Wheaton, President Charles A. Blanchard.
High School, c. m., Evanston, Principal W. F. Beardsley.
Evanston Academy of Northwestern University, c. m., Principal A. H. Wilde.
Manual Training School, c. m., Chicago, Director H. H. Belfield.
Harvard School, c. m., Chicago, Principal John J. Schobinger.
Lake Forest School, Lake Forest, Head Master J. C. Sloan.
West Division High School, '96, Chicago, Principal C. M. Clayberg.
Lake View High School, '96, Chicago, Principal B. F. Buck.
Englewood High School, '96, Chicago, Principal J. E. Armstrong.
Ottawa Tp. High School, '96, Ottawa, Principal J. O. Leslie.
Lyons Tp. High School, '96, La Grange, Principal S. R. Cole.
Lewis Institute, '95, Chicago, Director G. N. Carman.
Streator Tp. High School, '97, Streator, Principal Ralph R. Upton.
Bradley Polytechnic Institute, '97, Peoria, Director T. C. Burgess.
High School, '98, Elgin, Principal W. S. Goble.
Lake High School, '99, Chicago, Principal Edward F. Stearns.
Marshall High School, '99, Chicago, Principal Louis J. Block.
West Aurora High School, Aurora, Principal C. P. Briggs.
Rock Island High School, Rock Island, Principal H. E. Brown.
New Trier High School, Kenilworth, Principal F. L. Sims.
Kewanee High School, '04, Kewanee, Principal J. B. Cleveland.
La Salle-Peru Tp. High School, '05, Principal T. J. McCormack.
East Side High School, '05, Aurora, Principal C. L. Phelps.
Township High School, '05, Joliet, Principal J. Stanley Brown.
J. Sterling Morton High School, '05, Clyde, Principal H. V. Church.
Township High School, '06, Sterling, Principal E. T. Austin.
Rockford College, '06, Rockford, President Julia Gulliver.
High School of the University of Chicago, '06, Principal W. B. Owen.
Grand Prairie Seminary, '08, Onarga, President H. H. Frost.

WISCONSIN.

University of Wisconsin, c. m., Madison, President Charles R. Van Hise.
Beloit College, c. m., Beloit, President Edward D. Eaton.
Ripon College, '04, Ripon, President Richard C. Hughes.

Milwaukee-Downer College, '97, Milwaukee, President Ellen C. Sabin.
Milwaukee Academy, '97, Milwaukee, Principal J. H. Pratt.
North Division High School, '04, Milwaukee, Principal R. E. Krug.
Lawrence University, '05, Appleton, President Samuel Plantz.
South Division High School, '06, Milwaukee, Principal E. Rissman.
Wayland Academy, '06, Beaver Dam, Principal E. P. Brown.
East Division High School, '07, Principal George A. Chamberlain.

MINNESOTA.

University of Minnesota, '90, Minneapolis, President Cyrus Northrup.
Humboldt High School, St. Paul, Principal H. S. Baker.
Central High School, '04, St. Paul, Principal V. K. Froula.
Cleveland High School, St. Paul, Principal Milo Stewart.
Carlton College, '06, Northfield, President W. H. Sallmon.

IOWA.

State University of Iowa, c. m., Iowa City, President Geo. E. MacLean.
Cornell College, c. m., Mt. Vernon, President Wm. F. King.
State Normal School, c. m., Cedar Falls, President D. S. Wright.
Iowa College, '95, Grinnell, President J. H. T. Main.
Drake University, '06, Des Moines, President H. M. Bell.
Coe College, '08, Cedar Rapids, President N. N. Smith.
High School, '06, Council Bluffs, Principal S. L. Thomas.
High School, '06, Dubuque, Principal F. L. Smart.
West High School, '06, Des Moines, Principal Maurice Ricker.
Simpson College, '06, Indianola, President Charles E. Shelton.

MISSOURI.

University of Missouri, c. m., Columbia, President Richard H. Jesse.
Washington University, c. m., St. Louis, Chancellor Winfield S. Chaplin.
Drury College, '98, Springfield, President Homer T. Fuller.
Missouri Valley College, '98, Marshall, President Wm. H. Black.
Central High School, '96, St. Louis, Principal W. J. S. Bryan.
Westminster College, '00, Fulton, President David R. Kerr.
Mary Institute, '00, St. Louis, Principal E. H. Sears.
Kirkwood High School, '00, Kirkwood, Superintendent R. G. Kinkead.

Park College, '02, Parkville, President Lowell M. McAfee.
Wm. McKinley High School, St. Louis, '05, Principal G. B. Morrison.

NEBRASKA.

University of Nebraska, '96, Lincoln, President E. Benj. Andrews.
Lincoln High School, '98, Lincoln, Principal F. W. Sanders.

KANSAS.

University of Kansas, '96, Lawrence, Chancellor Frank Strong.
Washburn College, '06, Topeka, President Norman Plass.
Baker University, '08, Baldwin, President Lemuel H. Murlin.

COLORADO.

University of Colorado, '96, Boulder, President Jas. H. Baker.
Colorado College, '96, Colorado Springs, President W. F. Slocum.
The Miss Wolcott School, '06, Denver.

OKLAHOMA.

University of Oklahoma, '01, Norman, President David R. Boyd.

SOUTH DAKOTA.

University of South Dakota, '08, Vermillion, President F. B. Gault.
High School, Sioux Falls, '08, Principal W. J. Earley.
High School, Yankton, Principal R. C. Shellenbarger.
High School, Aberdeen, '07, Principal W. L. Cochrane, Aberdeen.

NORTH DAKOTA.

High School, Fargo, '08, Principal N. E. Hoover.

INDIVIDUAL MEMBERS.

OHIO.

Charles S. Howe, '02, President of Case School of Applied Science, Cleveland.
Jos. V. Denney, '03, Dean of the College of Arts, Philosophy and Science, Ohio State University, Columbus.
W. W. Boyd, '03, High School Visitor, Ohio State University, Columbus.
G. M. Jones, '05, Secretary of Oberlin College, Oberlin.
F. C. Hicks, '06, Professor in the University of Cincinnati, Cincinnati.

F. W. Ballou, High School Inspector, University of Cincinnati, Cincinnati.
J. W. Carr, '08, Superintendent of Schools, Dayton.

MICHIGAN.

Fred N. Scott, '98, Professor in the University of Michigan, Ann Arbor.
L. H. Jones, '95, President of the State Normal School, Ypsilanti.
A. S. Whitney, '03, High School Inspector, University of Michigan, Ann Arbor.
W. W. Beman, '95, University of Michigan, Ann Arbor.
Wm. A. Greeson, '97, Superintendent of Schools, Grand Rapids.

INDIANA.

Clarence A. Waldo, '95, Professor in Purdue University, Lafayette.
Carl Leo Mees, '90, President of Rose Polytechnic, Terre Haute.
W. W. Parsons, '99, President of the State Normal School, Terre Haute.

ILLINOIS.

A. V. E. Young, '95, Professor in Northwestern University, Evanston.
Thomas C. Chamberlin '95, Professor in the University of Chicago, Chicago.
Harry P. Judson, '95, Professor in the University of Chicago, Chicago.
Marion Talbot, '97, Dean of Women, University of Chicago, Chicago.
Thomas F. Holgate, '99, Professor in Northwestern University, Evanston.
A. F. Nightingale, c. m., County Superintendent, 1997 Sheridan Road, Chicago.
R. E. Hieronymus, '03, President of Eureka College, Eureka.
H. A. Hollister, '03, High School Inspector, University of Illinois, Champaign.
H. F. Fisk, '05, Professor in Northwestern University, Evanston.
Walter Libby, High School Inspector, Northwestern University, Evanston.
T. A. Clark, '06, Dean of Undergraduates, University of Illinois, Urbana.
E. J. Townsend, '07, Professor in University of Illinois, Champaign.

WISCONSIN.

Edward A. Birge, '96, Professor in the University of Wisconsin, Madison.
A. W. Tressler, '03, High School Inspector, University of Wisconsin, Madison.
H. L. Terry, '06, State High School Inspector, Madison.
W. O. Carrier, '06, President of Carroll College, Waukesha.
F. G. Hubbard, '08, Professor in the University of Wisconsin.
C. P. Cary, '08, State Superintendent of Schools.

MINNESOTA.

George B. Aiton, '97, State Inspector of High Schools, Minneapolis.

IOWA.

F. C. Ensign, '06, High School Inspector, State University, Iowa City.
Charles E. Shelton, '06, President of Simpson College, Indianola.
Richard C. Barrett, '08, Professor Iowa State College, Ames.
E. W. Stanton, '08, Dean Iowa State College, Ames.

MISSOURI.

John R. Kirk, '98, President of the State Normal School, Kirksville.
C. M. Woodward, '99, Professor in Washington University, St. Louis.
A. Ross Hill, '04, Dean of Teachers' College, University of Missouri, Columbia.
Joseph D. Elliff, '05, High School Inspector, University of Missouri, Columbia.
Ben Blewett, '08, Assistant Superintendent of Schools, St. Louis.

NEBRASKA.

J. W. Crabtree, '04, University of Nebraska, Lincoln.
A. A. Reed, '07, High School Inspector, University of Nebraska, Lincoln.

KANSAS.

W. H. Johnson, '06, High School Inspector, University of Kansas, Lawrence.

COLORADO.

H. G. J. Coleman, High School Inspector, University of Colorado, Boulder.

Frank E. Thompson, '08, Professor, University of Colorado, Boulder.

SOUTH DAKOTA.

C. E. Swanson, Assistant State Superintendent of Public Instruction, Pierre.

F. B. Gault, '08, President, University of South Dakota, Vermillion.

NORTH DAKOTA.

Webster Merrifield, '07, President, University of North Dakota, Grand Forks.

Richard Heyward, '08, Inspector of Schools, Grand Forks.

C. C. Schmidt, '08, Superintendent, Jamestown.

CONSTITUTION OF THE NORTH CENTRAL ASSOCIATION OF COLLEGES AND SECONDARY SCHOOLS.

AS AMENDED AT THE THIRTIETH ANNUAL MEETING, MARCH 27, 1908.

ARTICLE I.

NAME.

The name of the Association shall be the North Central Association of Colleges and Secondary Schools.

ARTICLE II.

OBJECT.

The object of the Association shall be to establish closer relations between the colleges and secondary schools of the North Central States.

ARTICLE III.

MEMBERSHIP.

Section 1.—The members of the Association shall consist of the following two classes: First, colleges and universities, and secondary schools. Secondly, individuals identified with educational work within the limits of the Association.

Section 2.—Election to membership shall require a two-thirds vote of the members present at any meeting, and shall be made only upon the nomination of the Executive Committee.

Section 3.—An institutional member shall be represented at the meeting of the Association by its executive head, or by some one designated by him in credentials addressed to the secretary.

Section 4.—No college or university shall be eligible to membership whose requirements for admission represent less than fifteen units of secondary work as defined by the Commission on Accredited Schools.

Section 5.—No college or university shall be eligible to membership which confers the degree of Doctor of Philosophy or Doctor of Science except after a period of three years of graduate study, not less than two of which shall be years of resident study, one of which shall be at the institution conferring the degree.

Section 6.—No secondary school shall be eligible to membership which does not provide fifteen units of secondary work as defined by the Commission on Accredited Schools.

ARTICLE IV.

POWERS.

All the decisions of the Association bearing upon the policy and management of higher and secondary institutions are understood to be advisory in their character.

ARTICLE V.

OFFICERS AND COMMITTEES.

Section 1.—The officers of the Association shall be a President, two Vice-Presidents from each state represented in the Association, a Secretary, a Treasurer, and an Executive Committee consisting of the President, the Secretary, the Treasurer, and four other members elected by the Association.

Section 2.—The officers shall be chosen at the annual meeting for the term of one year, or until their successors are elected. The election shall be by ballot.

Section 3.—The Executive Committee shall have power to appoint committees for conference with other bodies, whenever in their judgment it may seem expedient.

Section 4.—In case an officer holding office as representative of an institutional member severs his connection with the institution represented, he shall at his discretion hold his office until the close of the next regular meeting of the Association.

Section 5.—The Executive Committee shall have authority to fill a vacancy in any office, the officer elected by the committee to hold office until the close of the next annual meeting.

ARTICLE VI.

DUTIES OF OFFICERS.

Section 1.—The President, or in his absence, one of the Vice-Presidents selected by the Executive Committee, shall preside at the meetings of the Association, and shall sign all orders upon the Treasurer.

Section 2.—The Secretary shall keep a record of the Proceedings of the Association and attend to all necessary correspondence and printing.

Section 3.—The Treasurer shall collect and hold all moneys of the Association, and pay out the same upon the written order of the President.

Section 4.—The Executive Committee shall make all nominations for membership in the Association, fix the time of all meetings not otherwise provided for, prepare programs, and act for the Association when it is not in session. All the acts of the Executive Committee shall be subject to the approval of the Association.

ARTICLE VII.

MEETINGS.

There shall be an annual meeting of the Association and such special meetings as the Association may appoint.

ARTICLE VIII.

MEMBERSHIP FEE.

To meet expenses, an annual fee of $10 shall be paid by each university, $5 by each college, and $3 each by all other members, and each member shall have one vote. If the dues of any member shall remain unpaid for two years, such membership shall lapse.

ARTICLE IX.

QUORUM.

One-fourth of the members of the Association shall constitute a quorum.

ARTICLE X.

AMENDMENTS.

This constitution may be amended by a three-fourths vote at any regular meeting, provided that a printed notice of the proposed amendment be sent to each member two weeks before said meeting.

REGISTRATION.

Allen, Miss Clara B., Englewood High, Chicago, Illinois.
Anthony, Brayman N., President, Adrian College, Adrian, Michigan.
Armstrong, J. E., Principal, Englewood High, Chicago, Illinois.
Austin, C. B., Professor, Ohio Wesleyan University, Delaware, Ohio.
Babcock, E. J., Professor, University of North Dakota, Grand Forks, North Dakota.
Bacon, Paul V., 378 Wabash Avenue, Chicago, Illinois.
Baker, James H., President, University of Colorado, Boulder, Colorado.
Ballou, Frank W., Professor, University of Cincinnati, Cincinnati, Ohio.
Banersfeld, A. G., Thomas Hoyne Manual Training High, Chicago, Illinois.
Barrett, Charles S., Principal, South High, Columbus, Ohio.
Barrett, Richard C., Professor, Ames, Iowa.
Barto, D. O., Instructor, University of Illinois, Urbana, Illinois.
Beardsley, Wilfred F., Principal, Evanston Township High, Evanston, Illinois.
Bell, Hill M., President, Drake University, Des Moines, Iowa.
Beman, W. W., Professor, University of Michigan, Ann Arbor, Michigan.
Benton, George W., Principal, Shortridge High, Indianapolis, Indiana.
Berens, Helmut, Lewis Institute, Chicago, Illinois.
Bevier, Miss Isabel, Professor, University of Illinois, Urbana, Illinois.

Birge, Edward A., Dean, University of Wisconsin, Madison, Wisconsin.
Bliss, Frederick L., Principal, Detroit University School, Detroit, Michigan.
Bolton, Frederick E., Professor, State University of Iowa, Iowa City, Iowa.
Bone, H. A., Superintendent, Sycamore, Illinois.
Bosquet, Maurice L., American School of Home Economics, Chicago, Illinois.
Boyd, W. W., Inspector of Schools, Ohio State University, Columbus, Ohio.
Bray, George E., New Township High, Kenilworth, Illinois.
Bridgman, G. H., President, Hamline University, St. Paul, Minnesota.
Briggs, C. P., Principal, West Aurora High, Aurora, Illinois.
Brookfield, A. D., Muskegon High and Hackle Normal Training School, Muskegon, Michigan.
Brown, Edwin P., Principal, Maryland Academy, Beaver Dam, Wisconsin.
Brown, H. E., Principal, Rock Island High, Rock Island, Illinois.
Brown, J. S., Principal, Joliet Township High, Joliet, Illinois.
Bryan, W. J. S., Principal, Central High, St. Louis, Missouri.
Bryan, Mrs. W. J. S., St. Louis, Missouri.
Bryan, William L., President, University of Indiana, Bloomington, Indiana.
Buck, B. F., Lake View High, Chicago, Illinois.
Buswell, Clara, L., Principal, Polo High, Polo, Illinois.
Cable, J. E., Harvey, Illinois.
Caldwell, Otis W., Professor, University of Chicago, Chicago, Illinois.

Carman, George N., Director, Lewis Institute, Chicago, Illinois.
Carr, J. W., Superintendent, Dayton, Ohio.
Cary, C. P., State Inspector of Schools, Madison, Wisconsin.
Church, H. V., Principal, John Sterling Morton High, Clyde, Illinois.
Clark, A. L., Des Moines, Iowa.
Clark, Thomas Arkle, Dean, University of Illinois, Urbana, Illinois.
Clum, G. V., Superintendent, Earlville, Illinois.
Collie, George L., Dean, Beloit College, Beloit, Wisconsin.
Cook, John W., President, Northern Illinois Normal School, DeKalb, Illinois.
Cooper, C. George, Hinsdale, Illinois.
Coville, Roy L., Township High, Harvey, Illinois.
Coy, E. W., Principal, Hughes High, Cincinnati, Ohio.
Crossland, George M., Instructor, Township High, Harvey, Illinois.
Downey, John F., Professor, University of Minnesota, Minneapolis, Minnesota.
Duvall, J. G., Ohio Wesleyan University, Delaware, Ohio.
Eaton, Edward D., President, Beloit College, Beloit, Wisconsin.
Ehrman, S. W., Principal, Decatur High, Decatur, Illinois.
Elliff, D. J., Inspector, University of Missouri, Columbia, Missouri.
Elson, W. H., Superintendent, Cleveland, Ohio.
Ensign, Forest C., State University of Iowa, Iowa City, Iowa.
Fischer, Augustus R., Englewood High, Chicago, Illinois.
Fisk, Herbert F., Evanston, Illinois.
Foerste, August F., Steele High, Dayton, Ohio.
Fordyce, Charles, Dean, University of Nebraska, Lincoln, Nebraska.

Frost, Henry Hoag, President, Grand Prairie Seminary, Onarga, Illinois.
Froula, V. K., Principal, Central High, St. Paul, Minnesota.
Gault, F. B., President, Vermillion, South Dakota.
German, W. L., Superintendent, Polo, Illinois.
Giles, H. E., Principal, Hinsdale High, Hinsdale, Illinois.
Goble, W. L., Principal, Elgin High, Elgin, Illinois.
Goodier, F. T., Bloomington High, Bloomington, Illinois.
Gorrell, Harry R., Bloomington High, Bloomington, Illinois.
Grant, W. S., Acting Dean, Northwestern University, Evanston, Illinois.
Greeson, W. A., Superintendent, Grand Rapids, Michigan.
Greene, Everts B., Dean, University of Illinois, Urbana, Illinois.
Gulliver, Miss Julia H., President, Rockford College, Rockford, Illinois.
Gurney, Charles Henry, Professor, Hillsdale College, Hillsdale, Michigan.
Hall, Edward J., Calumet, Michigan.
Hamsher, Frank, Principal, Smith Academy, St. Louis, Missouri.
Harris, Edward L., Principal, Central High, Cleveland, Ohio.
Hart, Joseph K., Professor, University of Chicago, Chicago, Illinois.
Hartwell, L. O., Kalamazoo High, Kalamazoo, Michigan.
Hatfield, James Taft, Professor, Northwestern University, Evanston, Illinois.
Heil, J. H., Superintendent, Morgan Park, Illinois.
Herrich, Horace N., Instructor, Waller High, Chicago, Illinois.
Heyward, Richard, Principal, Grand Forks, North Dakota.
Hieronymus, R. E., President, Eureka College, Eureka, Illinois.

Hill, Thomas C., Principal, Curtis High, Chicago, Illinois.
Hoffman, Horace A., Professor, University of Indiana, Bloomington, Indiana.
Hollister, H. A., High School Visitor, University of Illinois, Urbana, Illinois.
Holland, E. O., Bloomington, Indiana.
Hubbard, F. G., Professor, University of Wisconsin, Madison, Wisconsin.
Hunt, Miss Caroline, University of Wisconsin, Madison, Wisconsin.
James, Edmund J., President, University of Illinois, Urbana, Illinois.
James, J. A., Professor, Northwestern University, Evanston, Illinois.
Johnson, Franklin W., Dean, University of Chicago, Chicago, Illinois.
Johnson, W. H., University High School Inspector, University of Kansas, Lawrence, Kansas.
Jolly, A. T., Evanston, Illinois.
Jones, George M., Secretary, Oberlin College, Oberlin, Ohio.
Jones, J. C., Dean, University of Missouri, Columbia, Missouri.
Jones, Miss Jessie Louise, Assistant Professor, Lewis Institute, Chicago, Illinois.
Kendall, Miss Marion A., Marshall High, Chicago, Illinois.
Kerr, David R., President, Westminster College, Fulton, Missouri.
King, Henry Churchill, President, Oberlin College, Oberlin, Ohio.
King, Wm., Professor, Cornell College, Mt. Vernon, Iowa.
Kirchner, Elida C., St. Louis, Missouri.
Kirk, John R., President, State Normal School, Kirksville, Missouri.

Lancaster, E. G., President, Olivet College, Olivet, Michigan.
Leavenworth, W. S., Professor, Olivet College, Olivet, Michigan.
Lee, L. B., Oak Park, Illinois.
Libby, Walter, Professor, Northwestern University, Evanston, Illinois.
Loomis, Hiram B., Hyde Park High, Chicago, Illinois.
Lorelle, Miss Ellen, Dean, Milwaukee-Downer College, Milwaukee, Wisconsin.
Mackenzie, David, Central High, Detroit, Michigan.
MacLean, George E., President, State University of Iowa, Iowa City, Iowa.
MacLeod, Miss Mary L., Cornell College, Mount Vernon, Iowa.
McAfee, Lowell M., Professor, Parkville, Missouri.
McClelland, Thomas, President, Knox College, Galesburg, Illinois.
Main, J. H. T., President, Iowa College, Grinnell, Iowa.
Mann, C. R., Professor, University of Chicago, Chicago, Illinois.
Marshall, George Edward, High School, Davenport, Iowa.
Marshall, L. C., University of Chicago, Chicago, Illinois.
Martin, Edwin D., 9 Jackson Boulevard, Chicago, Illinois.
Mays, Vernon G., Superintendent, Dixon, Illinois.
McConn, Charles Maxwell, Principal, Academy of the University of Illinois, Urbana, Illinois.
McKinney, Winfield S., Englewood High, Chicago, Illinois.
Millar, Frank E., Clinton, Iowa.
Miller, E. A. Dean, Oberlin College, Oberlin, Ohio.
Miller, H. A. Professor, Olivet College, Olivet, Michigan.
Miller, S. M., Aurora, Illinois.
Mitchell, W. L., Hyde Park High, Chicago, Illinois.
Mozier, W. F., Acting Principal, Ottawa Township High, Ottawa, Illinois.

Frank E. Thompson, '08, Professor, University of Colorado, Boulder.

SOUTH DAKOTA.

C. E. Swanson, Assistant State Superintendent of Public Instruction, Pierre.

F. B. Gault, '08, President, University of South Dakota, Vermillion.

NORTH DAKOTA.

Webster Merrifield, '07, President, University of North Dakota, Grand Forks.

Richard Heyward, '08, Inspector of Schools, Grand Forks.

C. C. Schmidt, '08, Superintendent, Jamestown.

CONSTITUTION OF THE NORTH CENTRAL ASSOCIATION OF COLLEGES AND SECONDARY SCHOOLS.

AS AMENDED AT THE THIRTIETH ANNUAL MEETING, MARCH 27, 1908.

ARTICLE I.

NAME.

The name of the Association shall be the North Central Association of Colleges and Secondary Schools.

ARTICLE II.

OBJECT.

The object of the Association shall be to establish closer relations between the colleges and secondary schools of the North Central States.

ARTICLE III.

MEMBERSHIP.

Section 1.—The members of the Association shall consist of the following two classes: First, colleges and universities, and secondary schools. Secondly, individuals identified with educational work within the limits of the Association.

Section 2.—Election to membership shall require a two-thirds vote of the members present at any meeting, and shall be made only upon the nomination of the Executive Committee.

Section 3.—An institutional member shall be represented at the meeting of the Association by its executive head, or by some one designated by him in credentials addressed to the secretary.

Section 4.—No college or university shall be eligible to membership whose requirements for admission represent less than fifteen units of secondary work as defined by the Commission on Accredited Schools.

Section 5.—No college or university shall be eligible to membership which confers the degree of Doctor of Philosophy or Doctor

Slone, Clyde, Superintendent, Huron, South Dakota.
Smart, Frank L., Davenport High, Davenport, Iowa.
Snow, Marshall S., Dean, Washington University, St. Louis, Missouri.
Stanton, E. W., Dean, Iowa State College, Ames, Iowa.
Steele, Harold, Principal, South Haven High, South Haven, Michigan.
Stoops, J. D., Iowa College, Grinnell, Iowa.
Stout, L. A. Chicago, Illinois.
Swann, John N., Professor, Monmouth College, Monmouth, Illinois.
Swanson, C. E., Deputy Superintendent of Public Instruction, Pierre, South Dakota.
Talbot, Miss Marion, Dean, University of Chicago, Chicago, Illinois.
Terry, H. L., State High School Inspector, Madison, Wisconsin.
Thomas, Charles S., Shortridge High, Indianapolis, Indiana.
Thompson, W. O., President, Ohio State University, Columbus, Ohio.
Townsend, E. J., Dean, University of Illinois, Champaign, Illinois.
Townsend, W. M., Principal, Central High, Columbus, Ohio.
Tressler, A. W., Professor, University of Wisconsin, Madison, Wisconsin.
Twiss, George R., Instructor. Central High, Cleveland, Ohio.
Voss, Walter C., Instructor, Von Humboldt School, Chicago, Illinois.
Waldo, C. A., Professor, Purdue University, LaFayette, Indiana.
Watson, R., Hinsdale, Illinois.

Weida, George F., Professor, Kenyon College, Gambier, Ohio.
Westcott, Oliver S., Principal, Waller High, Chicago, Illinois.
Whipple, George A., Evanston High, Evanston, Illinois.
White, J. M., Superintendent of City Schools, Carthage, Missouri.
Whitmore, Miss Cora R., Hinsdale High, Hinsdale, Illinois.
Whitney, A. S., Inspector, University of Michigan, Ann Arbor, Michigan.
Wilde, Arthur S., Principal, Evanston Academy of Northwestern University, Evanston, Illinois.
Wildman, Murray S., Professor, University of Missouri, Columbia, Missouri.
Wilson, Harry G., Chicago, Illinois.
Wreidt, E. A., University of Chicago, Chicago, Illinois.
Wright, H. C., J. Sterling Morton High, Clyde, Illinois.
Woodward, Calvin M., Dean, Washington University, St. Louis, Missouri.
Zapf, A. E. Secretary, American School of Correspondence, Chicago, Illinois.
Ziegler, W., Principal, Riverside High, Riverside, Illinois.

GENERAL INDEX.

Academic Degrees, report on granting of, H. W. Rogers, II., 120.
Accredited High Schools, Commission on, VI., 71.
    Amendment in report of (carried), G. N. Carman, VII., 43.
    Amendment in report of (lost), J. R. Kirk, VII., 43.
    Executive Committee, VII., appendix, 6.
    Members of Commission, VI., 71; VII., appendix, 6; IX., 94.
    Minutes of meeting of, IX., 50.
    Minutes of meeting of, G. N. Carman, XI., 109.
    Organization of Commission on, VII., appendix, 3.
    Report of, H. P. Judson, VII., 37; appendix, 8; VII., appendix, 1.
    Discussion on report of A. F. Nightingale, VII., 37; J. H. Baker, VII., 41; R. D. Harlan, VII., 41; A. S. Draper, VII., 41; A. S. Whitney, VII., 42.
    Report of, VIII., 175; G. N. Carman, VIII., 54; appendix, 4; X., 52; H. P. Judson, XI., 107; H. P. Judson, XII., 55.
    Resolution on Report of, A. S. Draper, VII., 43.
    Resolution on Secretary's reort of, W. R. Bridgeman, IX., 51.
    Unit Courses, VII., appendix, 8.
    In North Central Association, XI., 127.
    In North Central Association, XII., 58.
        XIII., 68-114.
Accrediting Colleges and Universities, Report of Committee on, Discussion on "Curriculum in Secondary Schools," II., 116.
    Discussion on "Teaching of Freshmen," II., 27, 29.
Adams, Charles Kendall, "Higher Education in the North Central States," II., 3-9.
Adams, Henry Carter, "Influence of Higher Commercial Education upon the Curriculum of the High School," VIII., 19, 30.
    Discussion on "Influence of Higher Education upon the Curriculum of the High School," VIII., 49.
Address of Welcome, G. N. Carman, II., 1; W. R. Harper, I., 7; L. H. Jones, VII., 3; H. S. Taylor, IV., 1.
Admission Requirements, Modification of, V., 19.
    Modification of, A. F. Nightingale, V., 20.

Resolutions on, V., 55.
Standards of, A. S. Whitney, XI., 124.
Standards of, A. S. Whitney, XII., 56.
Admission to College, Chicago Plan, H. P. Judson, I., 57.
Examination System of, C. H. Moore, I., 59.
University of Michigan, diploma system, B. A. Hinsdale, I., 51.
Systems of, I., 51.
Admission to Membership in the Board, report of committee on, Hurlbut, XII., 22.
"Advisability of Giving Credit for Work Done Outside of the Regular Courses," Homer H. Seerley, IX., 19-26.
Aiton, George B., "Address on Shaw's Garden," V., 57.
Discussion on Report of Definition of Unit in Physical Training, IX., 62.
Discussion on "State Universities and Public Schools," V., 15.
Allen, Dudley P., "Should the Terms University, College and School be Limited by Law?" VII., 72-89.
Amendments to the Constitution, III., 2; IV., 13; proposed, IV., 48.
American Federation of Learning, Geo. E. MacLean, XI., 3-25.
American Universities, Tendencies of, David Starr Jordan, VIII., 92-101.
American Universities, government of, A. S. Draper, IX., 3.
Andrews, E. B., discussion on "Common Schools in the Larger Cities," IV., 37.
Angell, James B., President's Address, I., 8.
Annual dues, XII., 24.
Armstrong, James E., Treasurer's report, VIII., 18; for year ending March 29, 1907, XII., 17.
"Co-Education, the Englewood Plan," XII., 150, 160.
"The Use and Abuse of Interscholastic Athletics," VII., 95, 103.
Discussion on "College Entrance Requirements in English," VI., 49.
Discussion on "Fees and Membership," IV., 19.
Discussion on "The High School Problem," VII., 30.
Discussion on "Social Ethics in High School Life," X., 138.
Discussion on "Systems of Admission," I., 79.
Discussion on "The Treatment of Incoming Freshmen," XIII., 59.

Athletic, Eligibility Certificate, VIII., 143.
Athletic and Institutional Career, Outline of, VIII., 144.
Athletic, Interscholastic and Intercollegiate Contests, Committee on, VII., 104.
Athletic Committee, report of, VIII., 103; IX., 28.
> Discussion on report of E. V. Robinson, IX., 34; C. A. Waldo, IX., 34; R. D. Harlan, IX., 36; C. M. Woodward, IX., 39; E. G. Cooley, IX., 40; C. S. Howe. IX., 41; A. A. Stagg, IX., 40.
> Report of, X., 25; (quoted), X., 28; C. A. Waldo, XI., 26; E. L. Harris, XII., 20.

Athletics, Discussion on. T. F. Holgate, VIII., 155.
Athletics, Intercollegiate, discussion on, Richard H. Jesse, VIII., 151.
Athletics, Intercollegiate and Secondary, discussion on, E. V. Robinson, VIII., 154.
Athletics, Table of Receipts and Expenses, IX., 32.
Auditing Committee, report on, IV., 25.
Auditing Committee, report on, XI., 165.
Ayers, discussion on Uniform Entrance Requirements, VIII., 86.
Babcock, E. J., discussion on The Treatment of Incoming Freshmen, XIII., 67.
Bachelors' Degree, requirements for, X., 33; tabulation of re-requirements for in various colleges in North Central Association, X., 38.
Baker, James H., discussion on "Curriculum in Secondary Schools," II., 113.
> Discussion on "Report of Commission on Accredited Schools," VII., 41.
> Discussion on "Short Courses in Secondary Schools," II., 59.
> Address, "Electives in Secondary Schools," VI., 61-62.
> Resolution on Statement of Definition of Units, XI., 122.

Ballou, C. Y., Discussion on "Commercial Training and the Public High School," IV., 81.
> Discussion on "Teaching of Freshmen," II., 26.
> Letter quoted on "Electives in Secondary Schools," VI., 66.

Beeman, W. W., discussion on "Teaching of Freshmen, II., 21.
Bennett, Charles A., "The Manual Arts; to What Extent Shall they be Influenced by the Recent Movement Toward Industrial Education?" XII., 38-49.

Benton, George W., "Since High Schools are Costing so Much, What can Colleges do to Assist Them in Meeting the Demands of the Public?" XI., 46-63.
Biology, Unit Courses in, VII., appendix 33.
Birge, E. A., discussion on "Service that Inspection Should be Expected to Render School and Community," VI., 36.
    Discussion of report of Medical Committee, XIII., 29-33.
    Address, "Should Industrial and Literary Schools be Combined or Encouraged to Separate?" VI., 51-55.
    Discussion of the Treatment of Incoming Freshmen, XIII., 60.
Black, William H., discussion on "Commercial Training and the Public High School," IV., 76.
    Discussion on "Entrance Requirements," III., 106.
    Discussion on "Equivalent Entrance Requirements in North Central Universities and Colleges," VI., 22.
    Discussion on "Influence of Higher Education upon the Curriculum of the High School." VIII., 42.
Bliss, F. L., Presidential Address, X., 3.
Board Examination, College Entrance, communication from, IX., 60.
    Report of Delegate E. L. Harris, X., 153.
    Report of Delegate E. L. Harris, XI., 44.
    Report of Delegate E. L. Harris, XII., 21.
Board, General Education, discussion on, H. P. Judson, XII., 66.
Board of Inspectors, report for 1903-04, A. S. Whitney, IX., 45.
    Report for 1904-05, A. S. Whitney, X., 54.
    Report of 1905-06., A. S. Whitney, XI., 124.
Boltwood, H. L., discussion on "Common Schools in Larger Cities," IV., 43.
    Discussion on "Preparation in History," I., 21.
    Discussion on "Report on Definition of Unit in Physical Training, IX., 63.
    Discussion on "Teaching of Freshmen," II., 29.
    Discussion on "Uniform Entrance Requirements," VIII., 61.
Boone, R. G., letter quoted on "Electives in Secondary Schools," VI., 63.
Botany, Committee on Definition of Unit in, XI., 119.
    Report of Com. on Definition of Unit in, VIII., 190.
    Standing Committee on Definition of Unit in, XII., 105.
    Unit Courses in, VII., appendix 26.

Bourne, H. E., discussion on "Entrance Requirements," III., 104.

Bridgeman, W. R., Resolution on Secretary's Report of Commission on Accredited Schools, XI., 51.

Brown, Abram, discussion of Curriculum, III., 138.
    Discussion of "Commercial Training and the Public High School," IV., 79.

Brown, J. F., discussion on Report on Definition of Unit in Physical Training, IX., 63.

Brown, J. Stanley, "Commercial and Industrial High Schools vs. Commercial and Industrial Courses in High Schools," XIII., —.

Brumbaugh, E. V., "Co-Education, the Cleveland Plan," XII., 138-146.

Bryan, W. J. S., "Co-Education, the Boston Plan," XII., 160-169.
    "Influence of State Universities Upon the Public School System," V., 9-14.
    Discussion on the High School Problem, VII., 32.
    Discussion on "Influence of Higher Education Upon the Curriculum of the High School," VIII., 48.
    Discussion on Report of Com. on Manual Training for Girls, XIII., 82.

Bryan, W. L., discussion on Uniform Entrance Requirements, VIII., 80.
    Discussion on the Treatment of Incoming Freshmen, XIII., 61.

Buchanan, John T., discussion on "Preparation in History," I., 20.
    Discussion on "Systems of Admission," I., 77.

Butler, N. M., "College Problem in the United States," VII., 44.
    Extract from Annual Report to Trustees of Columbia University, VII., 44.

Butts, William H., discussion on "Short Courses in Secondary Schools," II., 44.

Canfield, James H., "Some Existing Conditions in Public Education," III., 16-31
    Discussion on "Chief Purposes in Secondary Education," II., 80.
    Discussion on "College Entrance Requirements in English," III., 56.
    Discussion on "Commercial Training and the Public High School," IV., 83.
    Discussion on "Short Courses in Secondary Schools," II., 39.
    Discussion on "Teaching of Freshmen," II., 21.
    Quoted on "Courses in Commerce," IV., 72.

Carman, George N., Address of Welcome, II., 1.
  Presidential Address, VIII., 3.
  Amendment in Report of Commission on Accredited High Schools (carried), VII., 43.
  "Object and Work of the Association," VIII., 3-18.
  "Shall We Accredit Colleges," XI., 81-96.
  Minutes of Meetings of Commission on Accredited Schools, XI., 109.
  Discussion on "Commercial Training and the Public High School," IV., 74; IV., 91.
  Discussion on "The Manual Arts," XII., 52.
  Discussion on Report of Unit in Physical Training, IX., 63.
  Discussion on Report of Committee on Manual Training for Girls, XIII., 82.
  Discussion on "Technical Education," IV., 118.
Carnegie, foundation for advancement of Teaching, H. C. King, XII., 62.
Carr, J. W., discussion on the Treatment of Incoming Freshmen, XIII., 62.
Certificate, athletic eligibility, VIII., 143.
Chamberlin, T. C., discussion on "Curriculum in Secondary Schools," II., 90.
  Discussion on "Preparation in English," III., 70.
  Discussion on "Short Courses in Secondary Schools," II., 60.
Chaplin, W. S., "Education and Success," VII., 5-18.
  Discussion on "Common Schools in the Larger Cities," IV., 42.
  Discussion on "Curriculum in Secondary Schools," II., 111.
  Discussion on "Fees and Membership," IV., 18.
Charter Members of the North Central Association, P. 10.
Chicago Plan of Admission to College, H. P. Judson, I., 57.
Chief Purposes in Secondary Education, O. S. Westcott, II., 67.
  Discussion on, James H. Canfield, II., 80.
  Discussion on, L. R. Fiske, II., 81.
  Discussion on, James E. Russell, II., 79.
Chemistry, Committee on Definition of Unit in, XI., 118.
Chemistry, Standing Committee on Definition of Unit in, XII., 104.
Chemistry, Unit Courses in, VII., appendix 24.
Clark, F. C., discussion on "Commercial Training and the Public High School, IV., 63.
Clark, J. Scott, discussion on "College Entrance Requirements in English," III., 57.

Clark, Thomas Arkle, "To What Extent and by What Methods Should the Work of First Year Men in Colleges and Secondary Schools be Supervised?" XI., 131-144.
    The Treatment of Incoming Freshmen, XIII., 48-59.
Cleveland Plan of Co-Education, discussion on, E. L. Harris, XII., 146.
Co-Education, Cleveland Plan, discussion on, E. L. Harris, XII., 146.
    Englewood Plan, James E. Armstrong, XII., 150-160.
    Northwestern Plan, Thomas F. Holgate, XII., 174-177.
Co-Education, The Boston Plan, W. J. S. Bryan, XII., 160-169.
Co-Education, The Chicago University Plan, Albion Small, XII., 169-174.
Co-Education, the Cleveland Plan, E. V. Brumbaugh, XII., 138-146.
Co-Education, The Englewood Plan, Jas. E. Armstrong, XII., 150-160.
Co-Education, The Northwestern Plan, Thomas F. Holgate, XII., 174-177.
Co-Education, Tendencies in, M. V. O'Shea, XII., 109-137.
Coffeen, E. L., "The Inspecting and Accrediting of Colleges and Universities," XI., 97-107.
Cogswell, Francis, letter quoted on "Electives in Secondary Schools," VI., 65.
College Credit in High School Work, Committee on, VII., appendix, 7.
College Entrance Examination Board, Communication from, IX., 60.
College Entrance Examination Board, report of delegate to, E. L. Harris, XI., 44; XI., 53; XII., 21.
College Entrance Requirements, Uniform, discussion on, R. H. Jesse, III., 88.
College Entrance Requirements in English, F. N. Scott, VI., 37-49.
College Entrance, Requirements in English, discussion on, James E. Armstrong, VI., 49.
    Discussion on, J. H. Canfield, III., 56.
    Discussion on, E. G. Cooley, III., 66.
    Discussion on, O. F. Emerson, III., 66.
    Discussion on, A. F. Nightingale, III., 61
    Discussion on, F. H. Snow, III., 65.

College Entrance, What Determines Fitness for, A. R. Hill, VI., 4.
  Discussion on, George E. MacLean, VI., 22.
College Problem in the United States, N. M. Butler, VII., 44
  Resolution on, A. S. Draper, VII., 56.
College, Shall the Term be Limited by Law? J. V. Denney, VII., 87.
Collegiate Courses, discussion on, IV., 113.
Columbia University, extract from Annual Report, VII., 44.
Commercial Training and the Public High School, E. J. Jones, IV., 50-63.
"Common Schools in the Larger Cities," A. S. Draper, IV., 25-37.
Commerce, Courses in, quoted on, J. H. Canfield, IV., 72.
Commercial High Schools, Committee on, IV., 120.
  Resolution on, IV., 94.
Commercial Subjects, Committee on, Definition of Unit in, XI., 121.
Commercial Training and the Public High School, discussion on, C. G. Ballou, IV., 81.
  Discussion on, Wm. H. Black, IV., 76.
  Discussion on, Abram Brown, IV., 79.
  Discussion on, J. H. Canfield, IV., 83.
  Discussion on, G. N. Carman, IV., 74; IV., 91.
  Discussion on, F. C. Clark, IV., 63.
  Discussion on, E. G. Cooley, IV., 82; IV., 93.
  Discussion on, Mrs. J. B. Hargrave, IV., 85.
  Discussion on, Edmund J. James, IV., 85.
  Discussion on, W. F. King, IV., 85.
  Discussion on, J. R. Knirk, IV., 93.
  Discussion on, A. F., Nightingale, IV., 89.
  Discussion on, E. V. Robinson, IV., 80.
Commission on Accredited Schools, Executive Committee of, VII., appendix 6.
  Members of, VI., 71; VII., appendix, 6; IX., 94.
  Minutes of meeting of, IX., 50.
  Minutes of meeting of, G. N. Carman, XI., 109.
  Organization of, VII., appendix, 3.
  Report of, VI., 71; VII., appendix, 1; H. P. Judson, VII., 37; VII., appendix, 8; XIII., appendix.
  Amendment in report of (carried), G. N. Carman, VII., 43.
  Amendment in report of (lost) J. R. Kirk, VII., 43.

Discussion on report of J. H. Baker, VII., 41; A. S. Draper, VII., 41; R. D. Harlan, VII., 41; A. F. Nightingale, VII, 37; A. S. Whitney, VII., 42.

Resolution on report of A. S. Draper, VII., 43.

Committee on Athletics, report of, VIII., 103.

    Report of, IX., 28.

    Discussion of report of E. G. Cooley, IX., 40.

    Discussion of report of R. D. Harlan, IX., 36.

    Discussion of report of C. S. Howe, IX., 41.

    Discussion of report of E. V. Robinson, IX., 34.

    Discussion of report of A. A. Stagg, IX., 42.

    Discussion of report of C. A. Waldo, IX., 34.

    Discussion of report of C. M. Woodward, IX.. 39.

    Report of, X., 25; quoted, X., 28.

    Report of C. A. Waldo, XI., 26-28.

Committee, Auditing, report of, IV., 25.

Committee on College Credit for High School Work, VII., appendix, 7.

Committee on Definition of Unit in Botany, report of, VIII., 190; Botany, XI., 119; Chemistry, XI., 118; Commercial Subjects, XI., 121; English, XI., 110; French and Spanish, XI., 115; German, XI., 114; History, XI., 112; Latin and Greek, XI., 113; Manual Training, XI., 121; Mathematics, report of, VIII., 181; Mathematics, XI., 111; Physical Geography, report of, VIII., 194; Physical Geography, XI., 117; Physics, report of, VIII., 185; Physics, XI., 115; Zoology, XI., 120.

Committee on Commercial High Schools, IV., 120.

Committee on Commercial Subjects, report of, XIII., 68-73.

Committee on Equitable Entrance Requirements in North Central Association, report of, S. A. Forbes, VI., 70.

Committee to report on Equivalent Entrance Requirements in Universities and Colleges, VI., 24.

Committee of Ten, VII., 36.

Committee on High School Inspection, VII., appendix 7.

Committee, Sub, on High School Inspection, recommendations of, VII., appendix 35.

Committee on Interscholastic and Intercollegiate Athletic Contests, VII., 104.

Committee on Technical Schools, IV., 120.

Committee on Unit Courses of Study, VII., appendix, 7.
Committee on Accredited Schools, report of, VIII., 175.
  Report of G. N. Carman, VIII., appendix, 54.
  Resolution on Secretary's report of, W. R. Bridgeman, IX., 51.
  Report of, X., 52.
  Report of, H. P. Judson, XI., 107.
Commission on Teaching of English, III., 73.
Commission on Uniform Entrance Requirements, III., 101.
"Common Schools in the Larger Cities," A. S. Draper, IV., 25.
  Discussion on, E. B. Andrews, IV., 37; H. L. Boltwood, IV., 43; W. S. Chaplin, IV., 42; W. S. King, IV., 43; Mrs. Sarah P. Rhode, IV., 45.
Composition, Relation to Literature, F. N. Scott, III., 60.
  In, College Entrance Requirements, J. S. Clark, III., 57; W. J. Pringle, III., 59.
Condition of Admission to University of Illinois On and After September, 1899, David Kinley, III., 97-98.
Conference on Uniform Entrance Requirements in English, F. N. Scott, X., 20.
Constitution of the Association, P. 8.
Constitutional Amendments, III., 2; IV., 13; discussion on, IV., 13; C. H. Thurber, proposed, IV., 48.
Co-Ordinate Plan in the Education of Women, Charles F. Thwing. XII., 147-150.
  Standing Committee on, Definition of Unit in, XII., 107.
Cook, Jno. W., discussion of Treatment of Incoming Freshmen, XIII., 63.
  Moral Character in the Recommendation and Certification of Teachers, XIII., 129-135.
Cooley, E. G., discussion on "College Entrance Requirements in English," III., 66.
  Discussion on "Commercial Training and the Public High School," IV., 82; IV., 93.
  Discussion on Report of Committee on Athletics, IX., 40.
Courses in Commerce, quoted on, J. H. Canfield, IV., 72.
Courses of Study, Unit, Committee on, VII., appendix, 7.
Coulter, John M., discussion on "Short Courses in Secondary Schools," II., 55.
Coy, E. W., discussion on "Preparation in History," I., 20.
  Discussion on "Report on Definition of Unit in Physical Training," IX., 62.

Discussion on "Small High Schools in Larger Cities," VII., 19.
Discussion on "Systems of Admission," I., 80.
Discussion on "What Constitutes a College and what a Secondary School.," I., 34.
Discussion on Report of Committee on Manual Training for Girls, XIII., 81.
Letters quoted on "Electives in Secondary Schools," VI., 66.
Credit, College, for High School Work, Committee on, VII., appendix, 7.
Crusinberry, W. A., discussion on "Supervision of Freshmen," XI., 160.
Curriculum, discussion on, A. F. Nightingale, III., 145.
Discussion on Balance in, M. V. O'Shea, III., 121.
Plan of, III., 137.
Resolution on (adopted), III., 160.
"Curriculum in Secondary Schools," C. K. Adams, II., 116.
Discussion on, J. H. Baker, II., 113; T. C. Chamberlin, II., 90; W. S. Chaplin, II., 111; N. C. Dougherty, II., 96; Paul Shorey, II., 97.
Curriculum, letter on, C. W. Eliot, III., 156; David S. Jordan, III., 156; J. G. Schurman, IV., 154.
Davenport, Eugene, discussion on "Combining Industrial and Literary Schools," VI., 56.
"Defects in the Teaching of the English Language," D. K. Dodge, V., 32-38.
"Defects in Instruction in English in Secondary Schools," Mrs. May Wright Sewall, V., 26-31.
Degrees, Academic, Report on Granting of, H. W. Rogers, II., 120.
Discussion on, conferring of, C. A. Schaeffer, I., 45.
Conferring Institutions, State Supervision of, resolutions on, IV., 49.
Denney, J. V., discussion on "Should the Use of the Terms University, College and School be Limited by Law?", VII., 87.
Discussion on "Study of English," III., 42.
Discussion on "Uniform Entrance Requirements," VIII., 84.
Desirability of so Federating the North Central Colleges and Equivalent Entrance Requirements, The, Dean S. A. Forbes, VI., 11-21.
Development of the "Powers of a Pupil," E. L. Harris, II., 67-72.
Deevey, John, discussion on "Preparation in History," I., 22.
Diploma, System to Admission to University of Michigan, B. A. Hinsdale, I., 51-57.

Dodge, Daniel K., "Defects in the Teaching of the English Language," V., 32-38.
Dougherty, N. C., discussion on "Curriculum in Secondary Schools," II., 96.
　Discussion on "System of Admission," I., 70.
Downey, Professor Jno. F., discussion of Report of Medical Committee, XIII., 33.
Draper, Andrew S., "Common Schools in the Larger Cities," IV., 25-37.
　"Government in American Universities," IX., 3-17.
　"Shall the State Restrict the Use of the Terms 'College' and 'University'?" VII., 57-71.
　Discussion on "Fees and Membership," IV., 20.
　Discussion on "The High School Problem," VII., 29.
　Discussion on "Preparatory School." V., 17.
　Discussion on "Teaching of Freshmen," II., 15.
　Discussion on "Teachers," IV., 46.
　Discussion on "Uniform Entrance Requirements," VIII., 63-66.
　Discussion on "What Constitutes a College and What a Secondary School?" I., 37.
　Discussion on "Report of Commission on Accredited Schools," VII., 41.
　Resolution on "College Problem in State Universities," VII., 56.
　Resolution on "Report of Commission on Accredited Schools." VII., 43.
Eaton, E. D., discussion on "Methods of Teaching History," I., 13.
Education, Board, general discussion on, H. P. Judson, XII., 66.
Education, Higher, in North Central States, Chas. K. Adams, II., 2.
"Education and Success," W. S. Chaplin, VII., 5-18.
Education, Technical, discussion on, G. N. Carman, IV., 118.
Education, Technical, discussion on, C. A. Waldo, IV., 107.
Education, Technical, and Collegiate Courses, IV., 113.
Education, Technical, resolution on, IV., 97, 101.
Education, Technical, resolution on, referred to committee, IV., 119.
"Efficiency of Teachers," remarks on, Mrs. Maye Jones, IV., 41.
"Electives in Secondary Schools," Jas. H. Baker, VI., 61-62.
Electives in Secondary Schools, letter quoted on, C. G. Ballou, VI., 66; R. G. Boone, VI., 63; Francis Cogswell, VI., 65; E. W.

190   PROCEEDINGS OF THE

    Coy, VI., 66; W. H. Elson, VI., 62; W. W. Grant, VI., 63; G. M. Greenwood, VI., 65; Jno. N. Greer, VI., 65; W. N. Hailmann, VI., 62; L. H. Jones, VI., 64; E. H. Mark, VI., 64; W. C. Martinville, VI., 63; Jas. E. Morrow, VI., 64; A. F. Nightingale, VI., 64; Chas. C. Ramsey, VI., 63; Edward V. Robinson, VI., 61; W. F. Slaton, VI., 64; M. F. F. Swartzell, VI., 66; Jas. H. Van Sickle, VI., 62; R. H. Webster, VI., 66; C. B. Wood, VI., 64.

Eligibility, Athletic Certificate, VIII., 143.

Eliot, C. W., Letter on Curriculum, III., 156.

Elson, W. H., discussion on "Manual Arts," XII., 49.

    Letter quoted on "Electives in Secondary Schools," VI., 62.

Emerson, O. F., discussion on "College Entrance Requirements in English," III., 66.

    Remarks on "Fees and Membership," IV., 19.

English College Entrance Requirements in, discussion on, James E. Armstrong, VI., 49.

    College Entrance Requirements in, report on, III., 51.

    For College Entrance, resolution on, F. N. Scott, III., 69.

    Committee on Definition of Unit in, XI., 110.

    Standing Committee on Definition of Unit in, XII., 96.

    National Commission on, discussion, III., 63-64.

    Conference on Uniform Entrance Requirements in, report of delegate F. N. Scott, X., 20.

    Flexibility and Thoroughness in Study of, resolution and discussion, III., 31.

    In Secondary Schools, R. H. Jesse, III., 68.

    Teaching of, Commission on, III., 73.

    Discussion on, C. H. Tolman, III., 68.

    Study of, discussion on, C. H. Thurber, III., 32.

    Uniform Requirements in for 1909-10-11, X., 22.

    Unit Courses in, VII., appendix, 8.

English Language, Defects in Teaching of, D. K. Dodge, V., 32-38.

"Entrance Requirements in English," F. N. Scott, VI., 37-49.

Entrance, College, requirements in English, report on, III., 51.

Entrance, College, Requirements in English, discussion on, James E. Armstrong, VI., 49.

Entrance, College, Requirements, discussion on, III., 104.

Entrance, College, Requirements, discussion on, W. H. Black, III., 106; H. E. Bourne, III., 104; David Kinley, III., 94; W. J. Pringle, III., 101; H. W. Rogers, III., 74.

Entrance Requirements, equitable, report of committee on, S. A. Forbes, VI., 70.
Entrance Requirements, commission on, III., 101; VI., 24.
Entrance Requirements, uniform, discussion on, Ayers, VIII., 86; H. L. Boltwood, VIII., 61; W. L. Bryan, VIII., 80; J. V. Denney, VIII., 84; A. S. Draper, VIII., 63-66; E. L. Harris, VIII., 54; J. A. James, VIII., 87; R. H. Jesse, VIII., 83; D. S. Jordan, VIII., 56; H. P. Judson, VIII., 65-67-80; J. R. Kirk, VIII., 85; G. E. MacLean, VIII., 55; E. V. Robinson, VIII., 81; Sachs, VIII., 58; A. S. Whitney, VIII., 82-86; C. M. Woodward, VIII., 85.
"Entrance Equivalent Requirements in North Central Universities and Colleges," S. A. Forbes, VI., 11.
Entrance Equivalent Requirements, commission on, VI., 24.
Entrance Requirements in North Central Association, discussion on, W. H. Black, VI., 22; John J. Halsey, VI., 22; W. R. Harper, VI., 24; T. F. Holgate, VI., 23; J. O. Leslie, VI., 23; Geo. E. MacLean, VI., 22.
Entrance Requirements to University of Illinois, III., 97.
Entrance to Western Universities and Colleges. Table of Statistics, VI., 41.
"European Problems as Affected by Technical Teaching," (abstract), Wm. F. Slocum, IX., 67-74.
Examination Board, College Entrance, report of Delegate E. L. Harris, X., 153; XI., 44.
Examination Board, College Entrance, communication from, IX., 60.
"Examination System of Entrance to College," Clifford H. Moore, I., 59-67.
Executive Committee of Commission on Accredited Schools, VII., appendix, 6.
Extract from N. M. Butler's annual report to Trustees of Columbia University, VII., 44.
Fees, remarks on, IV., 16-25.
Fees and Membership, remarks on, J. E. Armstrong, IV., 19; W. S. Chaplin, IV., 18; A. S. Draper, IV., 20; O. F. Emerson, IV., 19; W. F. King, IV., 20; Joseph Swain, IV., 19; C. H. Thurber, IV., 23; C. A. Waldo, IV., 21.
Fisk, H. F., discussion on "Freshman Supervision," XI., 164.
Discussion on "Systems of Admission," I., 72.

Fisk, L. R., discussion on "Chief Purpose in Secondary Education," II., 81.
    Discussion on "Teaching of Freshmen," II., 23.
"Flexibility and Thoroughness in the Study of English," resolution on, III., 31.
Forbes, Stephen A., "The Desirability of So Federating the North Central Colleges and Universities as to Secure Essentially Uniform, or at Least Equivalent, Entrance Requirements," VI., 11-21.
    "Equivalent Entrance Requirements in North Central Universities and Colleges," VI., 11.
    Discussion on report of definition of Unit in Physical Training, IX., 65.
    Report of Committee to report on Equitable Entrance Requirements in North Central Association, VI., 70.
Ford, J. W., discussion on "What Constitutes a College and What a Secondary School," I., 41.
French. C. H., discussion on "Teaching of Freshmen," II., 10.
French, C. W., discussion on "Methods of Teaching History," I., 16.
    Report on Joint Committee of College Entrance Requirements in English, III., 51.
French and Spanish, Committee on definition of Unit in, XI., 115.
    Standing Committee on definition of Unit in, XII., 101.
French, Unit course in, VII., appendix, 16.
"Freshman Supervision," discussion on, W. S. Chaplin, XI., 145; W. A. Crusinberry, XI., 160; H. F. Fisk, XI., 164; E. L. Harris, XI., 156; M. S. Snow, XI., 161; C. A. Waldo, XI., 157.
Freshmen, teaching of, discussion on, W. W. Beman, II., 21.
    Discussion on, H. L. Boltwood, II., 29.
    Discussion on, James H. Canfield, II., 21.
    Discussion on, A. S. Draper, II., 15.
    Discussion on, C. H. French, II., 10.
    Discussion on, A. F. Nightingale, II., 30.
    Discussion on, H. W. Rogers, II., 18.
General Commission on Accredited Schools, Unit Courses in, VII., appendix, 8.
German, committee on definition of Unit in, XI., 114.
    Standing committee on definition of Unit in, XII., 100.
    Unit courses in, VII., appendix, 18.

"Government in American Universities," A. S. Draper, IX., 3-17.
Grant, W. W., quoted on "Electives in Secondary Schools," VI., 63.
Greek and Latin, committee on definition of unit in, XI., 113.
    Standing committee on definition of unit in, XII., 99.
"Greek in High School Program," II., 51.
Greek, unit courses in, VII., appendix, 16.
Greenwood, J. M., letter quoted on "Electives in Secondary Schools," VI., 65.
Greer, John N., letter quoted on "Electives in Secondary Schools," VI., 65.
Greeson, William A., discussion on "Systems of Admission," I., 68.
Hailman, W. N., quoted from letter on "Electives in Secondary Schools," VI., 62.
Halsey, John J., discussion on "Equivalent Entrance Requirements in North Central Universities and Colleges," VI., 22.
Hargrave, Mrs. J. B., discussion on "Commercial Training and the Public High School,' IV., 85.
    Remarks on "Quality of Teachers," IV., 41.
Harlan, R. D., discussion on "Report of Committee on Athletics," IX., 36.
    Discussion on "Report of Commission on Accredited Schools," VII., 41.
    Discussion on "Report on definition of unit in Physical Training," IX., 63.
Harper, Wm. R., "Address of Welcome," I., 7.
    Discussion on "Equivalent Entrance Requirements in North Central Universities and Colleges," VI., 24.
    Discussion on "Teaching of Freshmen," II., 23.
Harris, E. L., "The Development of the Powers of a Pupil," II., 67-72.
    "The Public High School; Its Status and Present Development," XII., 3-16.
    Discussion on "Cleveland Plan of Co-Education," XII., 146.
    Discussion on "Service that Inspection Should Be Expected to Render the School and the Community," VI., 36.
    Discussion on "Supervision of Freshmen," XI., 156.
    Discussion on "Uniform Entrance Units," VIII., 54.
    Report of Committee on Athletics, XII., 20.
    Report of delegate to College Entrance Examination Board, X., 153; XI., 44; XII., 21.

Report of delegate to College Entrance Examination Board, XIII., 39-41.
Hartwell, S. O., discussion on "Study of English," III., 47.
Hatfield, Henry R., discussion on "Influence of Higher Education Upon the Curriculum of the High School," VIII., 30.
Hetherington, C. W., "Regulation in Missouri and Adjacent Territory," VIII., 133-148.
High Schools, accredited, executive committee of commission on, VII., appendix, 6; Commission on, VI., 71; Members of, VI., 71.
High Schools, Commercial, resolution on, IV., 94.
High School Inspection, committee on, VII., appendix, 7.
Recommendation of sub-committee, VII., appendix, 35.
"High School Problem," C. M. Woodward, VII., 21-29.
Discussion on, James E. Armstrong, VII., 30; W. J. S. Bryan, VII., 32; A. S. Draper, VII., 29; A. F. Nightingale, VII., 32.
High School, program with Greek, II., 51; without Greek, II., 50.
High Schools, Public and Commercial Training, discussion on, C. G. Ballou, IV., 81.
Discussion on, Wm. H. Black, IV., 76.
Discussion on, Abram Brown, IV., 79.
Discussion on, J. H. Canfield, IV., 83.
Discussion on, G. N. Carman, IV., 74, 91.
Discussion on, F. C. Clark, IV., 63.
Discussion on, E. G. Cooley, IV., 82.
Discussion on, Mrs. J. B. Hargrave, IV., 85.
Discussion on, Edmund J. James, IV., 85.
Discussion on, W. F. King, IV., 85.
Discussion on, J. R. Knirk, IV., 93.
Discussion on, A. F. Nightingale, IV., 89.
Discussion on, E. V. Robinson, IV., 80.
High Schools, Small, in Larger Cities, discussion on, E. W. Coy, VII., 19.
High School Life, Social Ethics in, discussion on, James E. Arm-Armstrong, X., 138; E. H. Lewis, X., 130; A. J. Volland, X., 139; C. A. Waldo, X., 140.
Higher Education in the North Central States, Chas. K. Adams, II., 3-9.

Higher Education, Influence of, Upon the Curriculum of the High School, discussion on, C. K. Adams, VIII., 49; W. H. Black, VIII., 42; W. J. S. Bryan, VIII., 48; Henry R. Hatfield, VIII., 30; T. F. Holgate, VIII., 45; A. F. Nightingale, VIII., 47; E. V. Robinson, VIII., 30, 39; E. O. Sisson, VIII., 41; C. A. Waldo, VIII., 39; C. M. Woodward, VIII., 40.

A. R. Hill, "What Determines Fitness for Entrance to College," VI., 4.

    Discussion on, G. E. MacLean, VI., 22.

    Discussion on "Should Normal Schools Undertake the Preparation of Teachers for Secondary Schools?" X., 148.

Hinsdale, B. A., "The Diploma System of Admission to the University of Michigan," I., 51-57.

History, committee on definition of unit in, XI., 112.

    Standing committee on definition of unit in, XII., 98.

History, Methods of Teaching, discussion on, E. D. Eaton, I., 13; C. W. French, I., 16.

History, Preparation In, discussion on, H. L. Boltwood, I., 21; John T. Buchanan, I., 20; E. W. Coy, I., 20; John Dewey, I., 22; J. O. Leslie, I., 21.

History, Unit Courses in, VII., appendix, 13.

Holgate, Thomas F., "Co-Education, the Northwestern Plan," XII., 174-177.

    Discussion on Athletics, VIII., 155.

    Discussion on "Equivalent Entrance Requirements in North Central Universities and Colleges," VI., 23.

    Discussion on "Influence of Higher Education Upon the Curriculum of the High School," VIII., 45.

Howe, C. S., discussion on "Moral Responsibility of the College," IX., 91.

    Discussion on "Report of Committee on Athletics," IX., 41.

Hurlbut ———, "Admission to Membership in the Board, Standard of," report of committee on, XII., 22.

Industrial and Literary Schools, Combining of, discussion on, Eugene Davenport, VI., 56; G. B. Morrison, VI., 55.

"Influence of Higher Commercial Education Upon the Curriculum of the High School," Henry Carter Adams, VIII., 19-30.

"Influence of the State University on the Public Schools," Richard Henry Jesse, V., 3.

"Influence of State Universities on the Public School System," Wm. J. S. Bryan, V., 9-14.
"Inspection and Accrediting of Colleges and Universities," E. L. Coffeen, XI., 97-107.
Inspection, High School, committee on, VII., appendix, 7.
Inspection, Service of to School and Community, discussion on, E. A. Birge, VI., 36; E. L. Harris, VI., 36.
Inspectors, Report of Board of, A. S. Whitney, XI., 124.
Institutional and Athletic Career, Outline of, VIII., 144.
Institutions, Degree Conferring, Resolution on State Supervision of, IV., 49.
Intercollegiate Athletics, discussion on, R. H. Jesse, VIII., 151.
Intercollegiate and Interscholastic Athletic Contests, Committee on, VIII., 104.
"Intercollegiate and Secondary Athletics," E. V. Robinson, VIII., 154.
Interscholastic and Intercollegiate Athletic Contests, committee on, VII., 104.
James, Edmund J., "Commercial Training and the Public High School," IV., 50-63.
  Discussion on "Commercial Training and the Public High School," IV., 85.
  Classification of our Higher Institutions of Learning, XIII., 3-28.
James, J. A., discussion on "Uniform Entrance Requirements," VIII., 87.
Jesse, Richard Henry, "English in Secondary Schools," III., 68.
  "The Influence of the State University on the Public Schools," V., 3.
  "What Constitutes a College and What a Secondary School?" I., 24-26.
  Discussion on "Intercollegiate Athletics," VIII., 151.
  Uniform College Entrance Requirements," III., 88; VIII., 83.
Johnson, J. B., "Technical Education," IV., 95.
"Joint Report of the Six Committees on the Definition of the Units in Secondary Science," XII., 85.
Jones, L. H., Address of Welcome, VII., 3.
  Discussion on "Should Normal Schools Undertake the Preparation of Teachers for Secondary Schools," X., 142.
  Letter quoted on "Electives in Secondary Schools," VI., 64.

Jones, Miss M., Remarks on "Efficiency of Teachers in Cities," IV., 41.
Jordan, David Starr, "American University Tendencies," (abstract), VIII., 92-101.
    Discussion on "Uniform Entrance Requirements," VIII., 56.
    Discussion on "Curriculum," IV., 156.
Judson, Harry Pratt, "Co-Education, the Chicago Plan," I., 57-59.
"The Outlook for the Commission," IX., 59-60.
    Discussion on "General Education Board," XII., 66.
    Discussion on "Report of Definition of Unit in Physical Training." IX., 66.
    Discussion on "Uniform Entrance Requirements," VIII., 65, 67, 80.
    Report on Commission on Accredited Schools,' VII., 37; VII., appendix, 8; XI., 107; XII., 55.
Keeler, Harry, "The Secondary Situation—Accountability and Publicity in the Management of Athletics and in the Handling of Funds," VIII., 106-111.
King, Henry C., "The Moral Responsibility of the College," IX., 75-90.
    Statement on Carnegie Foundation for Advancement in Teaching. XII., 62.
King., W. F., discussion on "Commercial Training and the Public High School," IV., 85.
    Discussion on "Common Schools in the Larger Cities," IV., 43.
    Discussion on "Teaching of Freshmen," II., 25.
    Remarks on "Fees and Membership," IV., 20.
Kinley, David, "Conditions of Admission to the University of Illinois on and after September, 1899," III., 97-98.
    Discussion on "Commercial Training and the Public High School," IV., 93.
    Discussion on "Uniform Entrance Requirements," III., 94.
Kirk, J. R., Amendment in Report of Commission on Accredited Schools (lost), VII., 43.
    Discussion on "Uniform Entrance Requirements," VIII., 85.
Kirk, John S., "The Service that Inspection Should be Expected to Render the School and the Community," VI., 26-36.
Language, Place in the Curriculum, III., 131.
Latin, unit courses in, VII., appendix, 15.
Latin and Greek, Committee on Definition of Unit in, XI., 113.
    Standing Committee on Definition of Unit in, XII., 99.

Leslie, J. O., discussion on "Equivalent Entrance Requirements in North Central Universities and Colleges," VI., 23.
    Discussion on "Manual Arts," XII., 51.
    Discussion on "Moral Responsibility of the College," IX., 93.
    Discussion on "Preparation in History," I., 21.
Lewis, E. H., discussion on "Social Ethics in High School Life," X., 130.
Linjer, O. E., letter on "Minnesota State Board of Medical Examiners," XI., 64.
List of Accredited Schools in North Central Association Territory, XII., 58.
List of Members, 1901-2, VI., 77; 1902-3, VII., 108; 1903-4, VIII., 160; 1906-7, XI., 170; 1907-8, XII., 184; 1908-9, XIII., 157.
Literary and Industrial Schools, discussion on combining, Eugene Davenport, VI., 56; G. B. Morrison, VI., 55.
Literature, Place in the Curriculum, III., 131.
MacLean, George Edwin, "An American Federation of Learning," XI., 3-25.
    "Some Aspects of Graduate Work in State Universities," X., 85-115.
    Discussion on "Equivalent Entrance Requirements in North Central Universities and Colleges," VI., 22.
    Discussion on "The Manual Arts," XII., 53.
    Discussion on "Short Courses in Secondary Schools," II., 52.
    Discussion on "Uniform Entrance Units, University of Iowa," VIII., 55.
    Discussion on "What Determines Fitness for Entrance to College?" VI., 22.
    Discussion on Report of Medical Committee, XIII., 33.
    Report of Delegate to National Conference Committee of the Association of Colleges and Preparatory Schools, XIII., 41.
Main, J. H. T., "Are State Boards of Medical Examiners Justified in Excluding from Examinations the Graduates of Medical Colleges that Allow Advanced Credit for Work Done in Colleges of Liberal Arts?" XI., 66-73.
Mann, C. R., "The Meaning of the Movement for the Reform of Science Teaching," XII., 68-85.
Manual Arts; To What Extent Shall They be Influenced by the Recent Movement Toward Industrial Education? Chas. A. Bennett, XII., 38-49.

Discussion on, G. N. Carman, XII., 52.
Discussion on, W. H. Elson, XII., 49.
Discussion on, J. O. Leslie, XII., 51.
Discussion on, G. E. MacLean, XII., 53.
Discussion on, C. A. Waldo, XII., 53.
Manual Training, Committee on Definition of Unit in, XI., 121.
  Standing Committee on Definition of Unit in, XII., 107.
Maual Training, Place in Curriculum, III., 136.
Manual Training, Report of Committee on Definition of Unit in, XII., 90.
Mark, E. H., letter quoted on "Electives in Secondary Schools," VI., 64.
Martindale, W. C., letter quoted on "Electives in Secondary Schools," VI., 63.
Mathematics, Committee on Definition of Unit in, XI., 111.
  Standing Committee on Definition of Unit in, XII., 97.
Mathematics, Place in Curriculum, III., 136.
Mathematics, Report of Committee on Definition of Unit in, VIII., 181.
Mathematics, Unit Courses in, VII., appendix.
"Meaning of the Movement for the Reform of Science Teaching," C. R. Mann., XII., 68-85.
Medical Committee, Report of, XIII., 29-34.
Members, Charter of N. C. A., P. 10.
Members, Commission on Accredited Schools, VI., 71; VII., appendix, 6; IX., 94.
Members, list of for April 1, 1896, I., 5-6.
  List of, II., 4-6.
  Tabulated list of, IV., 17.
  List of for 1901-02, VI., 77.
  List of for 1902-03, VII., 108.
  List of for 1903-04, VIII., 160.
  List of for 1906-07, XI., 170.
  List of for 1907-08, XII., 184.
  List of for 1908-9, XIII., 157.
Membership and Fees, remarks on, James E. Armstrong, IV., 19; W. S. Chaplin, IV., 18; A. S. Draper, IV., 20; O. F. Emerson, IV., 19; W. F. King, IV., 20; Joseph Swain, IV., 19; C. H. Thurber, IV., 23; C. A. Waldo, IV., 21.
Membership in N. C. A., recommendation for, XI., 25.

Minnesota State Board of Medical Examiners, letter on, O. E. Linjer, XI., 64.

Minutes of Meetings of Commission on Accredited Schools, G. N. Carman, IX., 50; XI., 100.

Minutes of the Conference from the following Associations of Delegates Assembled at Williamstown, August 3 and 4, 1906, XII., 31.

Modification of Admission Requirements, discussion on, V., 19.

Moore, Clifford H., "The Examination System of Admission to College," I., 59-67.

"Moral Responsibility of the College," Henry C. King. IX., 75-90.
    Discussion on, C. S. Howe, IX., 91; J. O. Leslie, IX., 93; A. W. Small, IX, 88; M. Talbott, IX., 90; C. F. Thwing, IX., 88; C. M. Woodward, IX., 91.

Morrison, Gilbert B., "Social Ethics in High School Life," X., 116-130.
    Discussion on "Combining Industrial and Literary Schools," VI., 55.

Morrow, James E., letter quoted on "Electives in Secondary Schools," VI., 64.

National Commission on English, discussion on, III., 63-64.
    Remarks on, F. N. Scott, III., 64.

Nightingale, A. F., "Modification of Admission Requirements," V., 20.
    Presidential address, IV., 6.
    "What Studies Should Predominate in Secondary Schools," II., 82-86.
    Discussion on "College Entrance Requirements in English,' III., 61.
    Discussion on "Commercial Training and the Public High School," IV., 89.
    Discussion on "Curriculum," III., 145.
    Discussion on "The High School Problem," VII., 32.
    Discussion on "Influence of Higher Education Upon the Curriculum of the High School," VIII., 47.
    Discussion on "Report of Commission on Accredited Schools," VII., 37.
    Discussion on "State Universities and Public Schools," V., 14.
    Discussion on "Systems of Admission," I., 80.
    Discussion on "Teaching of Freshmen," II., 30.

Letter quoted on "Electives in Secondary Schools," VI., 64.
Resolution on "Short Courses in Secondary Schools," II., 63-64.
Normal Schools—Preparation of Teachers for Secondary Schools, discussion on, A. R. Hill, X., 148; L. H. Jones, X., 142; F. N. Scott, X., 152.
North Central States, Higher Education in, C. K. Adams, II., 2.
"Object and Work of the Association," G. N. Carman, VIII., 3-18.
Officers for 1895-6, P. 3; I., iii.
    Officers for 1897-8, II., iii.
    Officers for 1903-4, VII., 104.
    Officers for 1904-5, IX., 96.
    Officers for 1905-6, X., 159.
    Officers for 1906-7, XI., 167.
    Officers for 1907-8, XII., 180.
    Officers for 1908-9, XIII., 153.
Organization of Association, P. 5.
Organization of Commission on Accredited Schools, VII., appendix, 3.
Organization of Teachers, A. S. Draper, IV., 46.
O'Shea, M. V., "Balance in the Curriculum," discussion on, III., 121.
    "Tendencies in Co-Education," XII., 109-137.
Outline of Institutional and Athletic Career, VIII., 144.
Outlook for the Commission (abstract), H. P. Judson, IX., 59-60.
Paris Exposition, resolution regarding, II., 122.
Pearson, F. B., "Supervision of College Freshmen," XI., 147-153.
Physical Culture, report on definition of unit in, IX., 52.
Physical Geography, committee on definition of unit in, XI., 117.
Physical Geography, standing committee on definition of unit in, XII., 103.
Physical Geography, Unit Courses in, VII., appendix, 26.
Physical Geography, report of committee on definition of unit in, VIII., 194.
Physical Training, discussion on report of, G. B. Aiton, IX., 62; H. L. Boltwood, IX., 63; J. F. Brown, IX., 63; E. W. Coy, IX., 62; G. N. Carman, IX., 63; S. A. Forbes, IX., 65; R. D. Harlan, IX., 63; H. P. Judson, IX., 66; E. V. Robinson, IX., 81.
    Physical Training, resolution on report of definition in unit in, C. M. Woodward, IX., 67.

Physics, committee on definition of unit in, XI., 115.
Physics, standing committee on definition of unit in, XII., 102.
Physics, unit courses in, VII., appendix, 22.
Physics, report of committee on definition of unit in, VIII., 185.
Pierson, C. W., Resolution on Simplified Spelling, III., 119.
Preliminary Report of Committee on Shop Work and Drawing in Secondary Schools, C. M. Woodward, XII., 90.
"Preparation of Teachers for Secondary Schools," discussion on, L. H. Jones, X., 142; A. R. Hill, X., 148; F. N. Scott, X., 152.
Preparatory English, discussion on, T. C. Chamberlain, III., 70.
Preparatory School, discussion on, A. S. Draper, V., 17.
Presidential Address, James B. Angell, I., 8; F. L. Bliss, X., 3; G. N. Carman, VIII., 3; A. F. Nightingale, IV., 6.
Pringle, W. J., "Composition in College Entrance Requirements," III., 59.
    Discussion of Entrance Requirements, III., 101.
"Problem of Harmonizing State Inspection by Numerous Colleges, so as to Avoid Duplication of Work and Secure the Greatest Efficiency," (abstract), A. S. Whitney, VI., 25-26.
"Public High School; Its Status and Present Development," Edward L. Harris, XII., 3-16.
Ramsey, Charles C., letter quoted on "Electives in Secondary Schools," VI., 63.
Rankin, A. W., discussion on the Treatment of Incoming Freshmen, XIII., 65.
Recent Changes in the School System of St. Louis, V., 38.
Recommendation for Membership in N. C. A., XI., 25.
Recommendation of sub-committee on High School Inspection, VII., appendix, 35.
"Regulation of Athletics in College—What Next?" C. A. Waldo, VIII., 111-123.
"Regulation in Missouri and Adjacent Territory," C. W. Hetherington, VIII., 133-148.
Reighard, Jacob E., Report on Zoology, X., 60.
Relation of Composition to Literature," F. N. Scott, III., 60.
Report of Board of Inspectors for 1903-04, A. S. Whitney, IX., 45.
Report of Board of Inspectors for 1905, X., 54.
Report of Board of Inspectors for 1906, A. S. Whitney, XI., 124.
Report of Commission on Accredited Schools, H. P. Judson, VII., 37; VII., appendix, 8.

Report of Commission on Accredited Schools, VII., appendix, 1.
Report of Commission on Accredited Schools, amendment in (carried), G. N. Carman, VII., 43.
Report of Commission on Accredited Schools, amendment in (lost), J. R. Kirk, VII., 43.
Report of Commission on Accredited Schools, discussion on, J. H. Baker, VII., 41; A. S. Draper, VII., 41; R. D. Harlan, VII., 41; A. F. Nightingale, VI., 37; A. S. Whitney, VII.. 42.
Report of Commission on Accredited Schools, resolution on, A. S. Draper, VII., 43.
Report of Commission on Accredited Schools, VIII., 175.
Report of Commission on Accredited Schools, VIII., appendix, 54. G. N. Carman, X., 52.
Report of Commission on Accredited Schools, H. P. Judson, XI., 107.
Report of Commission on Accredited Schools, H. P. Judson, XII., 55.
Report of Commission on Accredited Schools, XIII., appendix.
Report of Committee on Athletics, VIII., 103.
Report of Committee on Athletics, IX., 28.
Report of Committee on Athletics, X., 25.
Report of Committee on Athletics (quoted), X., 28.
Report of Committee on Athletics, C. A. Waldo, XI., 26-8.
Report of Committee on Athletics, E. L. Harris, XII., 20.
Report of Joint Committee on College Entrance Requirements in English, III., 51.
Report of Committee on Definition of Unit in Botany, VIII., 190.
Report of Committee on Definition of Unit in Manual Training, C. M. Woodward, XII., 90.
Report of Committee on Definition of Unit in Mathematics, VIII., 181.
Report of Committee on Definition of Unit in Physical Culture, IX., 52.
Report of Committee on Definition of Unit in Geography, VIII., 194.
Report of Committee on Definition of Unit in Physics, VIII., 185.
Report of Committee on Definition of Unit in Zoology, J. E. Reighard, X., 60.
Report of Committee on Standard for Admission to Membership in the Board, Hurlbut, XII., 22.

Report of Committee to Report on Equitable Entrance Requirements in North Central Universities and Colleges, S. A. Forbes, VI., 70.
Report of Delegate to the Conference on Uniform Entrance Requirements in English, F. N. Scott, X., 20.
Report of Delegate from N. C. A. to College Entrance Examination Board, E. L. Harris, X., 153; XII., 21; XIII., 39.
Report on granting of Academic degrees, H. W. Rogers, II., 120.
Report(special), on granting of degrees, III., 111.
Report, Treasurer's, VI., 3.
Report, Treasurer's, VII., 18.
Report, Treasurer's, IX., 17.
Report, Treasurer's, XI., 25.
Report, Treasurer's, XII., 17, J. E. Armstrong.
Report, Treasurer's, XIII., 28.
Requirements for Admission, resolution on, V., 55.
Requirements for the Bachelor's Degree, X., 33.
Requirements, Committee on Equivalent Entrance, in N. C. A., VI., 24.
Requirements, entrance, in North Central Universities and Colleges, discussion on, W. H. Black, VI., 22; John J. Halsey, VI., 22; W. R. Harper, VI., 24; T. F. Holgate, VI., 23; J. O. Leslie, VI., 23; Geo. E. MacLean, VI., 22.
Resident Students in Universities and Colleges, table of number of, since 1889-06, XII., 128.
Resolution on College Entrance, English, F. N. Scott, III., 69.
Resolution on Curriculum (adopted), III., 160.
Resolution on Statement of definition of Units, J. H. Baker, XI., 122.
"Revolution in Methods, or the New Departure," C. M. Woodward, VIII., 123-133.
Rhode, Mrs. Sarah P., discussion on "Common Schools in Larger Cities," IV., 45.
Robinson, E V., Report of Committee on Commercial Subjects, XIII., 68.
Robinson, E. V., discussion on "Commercial Training and the Public High School," IV., 80.
>Discussion on "Influence of Higher Education Upon the Curriculum of the High School," VIII., 30 and 39.
>Discussion on "Intercollegiate and Secondary Athletics," VIII., 154.

Discussion on Report of Committee on Athletics, IX., 34.
Discussion on Report on Definition of Unit in Physical Training, IX., 81.
Discussion on Uniform Entrance Requirements," VIII., 81.
Quoted from letter on "Electives in Secondary Schools," VI., 61.
Rogers, H. W., discussion on Uniform Entrance Requirements, III.. 74.
Discussion on "Entrance Requirements," III., 103.
Discussion on "Teaching of Freshmen," II., 18.
Report on Granting of Academic Degrees, II., 120.
Russell, James E., discussion on "Short Courses in Secondary Schools," II., 33.
Discussion on "Chief Purposes in Secondary Education," II. 79.
Sachs, discussion on Uniform Entrance Requirements, VIII., 58.
Schaeffer, C. A., discussion on "Conferring Degrees," I.. 45.
Schobinger, John J., discussion on "System of Admission," I., 74.
Schools, Accredited, General Commission on Unit Courses in, VII., appendix, 8; XIII., appendix.
Schools. Accredited in N. C. A., XI., 127.
Schools, Accredited in N. C. A. Territory, list of, XII., 58.
Schools, Accredited, report of commission on, VIII., 175.
Schools, Accredited, report of commission on, G. N. Carman, VII., 54, appendix; XIII., appendix.
Schools, Accredited, report of commission on, H. P. Judson, XII., 55.
School, College and University, should terms be limited by law? J. V. Denney, VII., 87.
Schurman, J. G., letter on Curriculum, III., 154.
Science, Place in Curriculum, III., 135.
Science, Secondary, joint report of six committees on the Definition of Units in, XII., 85.
Scott, F. N.. "College Entrance Requirements in English," VI., 37-49.
"Relation of Composition to Literature," III., 60.
Discussion on "Should Normal Schools Undertake the Preparation of Teachers for Secondary Schools?" X., 152.
Remarks on "National Commission on English," III., 64.
Report of Delegate to the Conference on Uniform Entrance Requirements in English, X., 20.

Resolution on College Entrance English, III., 69.

Report of Delegate to Conference on Uniform Entrance Requirements in English, XIII., 35.

Scott, W. A., Commercial and Industrial High Schools vs. Commercial and Industrial Courses in High Schools, XIII., —.

Secondary and Intercollegiate Athletics, discussion on, E. V. Robinson, VIII., 154.

Secondary Schools, Electives in Letters, quoted on, C. G. Ballou, VI., 66; R. G., Boone, VI., 63; Francis Cogswell, VI., 65; E. W. Coy, VI., 66; W. H. Elson, VI., 62; W. W. Grant, VI., 63; G. M., Greenwood, VI., 65; John N. Greer, VI., 65; W. N. Hailman, VI., 62; L. H. Jones, VI., 64; E. H. Mark, VI., 64; W. C. Martindale, VI., 63; James E. Morrow, VI., 64; A. F. Nightingale, VI., 64; Chas. C. Ramsay, VI., 63; E. V. Robinson, VI., 61; W. F. Slaton, VI., 64; M. F. F. Swartzell, VI., 66; James H. Van Sickle, VI., 62; R. H. Webster, VI., 66; C. B. Wood, VI., 64.

Secondary Schools, Shop Work and Drawing in, report on, C. M. Woodward, XII., 90.

Secondary Science, "Joint Report of the Six Committees on the Definition of Units in, XII., 85.

Secondary Situation, Accountability and Publicity in the Management of Athletics, and in the Handling of Funds, Harry Keeler, VIII., 106-111.

Seerley, Homer H., "The Advisability of Giving Credit for Work Done Outside of the Regular Courses," IX., 19-26.

"Service that Inspection Should be Expected to Render the School and the Community," John S. Kirk, VI., 26-36.

Sewall, Mrs. May Wright "Defects in Instruction of English in Secondary Schools," V., 26-31.

"Shall we Accredit Colleges?" G. N. Carman, XI., 81-96.

"Shall the State Restrict the Use of the Terms, College and University?" A. S. Draper, VII., 57-71.

Shaw's Garden, address on, G. B. Alton, V., 57.

Shelton, President C. E., discussion of report of Medical Committee, XIII., 33.

Shop Work and Drawing in Secondary Schools, report on, C. M. Woodward, XII., 90.

Shop Work, Syllabus of Units in, XII., 92.

Shorey, Paul, discussion of "Curriculum in Secondary Schools," II., 97.
"Short Courses in Secondary Schools," discussion on, James H. Baker, II., 59; Wm., H. Butts, II., 44; Jas. H. Canfield, II., 39; T. C. Chamberlin, II., 60; Jno. W., Coulter, II., 55; Geo. E. MacLean, II., 52; Jas. E. Russell, II., 33.
"Short Courses in Secondary Schools," resolution on, A. F. Nightingale, II., 63-64.
"Should Industrial and Literary Schools be Combined or Encouraged to Separate?" E. A. Birge, VI., 51-55.
"Should the Use of the Terms University, College and School, be Limited by Law?" Dudley P. Allen, VII., 72-89.
Simplified Spelling, resolution on, C. W. Pierson. III., 119.
"Since High Schools are Costing so Much, What can Colleges do to Assist Them in Meeting the Demands of the Public?" George W. Benton, XI., 46-63.
Sisson, E. O., discussion on "Influence of Higher Education Upon the Curriculum of the High School," VIII., 41.
Slaton, W. F., letter quoted on "Electives in Secondary Schools," VI., 64.
Slocum, Wm. F., "European Problems as Affected by Technical Teaching" (abstract), IX., 69-74.
Small, Albion, "Co-Education, the Chicago Plan," XII., 169-174.
  Discussion on "Moral Responsibility of the College, IX., 88.
Snow, F. H., discussion on "College Entrance Requirements in English," III., 65.
Snow, M. S., discussion on "Supervision of Freshmen," XI., 161.
"Social Ethics in High School Life," Gilbert B. Morrison, X., 116-130.
  Discussion on, James E Armstrong, X., 138; E. H. Lewis, X., 130; A. J. Volland, X., 139; C. A. Waldo, X., 140.
Soldan, F. L., resolutions of respect upon the death of, XIII., 135.
"Soldier of Peace," a poem, Howard S. Taylor, IV., 3-4.
"Some Aspects of Graduate Work in State Universities," G. E. MacLean, X., 85-115.
"Some Existing Conditions in Public Education," James H. Canfield, III., 16-31.
"Spanish and French, Committee on Definition of Unit in, XI., 115.
"Spanish and French, Standing Committee on Definition of Unit in, XII., 101.

Spanish, Unit Course in. VII., appendix, 21.
Spelling, Simplified, Resolution on, III., 119.
Stagg, A. A., "The Uses of Football," VII., 90-95.
Discussion on Report of Committee on Athletics, IX., 42.
"Standards of Admission," A. S. Whitney, XI., 124; XII., 56.
Standard of Admission to Membership in Board, report of Committee on, Hurlbut, XII., 22.
Standing Committee on Definition of Unit in Botany, XII., 105.
Standing Committee on Definition of Unit in Chemistry, XII., 104.
Standing Committee on Definition of Unit in Commercial Subjects, XII., 107.
Standing Committee on Definition of Unit in English, XII., 96.
Standing Committee on Definition of Unit in French and Spanish, XII., 101.
Standing Committee on Definition of Unit in German, XII., 100.
Standing Committee on Definition of Unit in History, XII., 98.
Standing Committee on Definition of Unit in Latin and Greek, XII., 99.
Standing Committee on Definition of Unit in Manual Training, XII., 107.
Standing Committee on Definition of Unit in Mathematics, XII., 97.
Standing Committee on Definition of Unit in Physical Geography, XII., 103.
Standing Committee on Definition of Unit in Physics, XII., 102.
Standing Committee on Definition of Unit in Zoology, XII., 106.
"State Boards of Medical Examiners—Are they Justified in Excluding from Examinations the Graduates of Medical Colleges that Allow Advanced Credit for Work Done in Colleges of Liberal Arts?" J. H. T. Main, XI., 66-73; Fred C. Zapffe, XI., 73-80.
"State Supervision of Degree Conferring Institutions," resolution on, IV., 49.
"State Universities, Influence on Public Schools," R. H. Jones, V., 3.
"State Universities and Public Schools," discussion on, G. B. Aiton, V., 15; A. F. Nightingale, V., 14.
Statement on Carnegie Foundation for Advancement of Teaching, H. C. King, XII., 62.
Statistics, table of, entrance to Western Universities and Colleges, VI., 41.

Study of English, discussion on, J. V. Denney, III., 42; S. O. Hartwell, III., 47.
"Supervision of Freshmen," discussion on, W. S. Chaplin, XI., 145.
"Supervision of College Freshmen," F. B. Pearson, XI., 147-153.
Swain, Joseph, remarks on "Fees and Membership," IV., 19.
Swartzell, M. F. F., letter quoted on "Electives in Secondary Schools," VI., 66.
Syllabus of Units in Shop Work, XII., 92.
Systems of Admission to Universities and Colleges, I., 51.
"Systems of Admission," discussion on, J. E. Armstrong, I., 79; John T. Buchanan, I., 77; E. W. Coy, I., 80; N. C. Dougherty, I., 70; H. F. Fisk, I., 72; Wm. A. Greeson, I., 68; A. F. Nightingale, I., 80; John J. Schobinger, I., 70.
Table of Athletic Receipts and Expenses, IX., 32.
Table of Institutions not Members of North Central Association, X., 42.
Table of Insitutions Requiring Language for Admission, X., 41; X., 45.
Table of Institutions Requiring Latin or Greek for Admission, X., 41.
Table of Institutions not Members of N. C. A. Requiring Latin or Greek for Admission, X., 45.
Table Showing Number of Undergraduate and Resident Students in Universities and Colleges from 1889-90 to 1905-06, XII., 128.
Table of Statistics, Entrance to Western Universities and Colleges, VI., 41.
Tabulation of Requirements for Bachelor's Degree in Various Colleges, X., 38.
Talbott, M., discussion on Moral Responsibility of the College, IX., 90.
Taylor, H. S., Address of Welcome, IV., 1.
"The Soldier of Peace," IV., 3-4.
Teachers, Quality of, remarks on, Mrs. J. B. Hargraves, IV., 41.
Teachers, Organization of, A. S. Draper, IV., 46.
Teaching of English, Commission on, III., 73.
Teaching of English, discussion on, C. K. Adams, II., 27-29.
Teaching of English, discussion on, A. H. Tolman, III., 68.
Teaching of Freshmen, discussion on, C. S. Ballou, II., 26; L. R. Fiske, II., 23; W. R. Harper, II., 23; W. F. King, II., 25.

Technical Education, J. B. Johnson, IV., 95.
  Discussion on, G. N. Carman, IV., 118.
  Discussion on, C. A. Waldo, IV., 107.
  Resolutions on, IV., 97; IV., 101.
  Resolution on, referred to Committee, IV., 119.
Technical Education and Collegiate Courses, IV., 113.
Technical Schools, Committee on, IV., 120.
Ten, Committee of, VII., 36.
"Tendencies in Co-Education," M. V. O'Shea, XII., 109-137.
Thompson, W. O., Moral Character in the Recommendation and Certification of Teachers, XIII., 123-129.
Thurber, C. H., discussion on "Constitutional Amendment," IV., 13.
  Remarks on "Fees and Membership," IV., 23.
  Discussion on "Study of English," III., 32.
Thwing, Chas. F., "The Co-Ordinate Plan in the Education of Women," XII., 147-150.
  Discussion on "Moral Responsibility of the College," IX., 88.
"To What Extent and by What Methods Should the Work of First Year Men in Colleges and Secondary Schools be Supervised?" Thomas Arkle Clark, XI., 131-144.
Treasurer's Report, IV., 5; VI., 3; VII., 18; J. E. Armstrong, VIII., 18; IX., 17; X., 156; XI., 25; J. E. Armstrong, XII., 17; XIII., 28.
"True and False Standards of Graduate Work," Andrew F. West, X., 71-85.
"Use and Abuse of Interscholastic Athletics," James E. Armstrong, VII., 95-103.
"Uses of Football," A. A. Stagg, VII., 90-95.
Undergraduates in Universities and Colleges, member of, table of from 1889-1906, XII., 128.
Uniform Requirements in English for 1909-10-11, X., 22.
Units, Definition of, Resolution on, J. H. Baker, XI., 122.
Unit Courses in Botany, VII., appendix, 26; Biology, VII., appendix, 33; Chemistry, VII., appendix, 24; English, VII., appendix, 8; French, VII., appendix, 16; German, VII., appendix, 18; Greek, VII., appendix, 16; General Commission on Accredited Schools, VII., appendix, 8; History, VII., appendix, 13; Latin, VII., appendix, 15; Mathematics, VII., appendix, 11; Physical Geography, VII., appendix, 26; Physics, VII., appendix, 22; Spanish, VII., appendix, 21.

Unit Courses of Study, Committee on, VII., appendix, 7.
"Universities, American, Government of," A. S. Draper, IX., 3.
Universities and Colleges, Systems of Admission to, I., 51.
University, College and School—Should Terms be Limited by Law? discussion on, J. V. Denney, VII., 87.
University of Illinois, Entrance Requirements, III., 97.
University of Michigan, Diploma System of Admission to, B. A. Hinsdale, I., 51.
Universities Requiring no Language for Admission, X., 41.
Van Sickle, James H., quoted from letter on "Electives in Secondary Schools," VI., 62.
Volland, A. J., discussion on "Social Ethics in High School Life," X., 139.
Waldo, C. A., discussion on report of Committee on Athletics, IX., 34.
  Discussion on "Influence of Higher Education Upon the Curriculum of the High School," VIII., 39.
  Discussion on "The Manual Arts," XII., 53.
  Discussion on "Social Ethics in High School Life," X., 140.
  Discussion on "Supervision of Freshmen," XI., 157.
  Discussion on "Technical Education," IV., 107.
  "Regulation of Athletics in College. What Next?" VIII., 111-123.
  Remarks on "Fees and Membership," IV., 21.
Webster, R. H., letter quoted on "Electives in Secondary Schools," VI., 66.
West, Andrew F., "True and False Standards of Graduate Work," X., 71-85.
Westcott, O. S., "Chief Purpose in Secondary Education," II., 67.
Western Universities and Colleges, Entrance to, table, VI., 41.
"What Constitutes a College and What a Secondary School?" R. H. Jesse, I., 24-46.
  Discussion on, J. W. Ford, I., 41.
"What Determines Fitness for Entrance to College?" A. R. Hill, VI., 4-11.
"What Studies Should Predominate in Secondary Schools?" A. F. Nightingale, II., 82-86.
Whitney, A. S., "The Problem of Harmonizing State Inspection by Numerous Colleges so as to Avoid Duplication of Work and Secure the Greatest Efficiency" (abstract), VI., 25-26.

Discussion on Report of Commission on Accredited Schools, VII., 42.
Discussion on Uniform Entrance Requirements, VIII., 82.
Discussion on Uniform Entrance Requirements, VIII., 86.
Report of Board of Inspectors for 1903-04, IX., 45.
Report of Board of Inspectors for 1905-06, XI., 124.
"Standards of Admission," XI., 124; XII, 56.

Wilde, A. S., discussion on the Treatment of Incoming Freshmen, XIII., 67.

Williamstown, Minutes of Conference, August 3, and 4, 1906, XII., 31.

Wood, C. B., letter quoted on "Electives in Secondary Schools," VI., 64.

Woodward, C. M., discussion on report of Committee on Athletics, IX., 39.
Discussion on "Influence of Higher Education Upon the Curriculum of the High School," VIII., 40.
Discussion on "Moral Responsibility of the College," IX., 91.
Discussion on "Uniform Entrance Requirements," VIII., 85.
"The High School Problem," VII., 21-29.
"The New Departure, or Revolution in Methods," VIII., 123-133.
Preliminary Report on Shop Work and Drawing in Secondary Schools, XII., 90.
Report of Committee on Definition of Unit in Manual Training, XII., 90.
Resolution on Report on Definition of Unit in Physical Training, IX., 67.
Report of Committee on Manual Training for Girls, XIII., 77.

Zapffe, Fred C., "Are State Boards of Medical Examiners Justified in Excluding from Examinations the Graduates of Medical Colleges that Allow Advanced Credit for Work Done in Colleges of Liberal Arts?" XI., 73-80.

Zoology, Committee on Definition of Unit in, XI., 120.
Zoology, Standing Committee on Definition of Unit in, XII., 106.
Zoology, Report of Committee on Definition of Unit in, X., 60; Jacob E. Reighard.

INDEX TO ADDRESSES.

Adams, Charles Kendall, "Higher Education in the North Central States, II., 3-9.

Adams, Henry Carter, "Influence of Higher Commercial Education Upon the Curriculum of the High School," VIII., 19-30.

Allen, Dudley P., "Should the Use of the Terms University, College, and School, be Limited by Law?" VII., 72-89.

Armstrong, James E., "The Use and Abuse of Interscholastic Athletics," VII., 95-103.

"Co-Education, the Englewood Plan," XII., 150-160.

Baker, James H., "Electives in Secondary Schools," VI., 61-62.

Bennett, Charles A., "The Manual Arts; To What Extent Shall they be Influenced by the Recent Movement Toward Industrial Education?" XII., 38-49.

Benton, George W., "Since High Schools are Costing so Much, What Can Colleges do to Assist Them in Meeting the Demands of the Public?" XI., 46-63.

Birge, E. A., "Should Industrial and Literary Schools be Combined, or Encouraged to Separate?" VI., 51-55.

Brown, J. Stanley, "Commercial and Industrial High Schools vs. Commercial and Industrial Courses in High Schools, XIII., 136-143.

Brumbaugh, E. V., "Co-Education, the Cleveland Plan," XII., 138-146.

Bryan, William J. S., "Influence of State Universities on the Public School System," V., 9-14.

"Co-Education, the Boston Plan," XII., 160-169.

Canfield, James H., "Some Existing Conditions in Public Education," III., 16-31.

Carman, George N., "Object and Work of the Association," VIII., 3-18.

"Shall We Accredit Colleges?" XI., 81-96.

Chaplin, W. S., "Education and Success," VII., 5-18.

Clark, Thomas Arkle, "To What Extent and by What Methods Should the Work of First Year Men in Colleges and Secondary Schools be Supervised?" XI., 131-144.

The Treatment of Incoming Freshmen, XIII., 48-59.

Coffeen, E. L., "The Inspecting and Accrediting of Colleges and Universities," XI., 97-107.

Cook, Jno. W., "Moral Character in the Recommendation and Certification of Teachers," XIII., 129-135.

Dodge, Daniel K., "Defects in the Teaching of the English Language," V., 32-38.

Draper, Andrew S., "Common Schools in the Larger Cities," IV., 25-37.

"Shall the State Restrict the Use of the Terms 'College' and 'University?'" VII., 57-71.

"Government in American Universities," IX., 3-17.

Forbes, Stephen A., "The Desirability of so Federating the North Central Colleges and Universities as to Secure Essentially Uniform, or at Least Equivalent Entrance Requirements," VI., 11-21.

Harris, Edward L., "The Development of the Powers of a Pupil," II., 67-72.

"The Public High School; Its Status and Present Development," XII., 3-16.

Hetherington, C. W., "Regulation in Missouri and Adjacent Territory," VIII., 133-148.

Hill, A. Ross, "What Determines Fitness for Entrance to College?" VI., 4-11.

Hinsdale, B. A., "The Diploma System of Admission to the University of Michigan," I., 51-57.

Holgate, Thomas F., "Co-Education, the Northwestern Plan," XII., 174-177.

James, Edmund Janes, "Commercial Training and the Public High School," IV., 50-63.

"Classification of our Higher Institutions of Learning," XIII., 3-28.

Jesse, Richard H., "What Constitutes a College and What a Secondary School?" I., 24-46.

"The Influence of the State University on the Public Schools," V., 3.

Johnson, J. B., "Technical Education," IV., 95.

Jordan, David Starr, "American University Tendencies" (abstract), VIII., 92-101.

Judson, Harry Pratt, "Co-Education; the Chicago Plan," I., 57-59.

"The Outlook for the Commission" (abstract), IX., 59-60.

Keeler, Harry, "The Secondary Situation; Accountability and Publicity in the Management of Athletics, and in the Handling of Funds," VIII., 106-111.

King, Henry C., "The Moral Responsibility of the College," IX., 75-90.

Kinley, David, "Conditions of Admission to the University of Illinois on and after September, 1899," III., 97-98.

Kirk, John S., "The Service that Inspection Should be Expected to Render the School and the Community," VI., 26-36.

MacLean, George Edwin, "Some Aspects of Graduate Work in State Universities," X., 85-115.

"An American Federation of Learning," XI., 3-25.

Main, J. H. T., "Are State Boards of Medical Examiners Justified in Excluding from Examinations the Graduates of Medical Colleges that Allow Advanced Credits for Work Done in Colleges of Liberal Arts?" XI., 66-73.

Mann, C. K., "The Meaning of the Movement for the Reform of Science Teaching," XII., 68-85.

Moore, Clifford H., "The Examination System of Admission to College," I., 59-67.

Morrison, Gilbert B., "Social Ethics in High School Life," X., 116-130.

Nightingale, A. F., "What Studies Should Predominate in Secondary Schools?" II., 82-86.

President's Address, IV., 6.

O'Shea, M. V., "Tendencies in Co-Education," XII., 109-137.

Pearson, F. B., "Supervision of College Freshmen," XI., 147-153.

Scott, F. N., "College Entrance Requirements in English," VI., 37-49.

Seerley, Homer H., "The Advisability of Giving Credit for Work Done Outside of the Regular Course," IX., 19-26.

Sewall, Mrs. Mae Wright, "Defects in Instruction in English in Secondary Schools," V., 26-31.

Slocum, William F., "European Problems as Affected by Technical Training," IX., 69-74.

Small, Albion, "Co-Education; the Chicago Plan," XII., 169-174.

Stagg, A. A., "The Uses of Football," VII., 90-95.

Taylor, Howard S., "The Soldier of Peace" (poem), IV., 3-4.

Thompson, W. O., "Moral Character in the Recommendation and Certification of Teachers," XIII., 123-135.

Thwing, Charles F., "The Co-Ordinate Plan in the Education of Women," XII., 147-150.

Waldo, C. A., "Regulation of Athletics in College—What Next?" VIII., 111-123.
West, Andrew F., "True and False Standards of Graduate Work," X., 71-85.
Whitney, A. S., "The Problem of Harmonizing State Inspection, so as to Avoid Duplication of Work, and Secure the Greatest Efficiency" (abstract), VI., 25-26.
Woodward, C. M., "The High School Problem," VII., 21-29.
    "The New Departure, or, Revolution in Methods," VIII., 123-133.
Zapffe, Fred C., "Are State Boards of Examiners Justified in Excluding from Examinations the Graduates of Medical Colleges that Allow Advanced Credit for Work Done in Colleges of Liberal Arts?" XI., 73-80.

APPENDIX TO THE PROCEEDINGS OF THE THIRTEENTH
ANNUAL MEETING OF THE ASSOCIATION OF COLLEGES AND
SECONDARY SCHOOLS OF THE NORTH CENTRAL STATES

1908

REPORT

OF THE

Commission on Accredited Schools and Colleges

PUBLISHED BY THE ASSOCIATION
1908

NOTICE.

The following pages form part of the Proceedings of the Thirteenth Annual Meeting of the North Central Association of Colleges and Secondary Schools. The price of this volume of the Proceedings entire is twenty-five cents. The price of the Appendix, printed separately, is ten cents. Copies of either may be obtained by addressing the Treasurer of the Association, Principal J. E. Armstrong, Englewood High School, Chicago.

THE COMMISSION ON ACCREDITED SCHOOLS AND COLLEGES.

The Commission on Accredited Schools of the North Central Association of Colleges and Secondary Schools was organized at the Sixth Annual Meeting of the Association held in Chicago in March, 1901.

The first annual report* of the Commission was adopted by the Association March 28th, 1902. The duty of preparing a list of accredited schools was assigned to a committee of the Commission known as the Board of Inspectors. The Board prepared its first list of schools in 1904. The list is revised yearly and printed at the time of the Annual Meeting of the Association. In 1906 standing committees, consisting of two members from each of the states, one representing the college and the other the secondary school, were appointed on definitions of units, to make such revisions and additions as may, from time to time, be necessary. At the same time the name of the Commission was changed to read "The Commission on Accredited Schools and Colleges," and the Commission was instructed to report at the next annual meeting on the advisability of adopting a plan for the inspection of colleges and universities and the standardizing of their work. A committee of the Commission consisting of the Chairman, the Vice-Chairman, and the Secretary, was appointed to prepare and present to the Commission a plan for inspecting and accrediting colleges. A report of the committee was presented in 1908, and the As-

---

*Printed in the Proceedings of the Seventh Annual Meeting of the Association, also separately as an Appendix.

sociation voted that the Commission should undertake the work of inspecting and accrediting colleges and universities, but the plan presented was referred back to the Commission for further consideration.

The Commission, as now constituted, is as follows:

OFFICERS.

Chairman, President George E. MacLean, Iowa State University.

Vice-Chairman, President James H. Baker, University of Colorado.

Secretary, Director George N. Carman, Lewis Institute, Chicago.

APPOINTED FOR 1906-1909.

President Harry Pratt Judson, University of Chicago.
Professor E. O. Holland, Indiana University.
Superintendent A. F. Nightingale, Chicago.
Principal George W. Benton, Shortridge High School, Indianapolis.

APPOINTED FOR 1907-1910.

President James H. Baker, University of Colorado.
Professor F. G. Hubbard, University of Wisconsin.
Inspector A. S. Whitney, University of Michigan.
Principal E. L. Harris, Central High School, Cleveland.

APPOINTED FOR 1908-1911.

President George E. MacLean, State University of Iowa.
President John R. Kirk, Normal School, Kirksville, Mo.
Director George N. Carman, Lewis Institute, Chicago.
Principal F. L. Bliss, University School, Detroit.

ADDITIONAL MEMBERS.

A delegate member may be appointed by each college or university belonging to the Association which has a freshman class of at least fifty members. The chair shall also appoint a sufficient number of members from the secondary schools to maintain a parity of representation as between the secondary schools and the colleges.

At a meeting of the Commission held immediately after the adjournment of the Association, March 28, 1908, the following committees were appointed:

Committee on Standards of Colleges and Universities: President MacLean, President Baker, Director Carman, President King of Cornell College, Iowa, and Principal Bliss, of Detroit University School.

Committee on Definition of Units: Principal Harris of Cleveland Central High School, President Hughes of Ripon College, Inspector Aiton of Minnesota, Principal Benton of Shortridge High School, Indianapolis, and Director Carman.

DEFINITIONS OF UNIT COURSES OF STUDY.

UNIT COURSES IN GENERAL.

1. A unit course of study is defined as a course covering a school year of not less than thirty-six weeks, with four or five periods of at least forty-five minutes each per week.

2. The graduation requirement of the high school and the entrance requirement of the college shall include fifteen units as above defined.

3. All high school curricula and all requirements for college entrance shall include as constants three units of English and two units of mathematics.

COLLEGE CREDIT FOR WORK DONE IN SECONDARY SCHOOLS.

1. The Commission favors the general principle that colleges should give advanced credit for secondary school work, when sufficient in amount and quality, done in addition to the fifteen units required for admission.

2. In the opinion of the Commission no advanced college credit should be given for less than one full year of secondary school work in any subject, except so far as half units are specified in the definitions of unit courses, or for any study that is not pursued later than the second year of the high school course.

3. The amount of advanced credit to be awarded in any subject should be determined by the college which the student enters.

UNIT COURSES IN PARTICULAR SUBJECTS.

ENGLISH.

COMMITTEE.

F. N. Scott (Chairman), Professor of Rhetoric, University of Michigan.
J. V. Denney, Professor of English and Dean of the College of Arts, Philosophy, and Science, Ohio State University.
J. W. McLane, Principal Lincoln High School, Cleveland, Ohio.
T. A. Clark, Professor of Rhetoric and Dean of Undergraduates, University of Illinois.
H. E. Giles, Principal, High School, Kewanee, Illinois.
W. F. Webster, Principal, East High School, Minneapolis, Minnesota.
H. M. Belden, Professor of English, University of Missouri.
E. M. Hopkins, Professor of Rhetoric and English Language, University of Kansas.
W. W. Stoner, Superintendent of City Schools, York, Nebraska.
F. G. Hubbard, Professor of the English Language, University of Wisconsin.
H. E. Coblentz, Head of the Department of English, South Division High School, Milwaukee, Wisconsin.
W. L. Cochrane, Superintendent of City Schools, Aberdeen, South Dakota.
C. F. Ansley, Professor of English, State University of Iowa.
G. P. Koebel, Teacher of English in High School, Clinton, Iowa.
B. F. Kizer, Director of English, Manual Training High School, Kansas City, Missouri.
E. S. Parsons, Dean of Department of Liberal Arts, Colorado College.
W. M. Shafer, Superintendent of Schools, Cripple Creek, Colorado.

Definitions (3 units).

The three units in English should cover the following subjects:

(a) *Grammar.* The student should have a sufficient knowledge of English grammar to enable him at need to point out the syntactical structure of any sentence which he encounters in the prescribed reading. He should also be able to state intelligently the leading grammatical principles when he is called upon to do so. Whether this knowledge is obtained in the elementary school and the secondary school combined or only in the elementary school is immaterial, provided the student have it; but in most cases it cannot be acquired except through regular study and practice in the lower grades and occasional reviews in the higher, and scarce through these. A progressive and regular development of the grammar-sense from the lowest grades to the highest is much to be preferred to a sudden and unprepared-for injection of formal grammar at a particular stage, as, for example, in the eighth grade.

(b) *Reading.* The books prescribed by the Joint Committee on Uniform Entrance Requirements in English form the basis for this part of the work. It is expected that all students shall read these books intelligently and appreciatively, but it is important to understand that the list is prescribed neither as a maximum nor as a minimum requirement. Rather these books are intended to serve as a common center from which each school shall proceed with such wider courses of English study as it may find profitable. It is taken for granted that each school will arrange for a considerable amount of outside reading supplementary to the prescribed readings.

The list, as arranged by the Joint Committee on Entrance Requirements in English, is divided into two parts, the first consisting of books to be read with attention to their contents rather than to their form, the second consisting of books to be studied thoroughly and minutely. The lists, thus divided, are as follows:

I. BOOKS PRESCRIBED FOR READING.

For 1909, 1910, and 1911 ten books, selected as prescribed below from the following list:

Group I (two to be selected).

Shakespeare's *As You Like It, Henry V, Julius Cæsar, The Merchant of Venice, Twelfth Night.*

Group II (one to be selected).

Bacon's *Essays;* Bunyan's *The Pilgrim's Progress, Part I; The Sir Roger de Coverly Papers* in the Spectator; Franklin's *Autobiography.*

Group III (one to be selected).

Chaucer's *Prologue;* Selections from Spenser's *Færie Queene;* Pope's *The Rape of the Lock;* Goldsmith's *The Deserted Village;* Palgrave's *Golden Treasury (First Series), Books II and III,* with especial attention to Dryden, Collins, Gray, Cowper and Burns.

Group IV (two to be selected).

Goldsmith's *The Vicar of Wakefield;* Scott's *Ivanhoe, Quentin Durward;* Hawthorne's *The House of the Seven Gables;* Thackeray's *Henry Esmond;* Mrs. Gaskell's *Cranford;* Dickens' *A Tale of Two Cities;* George Eliot's *Silas Marner;* Blackmore's *Lorna Doone.*

Group V (two to be selected).

Irving's *Sketch Book;* Lamb's *Essays of Elia;* De Quincey's *Joan of Arc* and *The English Mail Coach;* Carlyle's *Heroes and Hero Worship;* Emerson's *Essays* (Selected); Ruskin's *Sesame and Lilies.*

Group VI (two to be selected).

Coleridge's *The Ancient Mariner;* Scott's *Lady of the*

Lake; Byron's *Mazeppa* and *The Prisoner of Chillon;* Palgrave's *Golden Treasury (First Series), Book IV,* with special attention to Wordsworth, Keats and Shelley; Macaulay's *Lays of Ancient Rome;* Poe's *Poems;* Lowell's *The Vision of Sir Launfal;* Arnold's *Sohrab and Rustum;* Longfellow's *The Courtship of Miles Standish;* Tennyson's *Gareth and Lynette, Lancelot and Elaine,* and *The Passing of Arthur;* Browning's *Cavalier Tunes, The Lost Leader, How They Brought the Good News from Ghent to Aix, Evelyn Hope, Home Thoughts from Abroad, Home Thoughts from the Sea, Incident of the French Camp, The Boy and the Angel, One Word More, Hervé Riel, Pheidippides.*

II. BOOKS PRESCRIBED FOR STUDY AND PRACTICE.

For 1909, 1910, and 1911: Shakespeare's *Macbeth;* Milton's *Lycidas, Comus, L'Allegro,* and *Il Penseroso;* Burke's *Speech on Conciliation with America,* or Washington's *Farewell Address* and Webster's *First Bunker Hill Oration;* Macaulay's *Life of Johnson,* or Carlyle's *Essay on Burns.*

Changes for the year 1912:

1. Tennyson's *Gareth and Lynette, Lancelot and Elaine,* and *The Passing of Arthur* are inserted in the list of Books for Study as an alternative to Milton's poems.

2. *Lycidas* is dropped from the list of Milton's poems.

3. In group VI of the Reading List, Tennyson's *Princess* is substituted for the *Idylls* transferred to the Study List.

4. In Group V, Carlyle's *Heroes and Hero Worship* is changed to Carlyle's *The Hero as Poet, The Hero as Man of Letters,* and *The Hero as King.*

5. The number of books to be selected in Group V is changed from two to one.

6. In Group III (Book I), is substituted for (Selections) from *Færie Queene.*

7. In the preliminary statement of the requirement for

Reading and Practice, nine is substituted for ten as the number of books to be offered for examination.

With reference to the second list, the Joint Committee recommends that each of the books prescribed for study be taught with reference to subject matter, form and structure; and that, in addition, attention be given to the essentials of English grammar and to the leading facts in those periods of English literary history to which the prescribed works belong.

The above lists and requirements are intended to indicate in a general way the extent and character of the required work, and are not to be interpreted as limitations upon the teacher's choice. Books of equal merit, covering a similar range of literary types, will meet the requirements satisfactorily.

(c) *Composition.* Regular and persistent training in both written and oral composition should be given throughout the entire school course. In the high school, instruction in this subject should not be broken up into term or semester courses, but should be regarded as continuous throughout the four years. As regards the subjects for composition, they should be taken in the high school course partly from the list of books prescribed for study and practice, or from other literature which the class may read; partly from the student's own thought and experience. The topics should be so chosen as to give practice in the four leading types of prose discourse, namely, Description, Narration, Exposition and Argument.

(d) *Rhetoric.* It is expected that the student will be familiar with the essential principles of rhetoric. The instruction in this subject should begin early in the high school course in connection with the work in composition, and should include the following particulars: choice of words; structure of sentences and paragraphs; the principles of narration, description, exposition and argument. The teacher should distinguish between those parts of rhetorical theory which are retained in text-books merely through the influence of tradition and those which have direct bearing upon the composition work. The former may be safely omitted.

A thorough revision of the requirements in English is planned in 1909.

MATHEMATICS.

COMMITTEE.

C. E. Comstock (Chairman), Professor of Mathematics, Bradley Polytechnic Institute, Peoria, Illinois.

H. Hancock, Professor of Mathematics, University of Cincinnati.

J. L. Markley, Junior Professor of Mathematics, University of Michigan.

A. Darnell, Head of Department of Mathematics, Central High School, Detroit, Mich.

H. E. Slaught, Assistant Professor of Mathematics, University of Chicago.

J. F. Downey, Professor of Mathematics and Dean of the College of Science, Literature and Arts, University of Minnesota.

W. A. Bartlett, Principal High School, Winona, Minnesota.

E. R. Hedrick, Professor of Mathematics, University of Missouri.

I. I. Cammack, Principal Central High School, Kansas City, Missouri.

E. B. Skinner, Assistant Professor of Mathematics, University of Wisconsin.

A. L. Candy, Professor of Mathematics, University of Nebraska.

A. R. Congdon, Principal of High School, Fremont, Nebraska.

H. B. Newson, Professor of Mathematics, University of Kansas.

A. M. Bogle, Teacher of Mathematics, Kansas City (Kansas) High School.

G. W. Nash, President Northern Normal and Industrial School, Aberdeen, South Dakota.

J. D. Harlor, Head of Department of Mathematics, East High School, Columbus, Ohio.

S. W. Reaves, Professor of Mathematics, University of Oklahoma.

Florian Cajori, Dean of School of Engineering, Colorado College.

E. L. Brown, Principal, North Side High School, Denver, Colorado.

Definitions (4 units).

In mathematics the commission adopts the statement of the College Entrance Examination Board, except that a somewhat smaller portion in algebra is assigned to the first year, and a review of essentials is recommended in connection with the advanced course in algebra.

1. *Algebra.* The four fundamental operations for rational algebraic expressions, factoring, highest common factor, lowest common multiple, complex fractions, the solution of equations of the first degree containing one or more unknown quantities, radicals, including the extraction of the square root of polynomials and numbers, and fractional and negative exponents. Quadratic equations and equations containing one or more unknown quantities that can be solved by the methods of quadratic equations, problems depending upon such equations.

2. *Plane Geometry,* including the solution of simple original exercises and numerical problems.

3a. *Algebra.* A review of the essentials to be followed by ratio and proportion, and the binomial theorem for positive integral exponents. The progressions, the elementary treatment of permutations and combinations, and the use of four and five place tables of logarithms.

3b. *Solid Geometry,* including properties of straight lines and planes, of dihedral and polyhedral angles, of projections, of polyhedrons, including prisms, pyramids and the regular solids, of cylinders, cones and spheres, of spherical triangles, and the measurement of surfaces and solids.

4a. *Algebra.* Undetermined coefficients, the elementary treatment of infinite series, the binomial theorem for fractional and negative exponents, and the theory of logarithms.

Determinants, and the elements of the theory of equations, including Horner's method for solving numerical equations.

4b. *Trigonometry.* Plane Trigonometry, including the definitions and relations of the six trigonometrical functions as ratios, proof of important formulæ, theory of logarithms and use of tables, solution of right and oblique plane triangles. Spherical Trigonometry, including the proof of important formulæ and the solution of right and oblique spherical triangles with the proper interpretation of the ambiguous cases.

The colleges make no formal entrance requirement in arithmetic, but presuppose a thorough training in this subject—the four fundamental operations with whole numbers, decimal and common fractions, percentage and its simple applications—as antecedent to the formal study of geometry and algebra. In connection with the latter subjects the facility in computation gained in arithmetic should be exercised and strengthened; these subjects, on the other hand, round out the work of arithmetic and make possible a more careful proof of its theory. The aspect of algebra as generalized arithmetic should be constantly kept in mind, and the theorems of arithmetic contained as special cases in those of algebra should be pointed out, exemplified, and applied in numerical cases. The examinations in algebra and geometry may always and should usually test incidentally the candidate's theoretical and practical knowledge of arithmetic.

In integral connection with arithmetic geometric forms should be studied from the outset, their principal properties being learned by observation and experiment. Informal proofs of a deductive character may be gradually introduced, as the pupils feel, or may be led to feel, the need for such proofs.

Similarly, the advantages of the literal representation of numbers may be gradually made evident and utilized in the solution of problems, leading to simple equations, and in the compact and clear statement of results (formulæ). Initially the natural literal notations (for number of units of length, etc.) should be used exclusively.

Mathematics owes its genesis largely to the needs of measurement. As in the race, so in the individual, the generalizations, the abstract form should be developed late, though foreshadowed long. From the beginnings of arithmetic to the close of the secondary school at least, the march should always be from the concrete to the abstract. The concrete is itself variable; what is abstract at one stage is quite concrete at another. In the secondary school, many concrete starting points for mathematical work are to be found in the physical sciences; for algebra the specific numerical relations of arithmetic often furnish a concrete basis.

In the secondary school arithmetic, algebra, geometry, and trigonometry should be regarded and treated as different phases of one subject, mathematics, and not as different and mutually exclusive subjects. The geometric, the arithmetical, the algebraic, and the physical phases of mathematics should be presented from the beginning to the end of the secondary school course. To do this best and most freely would require some reshaping of curricula, which should come gradually. But the individual teacher can do much, pending this readjustment, by letting down the barriers, by using geometry in algebra, and algebra in geometry, by concrete physical, graphical, arithmetical work, by free use of whatever material or methods will help towards the main end.

The teacher's constant aim should be to train the pupil to *think*: to observe accurately; to describe accurately in language, in picture, in equation; to make inferences correctly; to act on his inferences; to formulate clearly what he has done. The pupil's attitude must be, in the main, that of an active worker, not that of a passive listener.

With the systematic restoration of the close relations between mathematics and the physical sciences, so long unnaturally severed in the instruction of the secondary school, it is well to consider the methods of instruction in the physical laboratory. Some of these methods, suitably modified, may be of value also in the instruction in mathematics.

It is desirable that teachers keep themselves informed concerning movements in progress for the improvement of the teaching of mathematical science.

HISTORY.

COMMITTEE.

J. A. James (Chairman), Professor of History, Northwestern University.
H. E. Bourne, Professor of History, Western Reserve University.
H. V. Hotchkiss, Superintendent of Public Schools, Akron, Ohio.
H. V. Church, Principal, J. Sterling Morton High School, Clyde, Illinois.
D. C. Munro, Professor of European History, University of Wisconsin.
W. C. Howe, Instructor in History, West Division High School, Milwaukee, Wisconsin.
W. M. West, Professor of History, University of Minnesota.
H. H. Freer, Professor of Economics and Sociology, Cornell College, Mt. Vernon, Iowa.
N. W. Lambkin, Teacher of History, High School, Clinton, Missouri.
H. W. Caldwell, Professor of American History, University of Nebraska.
Amanda J. Sundeau, Teacher of History, High School, Lincoln, Nebraska.
C. H. Rhodes, Principal, High School, Winfield, Kansas.
W. W. Girton, Teacher of Civics, State Normal School, Madison, South Dakota.
J. S. Ellis, Lake Preston, South Dakota.
J. S. Buchanan, Professor of History, University of Oklahoma.
J. F. Willard, Professor of History, University of Colorado.
M. C. Potter, Superintendent of Schools, Idaho Springs, Colorado.

Definitions (4 units).

1. Ancient history, with special reference to Greek and Roman history, and including also a short introductory study of the more ancient nations and the chief events of the early middle ages, down to the death of Charlemagne (814).

2. Mediæval and modern European history, from the death of Charlemagne to the present time.

3. English history.

4. American history, or American history and civil government.

The periods that are here indicated as constituting the four units were recommended by the Committee of Seven of the American Historical Association in their report to the Association in 1899. The full report is published under the title "The Study of History in Schools." It contains suggestions as to various methods of treating these periods, and gives further information likely to be of service to the teacher. A short course of one year in general history of the world has been in a great measure abandoned by the schools, because it does not give the opportunity for the more concrete study and for the training in historical thinking that can be obtained from the more intensive work. The plan of continuing ancient history to the time of Charlemagne or the establishment of the Holy Roman Empire has much to commend it, and is now adopted in many schools. Excellent books have been prepared which will enable the teachers to cover the field, as a whole, satisfactorily. By continuing the study of ancient history down into the early middle ages, a reasonable adjustment of time between the earlier and later periods is secured; and from the purely historical as well as the pedagogical point of view, there is much to be said in favor of connecting Roman history with the later times; the pupil is not left in the confusion of the fallen or the decadent empire. In connection with a year's work in American history much instruction can be given in civil government; a course dwelling on the development of American political ideals and the actual workings of institutions necessarily gives information concretely of the present governmental forms and methods.

No definite statement need be made concerning the mode of teaching or the apparatus that should be used. But it may be said that the mere learning of a text will not give the preparation that the colleges desire. Happily the time is gone when teachers are inclined to confine their classes to the memorizing of a single text. Some colleges in their entrance examination expect the candidate to present notebooks showing the amount and character of the work done in the schools. It is desirable that notebooks or cards should be kept as a record of the work done. They may contain copious extracts from primary and secondary authorities, references to important material, sketch maps made by the pupils as illustrations of their studies, and informal notes on reading that has been done in connection with the course. Such work is necessary if the historical courses are to give their best educational results. Effort should be made to cultivate the power of handling facts and of drawing proper inductions from data, to develop the faculty of discrimination, to teach the pupils the use of books and how to extract substance from the printed page. The acquisition of information alone can not be the chief aim of any school work; knowledge of how to acquire information and, above all, some skill in putting forth what one knows must always be of more than secondary importance; history therefore should be taught as a disciplinary and educational subject.

The teacher of history in the secondary school should have completed a four year college course or the equivalent. He should have completed courses in history aggregating *at least* twelve hours for one year, including one "intensive" or "research" course. In the selection of these courses, at least three fields of history represented in the secondary school units should be chosen. It is also strongly recommended that the teacher should have pursued elementary courses in economics and political science.

The school library or an accessible public library should be equipped with at least the following numbers of well-selected books on the different units: Ancient History, 25 volumes; Mediæval and Modern History, each 25 volumes; English History, 50 volumes, and United States History, 75 volumes.

In addition to a good text-book, the pupil should have read in connection with each unit of History, as a minimum, the following amounts of carefully selected collateral material, of which at least one-fourth should be source material: Ancient History, 200 pp.; Mediæval and Modern European History, each 150 pp.; English History, 300 pp.; American History, 350 pp. (It is understood that Civics is additional.) Especial care should be exercised by the teacher in testing the reports on outside reading, to see that the best results are obtained. The pupil should show ability also in map analysis and the completion of outline maps.

The history class-room should contain standard maps and the pupils should have access to good historical atlases. Photographs of historic scenes ought also to constitute a part of the school equipment for the use of the teacher of history.

LATIN AND GREEK.

COMMITTEE.

E. W. Coy (Chairman), Principal of Hughes High School, Cincinnati, Ohio.

J. H. Drake, Junior Professor of Roman and Latin Languages, University of Michigan.

David Mackenzie, Principal of Central High School, Detroit, Michigan.

W. R. Bridgman, Professor of Greek, Lake Forest College, Lake Forest, Illinois.

J. S. Brown, Superintendent of Township High School, Joliet, Illinois.

M. S. Slaughter, Professor of Latin, University of Wisconsin.

Nora Frye, Teacher of Latin, High School, Stillwater, Minnesota.

J. H. T. Main, President of Iowa College, Grinnell, Iowa.

L. M. McAfee, President of Park College, Parkville, Missouri.

G. E. Barber, Professor of Roman History and Literature, University of Nebraska.

Grace I. Bridge, Head of the Department of Latin, High School, Lincoln, Nebraska.

W. J. Greer, Professor of Latin, Washburn College, Topeka, Kansas.

R. R. Price, Superintendent of City Schools, Hutchinson, Kansas.

A. Strachan, Superintendent of Schools and Principal of High School, Deadwood, South Dakota.

Edward Rissman, Principal of the South Division High School, Milwaukee, Wisconsin.

George Norlin, Professor of Greek, University of Colorado.

A. H. Dunn, Principal of High School, Fort Collins, Colorado.

Definitions of Latin (4 units).

In Latin the commission adopts the first two units as defined by the American Philological Association, and the third and fourth units as defined by the College Entrance Examination Board.

1. Latin lessons, accompanied from an early stage by the reading of very simple selections. Easy reading: twenty to thirty pages of consecutive text.

In all written exercises the long vowels should be marked, and in all oral exercises pains should be taken to make the pronunciation conform to the quantities.

The student should be trained from the beginning to grasp the meaning of the Latin before translating, and then to render into idiomatic English; and should be taught to read the Latin aloud with intelligent expression.

2. Selections from Cæsar's Gallic War equivalent in amount to four books; selections from other prose writers, such as Nepos, may be taken as a substitute for an amount up to, but not exceeding, two books.

The equivalent of at least one period a week in prose composition based on Cæsar.

Reading aloud and translating, together with training in correct methods of apprehending the author's meaning, both prepared and unprepared passages being used as material. The memorizing of selected passages.

3, 4. Cicero: Any six orations from the following list, but preferably the first six mentioned:

The four orations against Catiline, Archias, the Manilian Law, Marcellus, Roscius, Milo, Sestius, Ligarius, the fourteenth Philippic.

Vergil: The first six books of the Aeneid.

The equivalent of at least one period a week in prose composition based on Cicero.

Note: In place of a part of Cicero an equivalent of

Sallust's Catiline, and in place of a part of Vergil an equivalent of Ovid will be accepted.

Definitions of Greek (3 units).

In Greek the definitions of the three units of the Philological Association are adopted.

1. Introductory lessons:
    Xenophon's Anabasis (20 to 30 pages).
    Practice in reading at sight and in writing Greek.
    Systematic study of grammar begun.

2. Xenophon's Anabasis (continued), either alone or with other Attic prose (75 to 120 pages).

Practice in reading at sight, systematic study of grammar, thorough grammatical review, and practice in writing Greek, both based on study of Books I and II of the Anabasis.

3. Homer (2,500 to 4,000 lines); e. g., Iliad, I-III (omitting II, 494-end), and VI-VIII.

Attic prose (33 to 40 pages), with practice in writing Greek; grammar, practice reading at sight.

GERMAN.

COMMITTEE.

Laurence Fossler (Chairman), Professor of Germanic Languages and Literatures, University of Nebraska.
W. W. Davies, Professor of German, Ohio Wesleyan University.
A. Keifer, Teacher of German, High School, Piqua, Ohio.
M. Winkler, Professor of German Language and Literature, University of Michigan.
P. Huber, Superintendent of School, Saginaw, W. S., Michigan.
P. O. Kern, Assistant Professor of Germanic Philology, University of Chicago.
Jessie L. Jones, Assistant Professor of German, Lewis Institute, Chicago.
A. R. Hohlfeld, Professor of German, University of Wisconsin.
Elizabeth A. Waters, Assistant Principal, High School, Fond du Lac, Wisconsin.
Elida C. Kirchner, Teacher of German, Central High School, St. Louis, Missouri.
Emilie S. Hamm, Teacher of German, High School, Beatrice, Nebraska.
W. H. Carruth, Professor of German Language and Literature, University of Kansas.
Harriet Kemp, Teacher of German, High School, Junction City, Kansas.
Elizabeth Reid, Instructor in German, Huron College, Huron, South Dakota.
Hermine R. König, Instructor in German, North Side High School, Minneapolis, Minnesota.
J. B. Knoepfler, Professor of German, Iowa State Normal, Cedar Falls, Iowa.
Dorothea K. Beggs, Professor of German, University of Denver.
Wilhelmina Mohr, Teacher of German, High School, Denver, Colorado.

Definitions (4 units).

1. During the first year the work should comprise:

(1) Careful and persistent drill upon connected pronunciation;

(2) The memorizing and frequent repetition of easy colloquial sentences;

(3) Drill upon the rudiments of grammar; viz. upon the inflection of the articles, of such nouns as belong to the language of everyday life, of adjectives, pronouns, weak verbs, and the more *usual* strong verbs; also upon the use of the more common prepositions, the simpler uses of the modal auxiliaries, and the elementary rules of syntax and word-order;

(4) Abundant easy exercises designed not only to fix in mind the forms and principles of grammar, but also to cultivate readiness in the reproduction of natural forms of expression;

(5) The reading of from 50 to 100 pages of graduated texts from a reader or other text, with constant practice in translating into German easy variations upon sentences selected from the reading lesson (the teacher giving the English). Besides parts of Readers available for first year's class-work, good selections may be made from Müller und Wenckebach's Glück Auf; Kern's (Grimm's) German Stories Retold; Guerber's Märchen and Erzählungen; Seeligmann's Altes and Neues.

It will be found, however, that the work as outlined in the above, can be done successfully only when the students of the class are either fairly mature (say, in the 11th or 12th grade), or have had some previous language training. It is only to such that the full reading requirements can profitably be made to apply as a part of the first year's work. *The chief consideration is thoroughness and accuracy, is to put the student upon firm and sure ground, and never to give up what has already been gained.*

2. During the second year the work should comprise:

(1) The reading of from 150 to 200 pages of suitable texts in the form of easy stories and plays;

(2) Accompanying practice, as before, in the translation into German and easy variations upon the matter read;

(3) Continued drill upon the essentials of the grammar, directed to the ends of enabling the pupil, first, to use his knowledge with facility in the formation of sentences and, secondly, to state his knowledge correctly in the technical language of grammar.

Reading material suitable for the elementary course, other than that already mentioned, can be selected from the following list: Andersen's Märchen and Bilderbuch ohne Bilder; Arnold's Fritz auf Ferien; Baumbach's Die Nonna and Der Schwiegersohn; Gerstaecker's Germelshausen; Heyse's L'Arrabbiata, Das Mädchen von Treppi, Die Blinden; Storm's Immensee and Geschichten aus der Tonne; In St. Jürgen; Auerbach's Brigitta; Keller's Legenden; Fulda's Under vier Augen; Wildenbruch's Der Letzte, or, Das edle Blut; Frommel's Eingeschneit; Seidel's Aus goldnen Tagen; Zschokke's Der zerbrochene Krug; Blüthgen's Das Peterle von Nürnberg.

The net results of the first two years of a high school German course should be:

(a) A correct and ready pronunciation.

(b) A ready, *exact*, and fairly complete working knowledge of grammar, especially on the formal (inflectional) side.

(c) At least some ability to speak and understand the foreign spoken language.

(d) A better understanding of the grammatical structure of the English language.

(e) The reading of some 200-250 pages of suitable texts and the mastery of the fundamental facts of the language involved and illustrated in them.

(f) The acquisition of a fair working vocabulary, involving the full mastery of some 80 per cent of the words occurring in the texts read and worked over.

(g) Ready familiarity with ordinary or common idiomatic phrases or other expressions, such as *es tut mir leid, Sie haben recht, nehmen Sie sich in acht, wo hat er das her?* etc.

(h) The ability to understand and translate (with the help of a vocabulary for uncommon terms) from German into English texts of similar degree of difficulty as the one worked over in class.

In words of one of the high school manuals "The ideals of enabling the student eventually to read German literature in German without translating should be ever before the teacher. . . . . . Modern German literature is so rich in novelistic, dramatic, historical, and lyrical productions of a high order that, even for the more elementary classes, good literary selections may be found well suited to the age and preparation of high school students. If this principle be strictly observed, the instruction of German will gain enormously in dignity and interest, and will greatly extend the range of knowledge and culture of the student."

3. The work of the third year should comprise:

(1) A thorough and systematic review of the fundamental facts, the grammar of the language in connection with suitable practice in composition. A text-book, such as Harris', Wesselhoeft's, or Bernhardt's, German Composition, should be used for his purpose. Neither the teacher nor the pupil should trust himself to the process of merely "incidental" grammar and composition exercises. At least two recitation periods per week should be devoted to this purpose.

(2) The reading of some 300-400 pages of moderately difficult prose. A selection may be made from the following texts: Ebner-Eschenbach's Die Freiherren von Gem-

perlein; Freytag's Die Journalisten or his Bilder aus der deutschen Vergangenheit—for example, Karl der Grosse, Aus den Kreuzzügen, Doktor Luther, Aus dem Staat Friedrich's des Grossen; Gerstaecker's Irrfahrten; Meyer's Der Schusz von der Kanzel, Goethe's Hermann und Dorothea, Hoffman's Historische Erzählungen; Lessing's Minna von Barnhelm; Meyer's Gustav Adolf's Page; Moser's Der Bibliothekar; Riehl's Novellen—for example, Burg Neideck; Der Fluch der Schönheit, Der stumme Ratsherr, Das Spielmannskind; Rosegger's Waldheimat; Schiller's Wilhelm Tell, Die Jungfrau von Orleans, Das Lied von der Glocke; Sudermann's Frau Sorge; selections from the poems of Uhland, Heine, Schiller, Goethe, etc., as found e. g. in Hatfield's collection of German Lyrics and Ballads.

4. The work of the fourth year should comprise the reading of about five hundred pages of good literature in prose and poetry, reference readings upon the lives and works of the great writers studied, the writing in German of numerous short themes upon assigned subjects, independent translation of English into German. Favored texts seem to be: Goethe's Sesenheim, Dichtung und Wahrheit, Egmont, Iphigenie; Schiller's Maria Stuart; Lessing's Minna von Barnhelm; Kleist's Michael Kohlhaas, Prinz von Homburg, Fulda's Der Talisman, Grillparzer's Der Traum ein Leben, Sappho, Ludwig's Zwischen Himmel und Erde, Hebbel's Agnes Bernauer, Scheffel's Ekkehard, Hauff's Lichtenstein.

The nature and scope of the fourth year's work may well be left to the direction of the authorities issuing the several high school Manuals, and to those in immediate charge of these advanced courses. It is possible that even here many teachers will feel the necessity of insisting upon the more formal aspects of the problem, others may feel that the advancement and maturity of the class will warrant a sympathetic and systematic study of literature proper.

FRENCH AND SPANISH.

COMMITTEE.

B. L. Bowen (Chairman), Professor of Romance Languages, Ohio State University.

C. W. Benton, Professor of French Language and Literature, University of Minnesota.

J. R. Effinger, Junior Professor of French, University of Michigan.

Eugénie Galloo, Professor of Romance Languages and Literatures, University of Kansas.

Alfred Nonnez, Teacher of French, Walnut Hills High School, Cincinnati, Ohio.

T. E. Oliver, Professor of Romance Languages, University of Illinois.

F. L. Smart, Assistant Superintendent and Principal of High School, Dubuque, Iowa.

Raymond Weeks, Professor of Romance Languages, University of Missouri.

C. C. Ayer, Professor of Romance Languages, University of Colorado.

Emeline Jensen, Assistant Principal, High School, Durango, Colorado.

Definitions of French (4 units).

The definitions of the four units in French are those recommended by the Committee of Twelve of the Modern Language Association.

1. During the first year the work should comprise: (1) careful drill in pronunciation; (2) the rudiments of grammar, including the inflection of the regular and the more common irregular verbs, the plural of nouns, the inflection of adjectives, participles, and pronouns; the use of personal pronouns, common adverbs, prepositions, and conjunctions; the order of words in the sentence, and the elementary rules of syntax; (3) abundant easy exercises, designed not only to fix in the memory the forms and principles of grammar, but also to cultivate readiness in the reproduction of natural forms of expression; (4) the reading of from 100 to 175 duodecimo pages of graduated texts, with constant practice in translating into French easy variations of the sentences read (the teacher giving the English), and in reproducing from memory sentences previously read; (5) writing French from dictation.

2. During the second year the work should comprise: (1) the reading of from 250 to 400 pages of easy modern prose in the form of stories, plays, or historical or biographical sketches; (2) constant practice, as in the previous year, in translating into French easy variations upon the texts read; (3) frequent abstracts, sometimes oral and sometimes written, of portions of the text already read; (4) writing French from dictation; (5) continued drill upon the rudiments of grammar, with constant application in the construction of sentences; (6) mastery of the forms and use of pronouns, pronominal adjectives, of all but the rare irregular verb forms, and of the simpler uses of the conditional and subjunctive.

Suitable texts for the second year are: About's *Le roi des montagnes,* Bruno's *Le tour de la France,* Daudet's easier short tales, La Bedolliere's *La Mère Michel et son chat,* Erckmann-Chatrian's stories, Foa's *Contes biographiques* and *Le Petit Robinson de Paris,* Foncin's *Le pays de France,* Labiche and Martin's *La poudre aux yeux* and *Le voyage de M. Perrichon,* Legouvé and Labiche's *La cigale chez les fourmis,* Malot's *Sans famille,* Mairet's *La tache du petit Pierre,* Merimee's *Colomba,* extracts from Michelet, Sarcey's *Le siége de Paris,* Verne's stories.

3. This should comprise the reading of from 400 to 600 pages of French of ordinary difficulty, a portion to be in the dramatic form; constant practice in giving French paraphrases, abstracts or reproductions from memory of selected portions of the matter read; the study of a grammar of moderate completeness; writing from dictation.

Suitable texts are: About's stories, Augier and Sandeau's *Le Gendre de M. Poirier,* Beranger's poems, Corneille's *Le Cid* and *Horace,* Coppee's poems, Daudet's *La Belle-Nivernaise,* La Brète's *Mon oncle et mon curé,* Madame de Sévigné's letters, Hugo's *Hernani* and *La chute,* Labiche's plays, Loti's *Pêcheur d'Islande,* Mignet's historical writings, Moliere's *L'avare* and *Le Bourgeois Gentilhomme,* Racine's *Athalie, Andromaque,* and *Esther,* George Sand's plays and stories, Sandeau's *Mademoiselle de la Seiglière,* Scribe's plays, Thierry's *Récits des temps mérovingiens.* Thiers' *L'expedition de Bonaparte en Egypte,* Vigny's *La canne de jonc,* Voltaire's historical writings.

4. This should comprise the reading of from 600 to 1,000 pages of standard French, classical and modern, only difficult passages being explained in the class; the writing of numerous short themes in French; the study of syntax. One unit.

Suitable reading matter will be: Beaumarchias's *Barbier de Seville;* Corneille's dramas; the elder Dumas's prose writings; the younger Dumas's *La question d'argent;* Hugo's *Ruy Blas,* lyrics and prose writings; La Fontaine's fables; Lamartine's *Graziella;* Marivaux's plays; Moliere's plays; Musset's plays and poems; Pellissier's *Mouvement littèraire au XIXe siécle;* Renan's *Souvenirs d'enfance et de jeunesse;* Rousseau's writings; Sainte-Beuve's essays; Taine's *Origines de la France contemporaine;* Voltaire's writings; selections from Zola, Maupassant, and Balzac.

Definitions of Spanish (2 units).

In Spanish the commission adopts the definitions of the two units of the College Entrance Examination Board, which are in close harmony with the definitions of French of the Modern Language Association.

1. During the first year the work should comprise (1) careful drill in pronunciation; (2) the rudiments of grammar, including the conjugation of the regular and the more common irregular verbs, the inflection of nouns, adjectives and pronouns, and the elementary rules of syntax; (3) exercises containing illustrations of the principles of grammar; (4) the reading and accurate rendering into good English of from 100 to 175 duodecimo pages of graduated texts, with translation into Spanish of easy variations of the sentences read; (5) writing Spanish from dictation.

2. During the second year the work should comprise: (1) the reading of from 250 to 400 pages of modern prose from different authors; (2) practice in translating Spanish into English, and English variations of the text into Spanish; (3) continued study of the elements of grammar and syntax; (4) mastery of all but the rare irregular verb forms and of the simpler uses of the modes and tenses; (5) writing Spanish from dictation; (6) memorizing of easy short poems.

Suitable texts for the second year are: Valera's *El pajaro verde;* Alarcon's *El final de Norma;* Valdes's *José;* Galdos's *Dona Perfecta, Marianela;* Padre Isla's version of *Gil Blas;* Carrion and Aza's *Zaragueta.*

PHYSICS.

COMMITTEE.

C. R. Mann (Chairman), Assistant Professor of Physics, University of Chicago, Chicago, Illinois.

A. D. Cole, Professor of Physics, Ohio State University.

Seth Hayes, Principal of High School, Lancaster, Ohio.

C. W. Greene, Professor of Physics, Albion College, Albion, Michigan.

C. F. Adams, Head of Department of Science, Central High School, Detroit, Mich.

C. H. Smith, Teacher of Physics, Hyde Park High School, Chicago.

C. W. Treat, Professor of Physics, Lawrence University, Appleton, Wisconsin.

H. L. Terry, State Inspector of High Schools, Madison, Wisconsin.

F. S. Jones, Professor of Physics and Dean of the College of Engineering, University of Minnesota.

E. F. Smith, Teacher of Physics, Humboldt High School, St. Paul, Minnesota.

K. E. Guthe, Professor of Physics, State University of Iowa.

S. L. Thomas, Principal, High School, Council Bluffs, Iowa.

O. M. Stewart, Professor of Physics, University of Missouri.

F. H. Ayres, Head of Department of Science in Central High School, Kansas City, Missouri.

J. E. Almy, Associate Professor of Physics, University of Nebraska.

H. M. Garrett, Teacher of Science in High School, Beatrice, Nebraska.

H. L. Woods, Professor of Physics and Astronomy, Washburn College, Topeka, Kansas.

A. J. Stout, Teacher of Science in High School, Topeka, Kansas.

L. E. Akeley, Professor of Physics, University of South Dakota.

W. A. Thompson, Superintendent of Public Schools, Webster, South Dakota.

H. A. Howe, Dean and Professor of Anatomy and Applied Science, University of Denver.

Carleton Aylard, Teacher of Physics, High School, Colorado Springs.

John Dewey, Professor of Philosophy, Columbia University, New York.

Paul H. Hanus, Professor of the History and Art of Teaching, Harvard University, Cambridge, Massachusetts.

George H. Mead, Professor of Philosophy, University of Chicago, Chicago, Illinois.

M. Vincent O'Shea, Professor of the Science and Art of Education, University of Wisconsin, Madison, Wisconsin.

Definition (1 unit).

1. The unit in physics consists of at least one hundred and eighty periods of forty-five minutes each (equal to 135 hours) of assigned work. Two periods of laboratory work count as one of assigned work.

2. The work consists of three closely related parts; namely, class work, lecture-demonstration work, and laboratory work. At least one-fourth of the time shall be devoted to laboratory work.

3. It is very essential that double periods be arranged for the laboratory work.

4. The class work includes the study of at least one standard text.

5. In the laboratory, each student shall perform at least thirty individual experiments, and keep a careful note-book record of them. Twenty of these experiments must be quantitative; each of these must illustrate an important physical principle which is one of the starred topics in the syllabus of required topics, and no two must illustrate the same principle.

6. In the class work the student must be drilled to an understanding of the use of the general principles which make up the required syllabus. He must be able to apply these principles intelligently to the solution of simple, practical, concrete problems.

7. Examinations will be framed to test the student's understanding of and ability to use the general principles in the required syllabus, as indicated in 6.

8. The teacher is not expected to follow the order of topics in the syllabus unless he wishes to do so.

Syllabus of Required Topics.

This list of required topics is not intended to include all the material for the year's work. It is purposely made short, in order that each teacher may be free to supplement it in a way that fits his individual environment. It does include those topics which all agree are essential to a first course in physics, and which are capable of comprehension, at least to the extent specified in number 6 of the definition of the unit, by boys and girls of high school age.

*1. Weight, center of gravity.
*2. Density.
*3. Parallelogram of forces.
4. Atmospheric pressure; barometer.
*5. Boyle's law.
6. Pressure due to gravity in liquids with a free surface; varying depth, density, and shape of vessel.
*7. Buoyancy; Archimedes' principle.
*8. Pascal's law; hydraulic press.
9. Work as force times distance, and its measurement in foot-pounds and gram-centimeters.
10. Energy measured by work.
*11. Law of machines: work obtained not greater than work put in; Efficiency.
*12. Inclined plane.
*13. Pulleys, wheel and axle.
*14. Measurement of moments by the product of force times arm; Levers.
15. Thermometers: Fahrenheit and Centigrade scales.
16. Heat quantity and its measurement in gram calories.
*17. Specific heat.
*18. Evaporation; heat of vaporization of water.
*19. Dew point; clouds and rain.
*20. Fusion and solidification; heat of fusion.
21. Heat transference by conduction and convection.
22. Heat transference by radiation.
23. Qualitative description of the transfer of energy by waves.

24. Wave length and period of waves.
25. Sound originates at a vibrating body and is transmitted by waves in air.
*26. Pitch and period of sound.
*27. Relation between the wave length of a tone and the length of a string or organ pipe.
*28. Resonance.
29. Beats.
30. Rectilinear propagation of light; pin-hole camera.
*31. Reflection and its laws; image in a plane mirror.
*32. Refraction, and its use in lenses; the eye, the camera.
*33. Prisms and dispersion.
34. Velocity of light.
35. Magnetic attractions and repulsions.
*36. Field of force about a magnet.
37. The Earth a magnet; compass.
38. Electricity by friction.
39. Conductors and insulators.
*40. Simple galvanic cell.
*41. Electrolysis; definition of the Ampere.
*42. Heating effects; resistance; definition of the Ohm.
*43. Ohm's law; definition of the volt.
*44. Magnetic field about a current; electromagnets.
*45. Electromagnetic induction.
*46. Simple alternating current dynamo of one loop.
*47. Electromagnetic induction by breaking a circuit; primary and secondary.
48. Conservation of energy.

CHEMISTRY.

COMMITTEE.

H. E. Griffith (Chairman), Professor of Chemistry, Knox College, Galesburg, Illinois.

D. C. Rybolt, Principal of High School, Akron, Ohio.

Delos Fall, Professor of Chemistry, Albion College, Albion, Michigan.

W. L. Whitney, Teacher of Chemistry in High School, Saginaw, E. S., Michigan.

G. B. Frankforter, Dean of the School of Chemistry, University of Minnesota.

W. S. Hendrixson, Professor of Chemistry, Iowa College, Grinnell, Iowa.

F. N. Peters, Teacher in Chemistry, Central High School, Kansas City, Missouri.

B. Dales, Professor of Chemistry, University of Nebraska.

H. A. Senter, Head of Department of Chemistry, High School, Omaha, Nebraska.

E. A. White, Teacher of Chemistry, High School, Kansas City, Kansas.

Margaret V. Maguire, Teacher of Science, High School, Mitchell, South Dakota.

G. L. Holter, Professor of Chemistry, Agricultural and Mechanical College, Stillwater, Oklahoma.

W. P. Headden, Professor of Chemistry and Geology, Colorado Agricultural Colllege.

J. W. Lakin, Teacher of Science, High School, Greeley, Colorado.

Definition (1 unit.)

Chemistry is an art as well as a science. Acquaintance with its elements includes ability to *do* certain things *intelligently* as well as remembrance of the bare results of chemical changes. An organized account of the latter is only a sort of dessicated residuum if it is not illuminated by the experience acquired along with skill in the former. The books usually—and necessarily—give prominence to the second (the systematic aspect), leaving instruction in the art to the teacher. A requirement in chemistry, on the other hand, must emphasize the art, for it is universal. It will lay less stress on any particular list of substances, reactions, or topics, in view of the extent of the available material, the briefness of the school course and the consequent differences between equally good individual selections. The art cannot, of course, be acquired without a fair systematic knowledge, while a semblance of the systematic knowledge may be acquired without the art. The art is therefore more worthy of emphasis.

It will be noted that the art of chemistry consists in the practical knowledge of the physical properties of all kinds of matter and the utilization of this knowledge in arranging intelligently the conditions before chemical change, in noting all physical indications during experiment and distinguishing the significant ones, and in interpreting the result of this observation. It thus deals almost exclusively with physical conceptions and facts. It demands, therefore, a careful training in physical facts, physical observation and physical inference. Conventionalized chemical work which can progress without skill in this art (for example, reiterated observation of precipitations) is valueless.

Disregarding questions of order, and simply classifying the essential principles of instruction, the pupil should be taught:

1. *Technique of experimentation.*

   Properties of common apparatus in respect to structure and material. For example, how to make an apparatus air-tight and why. Object of such operations as washing and drying gases and how the object is attained.

   Physical properties which may be used for recognition of each substance and for explanation of all observations.

   Judicious use of proportions and materials. Influence of conditions (temperature, homogeneous and heterogeneous mixture, etc.) on chemical change.

2. Physical phenomena, their recognition, description, and physical interpretation.

3. The more strictly *chemical application* of the results. For example, inference in regard to the nature of the chemical change which must have led to the results observed. Making of the chemical equation from adequate data.

The material basis for the above may be found for the most part in the employment of a restricted number of elements and a few of their chief compounds. Facts should be simplified and systematized by generalization, and generalizations ("laws") should be illustrated and applied to familiar things. The usual theoretical explanations should be given as the facts accumulate. Laws and theories derive their importance from the facts, not *vice versa*, and none should be given unless and until the corresponding facts have been encountered in laboratory or class-room experiments.

A knowledge of important chemical industries and ability to work simple problems will be expected.

PHYSICAL GEOGRAPHY.

COMMITTEE.

C. E. Peet (Chairman), Assistant Professor of Physiography, Lewis Institute, Chicago.

G. D. Hubbard, Assistant Professor of Geology, Ohio State University.

A. F. Foerste, Teacher of Science, Steele High School, Dayton, Ohio.

C. A. Jewell, Jr., Teacher of Science, Central High School, Grand Rapids, Mich.

W. W. Atwood, Instructor in Physiography and Geology, University of Chicago.

G. L. Collie, Professor of Geology and Dean, Beloit College, Beloit, Wisconsin.

C. W. Hall, Professor of Geology and Mineralogy, University of Minnesota.

W. H. Norton, Professor of Geology, Cornell College, Mt. Vernon, Iowa.

H. H. Savage, Superintendent of Schools, East Waterloo, Iowa.

C. F. Marbut, Professor of Geology and Mineralogy, University of Missouri.

P. Graves, Teacher of Physical Geography and Geology, Central High School, Kansas City, Missouri.

W. L. Enfield, Teacher of Science, High School, Wichita, Kansas.

E. C. Perisho, Professor of Geology of University of South Dakota, and State Geologist.

G. E. Condra, Professor of Geography and Economic Geology, University of Nebraska.

F. H. Hoff, Superintendent of Schools, Mitchell, South Dakota.

R. D. George, Professor of Geology, University of Colorado.

G. L. Cannon, Teacher of Physiography, East Side High School, Denver, Colorado.

Definition (1 unit).

The following outline includes only the most essential facts and principles of physical geography, which must be studied in the class room and laboratory:

THE EARTH AS A GLOBE.

Shape of earth: How proved; probable causes of.
Size: How measured.
Rotation: How proved; day and night; longitude and time; latitude.
Revolution: How proved; rate; path; direction.
Seasons and their causes.
Magnetism: Compass; variation in.
Map projection explained.

THE LAND.

Distribution. Graphic representation of topography.

Changes in land areas and in land forms: Effects of (1) elevation and depression, of (2) deposition of sediments, (3) of shore erosion.

Plains: Plains distinguished from the plateaus and mountains. Kinds of plains: classification based on genesis, on topography, on fertility, etc. Development of plains of different forms. Distribution of the great plains of the earth. The coastal plain of the Atlantic and Gulf coasts. The plains of the eastern interior. The plains of the western interior. Effect of climate and rock structure on topography of plains. Alluvial plains: their formation and importance. Relation of life to different forms of plains.

Plateaus: Relations to plains and to mountains. Stages in the history of a plateau; young plateaus, dissected plateaus, old plateaus, broken plateaus. Effect of climate, rock structure, etc., on topography of plateaus. Locations of the great plateaus. Life conditions on plateaus.

Mountains: Classes: block mountains; folded mountains; domed mountains; massive mountains; mountains of circumdenudation. History of mountains. Effects of climate, rock structure, etc., on mountain topography. Life conditions in mountains.

Volcanoes: Distribution. Phenomena of eruptions. History of a volcano. Influence of volcanoes on topography and life.

Rivers: Life history of a river from birth to old age. The work of rivers. The topography of surfaces shaped by river erosion at different stages of valley development. Revived rivers. Drowned rivers and valleys. The great drainage basins of the United States.

Lakes: The distribution of lakes, particularly in North America. The changes which they are undergoing. Their relations to rivers. Their effect on climate. Their relations to life in general. Salt lakes; their history. The origin of lake basins.

Glaciers: The nature of glacier ice. The distribution of glaciers. The conditions necessary for glaciers. Types of glaciers. The work of glaciers. Glaciated areas compared and contrasted with areas which have not been affected by ice; especially the glaciated and non-glaciated areas of North America.

THE ATMOSPHERE.

Composition and offices of atmosphere. Instruments used in study of atmosphere.

Temperature: Source of atmospheric heat, and variations of atmospheric temperatures. Isothermal charts of world, and of the United States, especially the January, July and annual charts, with special study of (1) isotherms of northern and southern hemispheres, (2) location of heat equator, (3) cold pole, (4) crowded isotherms, etc.

Pressure: Measurement of pressure. Determination of altitudes by atmospheric pressure. Relation to temperature. Study of isobars on U. S. weather maps. Distribution of pressure in general, in mid-winter (January), and in midsummer (July). Relation of pressure (isobars) and temperature (isotherms).

Circulation of atmosphere: Winds; their causes; their classes; and their effects.

Moisture: Sources. Conditions for precipitation. Forms of precipitation; rain and snow; dew and frost; distribution of rain and snow; principles governing. Relation of precipitation to life.

Storms: Cyclones of temperate and tropical latitudes. Paths and characters of storms of United States. Relation of storms to general weather conditions. Weather at different seasons; study and construction of weather maps. Relation of weather to climate. Relation of climate, weather, etc., to life and to human industries.

THE OCEAN.

Form, divisions and general characteristics of the oceans, and of ocean basins. Depth, density and temperature of ocean waters. Characteristics of ocean floor; topography, material, etc. The life of the oceans.

Movement of ocean waters: Waves; cause and effect. Currents; causes and their proofs; important currents; effects of currents on climate, life, etc. Tides; character of motion; causes of tides; variation of tides, and their causes; bores; effect of tides on navigation, harbors, etc.

Work of ocean: Erosion and deposition. Shore lines; the leading types, and their distribution. Influence of harbors and coast lines, now and in the past.

Summary. The outline given can but enumerate the larger topics to be covered, and in a way suggest the point of view desired. Each topic should be treated so as to show its causal relations to other topics. So far as possible, the effects of earth features on life (especially human life) conditions should be emphasized.

Throughout the work an effort should be made to develop the student's ability to use the data presented. The acquisition of the facts presented in the text-books is in itself of relatively little value. The student should be taught to apply, out-of-doors and in the laboratory, the principles developed in the class room. When he can do this, and when he can utilize and combine the data presented in the books in new ways and to new ends, one of the chief aims of the study will have been accomplished.

The candidate's preparation should include:

a. The study of one of the leading secondary text-books in physical geography, for the sake of essential principles, and of well-selected facts illustrating those principles.

b. Individual laboratory work should occupy from one-fourth to one-half of the time of the student in the class-room. Field trips should take the place of some of the laboratory work in autumn and spring. The results of laboratory work should be carefully recorded in writing, and in many cases should be made the basis of class-room discussion. Similarly the field work should be made the basis of written reports or of subsequent class-room discussion, or both. In general the laboratory and the field should be made to afford illustrations of as many principles and phenomena as possible.

BOTANY.

COMMITTEE.

O. W. Caldwell (Chairman), Associate Professor of Botany, University of Chicago.
F. C. Newcombe, Professor of Botany, University of Michigan.
L. Murbach, Head of the Department of Biology, Central High School, Detroit, Michigan.
C. R. Barnes, Professor of Plant Physiology, University of Chicago.
R. A. Harper, Professor of Botany, University of Wisconsin.
M. F. Arey, Professor of Natural Science, Iowa State Normal School, Cedar Falls, Iowa.
C. E. Bessey, Professor of Botany and Dean, University of Nebraska.
E. A. Bostrom, Superintendent of Schools, Osceola, Nebraska.
Alberta Cory, Teacher of Botany, High School, Kansas City, Kansas.
C. S. Parmenter, Vice President of Baker University, Baldwin, Kansas.
Eloise Butler, Teacher of Botany, South Side High School, Minneapolis, Minnesota.
M. F. Guyer, Professor of Biology, University of Cincinnati.
Francis Remaley, Professor of Biology, University of Colorado.
Ellsworth Bethel, Teacher of Botany, East Side High School, Denver, Colorado.

Definition (1 unit).

It is undesirable that the course in Botany should be given earlier than the second year (10th grade), but whenever given it is indispensable that the teacher should adapt the work carefully to the development of the pupils. Inasmuch as Botany is likely to be one of the first sciences studied it is of the utmost importance that the pupil should be guarded against hasty inferences and sweeping generalizations from insufficient data. No experiment should be conducted by him which is not checked by a control, and whenever possible the conditions should be such that only one variable factor marks the difference between the test and the control. Inasmuch as both the simple and the compound microscope must be used he should be shown how to use both to the best advantage. The simple microscope is much neglected. The compound microscope brings an entirely new set of experiences to the pupil and he needs to be taught how to interpret what he sees. When sections of larger objects are furnished him, the teacher should take care that he understands the position of the section with reference to the object from which it was cut. He should be taught by practice to interpret and combine sections so as to obtain a conception in three dimensions of structures seen in two. Drawing, and especially the making of clear diagrams, should be insisted upon, avoiding undue detail and repetition which consume time but illustrate no new structure or form. Well-made diagrams, with details carefully drawn in certain parts, are much more profitable than the most elaborate drawings without correct ideas behind them.

It is not contemplated that the student shall obtain a knowledge of Botany as a science, but that he shall know what plants are, how they work, and how they are related to the external world and to other living things. The objects to be kept in view should be: first, to impart to a student through his own observation and reading a conception of the extent and variety of the plant kingdom, relating the groups to one another by a thread of evolution; second, a conception of the ways in which plants "live and move and have their being," by exhibiting them as mechanisms with parts, each doing its own work, and all working together harmoniously because they are sensitive to changes in the surrounding world and because they have power to adapt themselves thereto; third, a conception of the social relations of plants to other plants and to animals, and of the way in which their distribution is determined by all the agents acting upon them. To the laboratory and field work there should be devoted not less than two, and preferably three, double periods per week. It should be accompanied by assigned readings in one or more modern texts, and quizzes, for which two or three single periods per week are needed. When only single periods are given to the course, it should be discretionary with colleges to accept such work as one-half unit.

The general aims and methods of botanical teaching are well set forth in Ganong's "Teaching Botanist," which is commended to the attention of teachers of botany. The teacher who is adequately prepared will be the best judge of the materials and the methods by which in his own school the foregoing objects can be attained. The following suggestions are made as an indication of the amount and character of the work desired. They disregard questions of order. It is especially desirable, for instance, that physiological and ecological work be taken up in connection with the study of the anatomy of the organs with which they are most intimately associated, or with the organisms exhibiting certain relations best; *e. g.*, sterilization and the economic relations of fungi should be presented when the fungi are under examination.

The synoptical view of the great natural groups of plants

should be based upon a study of the structure, reproduction, and adaptations of types from each group. Where living material is not available, preserved material may be used. The evolutionary history of the great groups should be presented as far as it is known. Evolutionary principles may also be illustrated in a study of floral development. The alternation of generations should be traced from its clear development in bryophytes and pteridophytes backward to the hints of it among the algae and forward to its complete disappearance among the angiosperms. In the pteridophytes attention should be devoted to heterospory and to the consequent development of the seed habit in gymnosperms and angiosperms.

In general the simplicity of the lowest plants requires only brief study, and progressively more should be given to the higher and more conspicuous forms, until in the angiosperms detailed study is made of the various organs, and their functions. The following types are suggested, but should be changed to suit local conditions:

ALGAE: Pleurococcus, Nostoc, Spirogyra, Cladophora, Vaucheria. Fucus, Nemalion or Polysiphonia or Coleochæte.

FUNGI: Bacteria, Mucor, Yeast, Puccinia or a powdery mildew, Mushroom.

LICHENS: Physcia or Parmelia.

BRYOPHYTES: (Hepaticæ) Radula or Porella or Marchantia; (Musci) Mnium or Funaria or Polytrichum.

PTERIODPHYTES: Aspidium or equivalent, including the prothallus.

GYMNOSPERMS: Pinus.

ANGIOSPERMS: A monocotyledon and a dicotyledon. Examination of the structure and function of the following parts in any convenient species.

The seed: Three types (dicotyledon, one without and one with endosperm, and a monocotyledon); structure and homologous parts. Food supply, experimental determination of its nature. Phenomena of germination and growth of embryo into a seedling (including escape from the seed coats and development of parts).

The shoot: Gross anatomy of a foliage shoot, including the relationships of position of leaf, stem (and root), the arrangement of leaves and buds on the stem, and deviations (through light adjustment, etc.) from symmetry. Buds, and the mode or origin of new leaf and stem; winter buds in particular. Annual growth; shedding of bark and leaves.

Specialized shoots, including the flower. Comparative study of the parts and their functions in six or more different types, such as the ranunculaceaus, cruciferous, leguminous, convolvulaceous, labrate, composite, liliaceous, and gramineous types. In connection with the study of the flower students should be shown how to discover the names of unknown plants by use of analytic keys and descriptive floras. In general they should be introduced to unknown plants by name.

The root: Gross anatomy and general structure of a typical root; position and origin of secondary roots; hair-zone; cap and growing point.

Specialized roots of various sorts.

The fruit: Comparative study of several types of fruit (dry capsule, legume, nut) and fleshy (pome, berry, drupe, etc.), especially with reference to changes from the flower, and from ovule to seeds.

In connection with the study of anatomy the following physiological topics should be presented:

Rôle of water in the plant: Absorption (osmosis), path of transfer, transpiration, turgidity and its mechanical value, plasmolysis.

Phytosynthesis: Dependence of starch formation upon chlorophyll, light and carbon dioxid; evolution of oxygen.

Respiration: Necessity of oxygen for growth, evolution of carbon dioxid.

Digestion: Action of diastase on starch and of lipase on fats.

Irritability: Geotropism, heliotropism, etc.; nature of stimulus and response.

Growth: Localization and rate in higher plants.

The following ecological topics should receive attention either in connection with the foregoing laboratory work or in special field excursions, for which students should be furnished as careful directions as for laboratory work.

Adaptations of parts for special functions.

Dissemination.

Cross-pollination.

Light relations of green tissues; leaf mosaics.

*Plant societies*s Mesophytes, hydrophytes, halophytes, xerophytes, climbers, epiphytes, parasites and saprophytes. Plant associations and zonal distribution.

ZOOLOGY.

COMMITTEE.

J. Reighard (Chairman), Professor of Zoology, University of Michigan.

E. L. Moseley, Teacher of Science, High School, Sandusky, Ohio.

W. A. Locy, Professor of Zoology, Northwestern University.

F. L. Charles, Instructor in Biology, Northern State Normal School, DeKalb, Illinois.

H. D. Densmore, Professor of Botany, Beloit College.

L. Atherton, Head of Department of Biology, High School, Oshkosh, Wisconsin.

H. F. Nachtrieb, Professor of Animal Biology, University of Minnesota.

H. W. Norris, Professor of Zoology, Iowa College, Grinnell, Iowa.

J. A. Anderson, Head of Department of Biology, High School, Dubuque, Iowa.

L. E. Griffin, Professor of Biology, Missouri Valley College, Marshall, Missouri.

J. W. Scott, Teacher of Biology, Westport High School, Kansas City, Missouri.

Caroline E. Stringer, Head of Department of Biology, High School, Omaha, Nebraska.

A. Pihlblad, Professor of Biology, Bethany College, Lindsborg, Kansas.

C. E. Johnson, Teacher of Science, Sumner County High School, Wellington, Kansas.

C. P. Lommen, Professor of Biology, University of South Dakota.

G. D. A. Cockerell, Professor of Systematic Botany, University of Colorado.

A. E. Beardsley, Professor of Biology, State Normal School, Greeley, Colorado.

Definition (1 unit).

A high school course in Zoology should have for its objects: (1) To acquaint the student with the common animals of his own neighborhood, with the various environments of these animals, with the structural adaptations which the animals show to their environment and with their habits and economic importance. (2) To afford training in critical methods of making and recording observations both by drawing and by writing, both in the laboratory and in the field. (3) To teach enough of the interpretation of the observed facts that the student may understand the current methods of interpretation from the morphological, physiological, and ecological standpoints. In other words, with the study of the structures there should go an interpretation of their use (physiology, ecology) and of their past history (evolution). An elementary training in both experimental and comparative methods should be sought, and the peculiar value of such training as a means of intellectual development should not be overlooked. Ability on the part of the student to observe and think independently is especially desired.

For a course extending through the year with four periods per week, it is recommended that the laboratory and field work consist of the study of at least ten type forms to be selected from the following lists:

1. An insect.
2. The crayfish.
3. An earthworm, leech, or fresh water oligochaete.
4. An Amoeba or other protozoan.
5. Hydra or a hydroid.
6. A mussel or snail.
7. A fish.
   A frog, or turtle.
9. A bird.
10. A mammal.

The animal to be taken as the type under each head may be selected by the teacher and will vary with the locality. It will usually be most convenient to begin with insects in the fall and to take up birds before the spring migration and mammals later in the spring. The order in which the other forms are taken up may vary according to convenience. In the above list the crayfish and the earthworm have been placed after the insect in order to bring like forms together. Those who find difficulty in beginning with a form as small as the grasshopper may prefer to spend the first two weeks on the crayfish, but any considerable delay in taking up insects in the fall should be avoided. The other forms are arranged in the usually accepted logical order which is preferred by most teachers. If, for practical reasons, it is deemed best to depart from this order, it will be found that the idea of evolution may be taught with quite as much force from material within the individual groups as by an adherence to the so-called logical order of the groups themselves.

If time permits the teacher may profitably add to the list of types an echinoderm and a sponge, to each of which one or two classes and laboratory periods may be devoted. The student's conception of the animal kingdom is thus greatly broadened.

A suitable laboratory and field equipment is assumed. Its precise character will vary with circumstances. In general the better the equipment the better the work that may be done. While it is true that a course in zoology may be given without the use of the compound microscope, in the opinion of your committee a much better course may be given by its moderate use.

As far as possible the work on each type should be begun by collecting by the students, chiefly of the type form but incidentally of as many as possible of other forms belonging to the same group. Some of the animals collected should be kept living and the subsequent study should, where practicable, be made on living material. The work on each type should include:

1. *Structure.* The structural work should consist chiefly of external morphology and the structures should be considered as adaptations. It is not intended to eliminate individual dissection, but it is thought that the amount of individual dissection may be much lessened and that internal structures may be studied in part by means of anatomical preparations made by the teacher and by means of models and charts. In connection with each system of organs the special physiology of the system should be taught and should be illustrated by experiments. Physiology should not be taught merely as an inference from structure. The physiological instruction may be profitably concentrated on two types, one invertebrate and one vertebrate, preferably the insect and the frog. By this plan physiological work on other types may be minimized.

2. *Behavior and Habits*: These should be considered in connection with the study of its structure and where practicable the behavior should be studied first and the structures necessary to the behavior considered afterward. It is believed that more interest will be aroused by finding out first what the animal does and then studying the structures which it uses; but it will often be found necessary to reverse this order.

3. *Study of related forms*: It is not meant that the course should be limited to the study of the type forms, but rather that, in each group, the type form should be the basis upon which to build an acquaintance with the commoner related forms in the local fauna. The scientific names and the classification of these forms need not be taught but rather sight recognition of many forms and their common names with a reference of each to the group represented by the laboratory type. Although it is not intended that

taxonomy should be taught, nevertheless individual students who show an aptitude for it should be provided with literature and should receive every encouragement from the teacher to carry on voluntary work in collecting and classifying animals.

4. *Ecology*: Animal ecology includes not only a study of the habits of animals referred to but also a study of the relations of animals to their environment. This branch of zoology, which must be in part carried on in the field, attempts to determine how animals maintain themselves in their environment and why animals in a given environment give place to others when the physical and other characteristics of the environment are altered. Few teachers are prepared to include this subject in their teaching, but attention should be called to the importance of the subject as a constituent part of a high school course in zoology and teachers should prepare themselves to do work of this sort. The amount of such work that may be done in elementary classes is indicated in the specific illustration which follows.

The plan recommended for laboratory and field work may be best made clear by a specific illustration. Thus the work on insects may be begun with the grasshopper with a collecting trip in which each individual student is required to bring into the laboratory as many kinds of grasshoppers as he can obtain, and together with these a certain number of insects belonging to other groups. Each student should then preserve most of the insects in his collection and after sorting them put them aside for future use. In this connection instruction may be given in methods of pinning and preserving insects and encouragement may be given the pupil to make his own collection. Many of the grasshoppers collected should be kept alive and their study now be undertaken. In this study function and structure should, as far as possible be considered in connection with one another. Thus the student may observe the ways of walking, hopping, and flying, and in connection with these may study on preserved material the structure of the legs and wings. At the same time he may be instructed in the class room and by the aid of models, preparations and diagrams concerning muscles and the movements produced by them. Similarly he may study the use of the mouth parts in feeding and may then observe the structure of the mouth parts in greater detail. From this he may proceed to a study of the structure of the digestive organs either from his own dissections or from preparations and charts. The teacher may then give them elementary instruction concerning the process of digestion. Again observations may be made on the breathing movements to be followed by an anatomical study of the spiracles and tracheae and an exposition of the nature of respiration. Thus in all cases, so far as practicable, close correlation should be made between the work on the function and that on the structure of the various parts of the body.

The work in which the student can actually see the working of the part observed will of course have to be followed by a study of the parts whose function is not so obvious, but the same principle of correlating structure and function may be followed throughout. It is advisable that the work in which the teacher supplies most of the physiological instruction should follow that in which the pupil is able to make his own observations.

The class should next make a comparative study of the different grasshoppers collected so as to be able to distinguish the different species in a second field excursion. When a good conception has been gained of the general structure of the body and of the chief functions of its part, and when a sight recognition of the local species of grasshoppers is assured, attention may be directed to the life of grasshoppers in the field and to the adaptations shown by the various species to their conditions of existence (ecology). To give an illustration of the nature of the ecological work that may be undertaken advantageously in the high school we may cite the following observations which may easily be made upon the grasshoppers which occur in nearly every neighborhood. The kind of situation should be noted in which each species occurs. The students should observe the relation between these habitats and the species found in them. The instinct of the roadside grasshopper to alight in barren spots of ground and of various species of green coloration to alight on grass stems and to keep on the side opposite the observer. The instinct of other species when alighting in the grass to drop down and remain quiet next the ground. These and many other features of behavior which show a marked adaptation to particular kinds of environment can easily be observed and interpreted. If the teacher directs the attention of the students to such phenomena and by carefully planned questions leads them to make and to record observations of their own, work cannot fail to prove of interest and value. Such work, if properly planned, can be controlled as well as tasks performed in the laboratory.

When the field work on the grasshopper has been completed the class should take up the insects on the first field excursion and should become familiar with the principal groups of insects. At this point attention may be directed to the economic value of certain species. Here, again, opportunity will be afforded to stimulate individual work and the making of collections.

The same plan of work may be followed in considerable detail with the mollusca. In the case of other groups the field work may need to be considerably modified. Thus birds and mammals may not be collected but both may be studied in the field. Protozoa and hydra may be collected but are not, of course, suitable for field study. In the case of each type the plan outlined should be followed in so far as the nature of the material permits. It is believed that in the laboratory the plan is feasible in nearly every case.

Both laboratory and field work is best carried on by means of written or printed directions prepared by the teacher. Just before each field excursion the teacher should visit the locality selected for the field work in order to be assured that the desired material is available and that the observations outlined are feasible.

The class room instruction should co-ordinate and extend the work done in the laboratory and further interpret it. It is believed that the further work carried on in the class room may be best done by means of topics to be studied in connection with those laboratory types which best illustrate them. Thus in connection with insects protective coloring and mimickry, as well as the general subject of metamorphosis, may be enforced and illustrated. In connection with the frog the development should be studied in the laboratory and general notions of development added to those of metamorphosis. In connection with mollusca variation and the ideas of species may be enforced. Instinct and intelligence may properly be considered in connection with several of the types. Toward the end of the course time should be left for a connected presentation of the doctrine of evolution and of natural selection.

The importance of proper field and laboratory notes and drawings should be emphasized. Notes, both in field and laboratory should be made while the work is in progress, not afterward. They should be criticized by the teacher with reference to their pertinence and completeness and should be permanently preserved. Such notes may be made the basis of more careful reports which should be criticized with a reference to the arrangement of their contents, the character of their conclusions and their English. It is suggested that teachers of English will often be found willing to co-operate in the correction of such reports. Drawing is of no less importance than note taking. Drawings should be made chiefly in the laboratory and always from the specimen. It should be the object of the teacher to see that the drawings are accurate and that their details have meaning. Meaningless or ambiguous lines or masses of shade have no more place in a scientific drawing than meaningless words in a sentence.

Attention should also be called to the importance of local school museums. These should contain primarily representatives of the local fauna attractively displayed. Students may be referred to specimens in such a museum as they are referred to books and may use the museum as they would a library. The Michigan Academy of Sciences maintains a bureau the purpose of which is to secure for teachers and others the identification of specimens collected by them and their exchange for other specimens. Information concerning the bureau may be had from the Secretary of the Academy, Professor Charles E. Marshall, Agricultural College, Mich.

The following recommendations are also made:

1. That the course be put in the second high school year, rather than in the first, and that it be preceded by a course in physiography. Such an arrangement should greatly help the teaching of field ecology.

2. Each week's work should consist of two class exercises and at least two laboratory exercises. Each laboratory exercise should consist of at least two school periods, and these should if possible be the last two periods of the afternoon. By this arrangement it will be possible to use the greater part of the afternoon for field excursion.

3. Where but half a year's work is offered in zoology the teacher should select the groups to be studied. Since the groups do not require equal periods of time, the number

to be studied in a half year's course will depend on the selection. It should not be less than five.

4. Where but a half year's work is offered in zoology, and where at the same time human physiology is taught the zoology should be followed at once by the physiology or the two subjects should be combined into a single course. It is believed that time will be saved by this arrangement and that interest will be added to both subjects.

COMMERCIAL SUBJECTS.

COMMITTEE.

E. V. Robinson (Chairman), Professor of Economics and Politics, University of Minnesota.

F. C. Hicks, Professor of Economics and Civics, University of Cincinnati.

D. Kinley, Dean of Graduate School, Director of Courses in Commerce, Professor of Economics, University of Illinois.

H. E. Brown, Principal, High School, Rock Island, Illinois.

M. M. Beddall, Principal, High School, Boone, Iowa.

I. A. Loos, Professor of Political Economy, State University of Iowa.

M. S. Wildman, Assistant Professor of Economics, University of Missouri.

P. B. S. Peters, Director of Business Course, Manual Training High School, Kansas City, Missouri.

G. A. Gregory, Superintendent of Schools, Crete, Nebraska.

N. M. Graham, Principal, High School, South Omaha, Nebraska.

D. T. Walker, President, Watertown Commercial College, Watertown, South Dakota.

B. O. Aylesworth, President, State Agricultural College, Fort Collins, Colorado.

J. A. Hutchinson, Teacher of Commercial Branches, West Side High School, Denver, Colorado.

Definitions (7 units).

Business Arithmetic (½ unit).

The object is first of all absolute accuracy, and secondly speed, in ordinary business computations. To secure these essentials, not less than half of each recitation should be devoted to mental drill on simple exercises. For the same reason, no credit whatever should be allowed on work involving any error in computation; and a rigid time limit should be set for all written work.

As to subject matter, complicated methods and obsolete subjects should be eliminated. This means cutting out about half of what the books contain. The topics to be *emphasized* are: (1) the fundamental operations with integers; (2) common fractions having as denominators 2, 3, 4, 6, 8, 12, or 16, and small decimals; (3) a few common weights and measures, but not the mass of uncommon ones, nor a mixture of denominations (e. g. no merchant sells cloth by yards, feet and inches, but by yards and fractions thereof); (4) percentage and its more important applications, especially interest and discount; (5) short methods, especially thorough drill in the use of interest and other calculation tables.

Text book, supplemented by numerous live exercises from current sources, such as stores, trade papers, etc. The methods should be planned so as to arouse and sustain interest. "The class work must touch life and breathe the spirit of business."

Elementary Bookkeeping (1 unit).

The technical business subjects, especially bookkeeping and stenography are vocational in purpose and must therefore be taught with a view to practical mastery. This fact should suggest and control the method. For example, no credit whatever should be allowed unless the work is done neatly, accurately, and at a satisfactory rate of speed. And there should be a combination of class and individual methods of instruction to secure maximum results. In order to establish sound habits, it is also well to provide double periods for elementary bookkeeping, and require all work to be done in the class room under the eye of the instructor.

The first requisite is a good, clear business handwriting. Unless pupils have it, which they rarely do, they should be required to do a prescribed amount of practice writing under the supervision of the instructor.

Definitions of double entry terms, with rules for debit and credit, kinds and uses of books. Conduct of a set including the journal, cash book, sales book ledger, check book, bank pass book and trial balance book, closing of books. Single entry set: changing from single to double entry.

Text book, with exercises so arranged that no two pupils will do exactly the same work.

Advanced Bookkeeping and Business Usage (1 unit).

Thorough drill on the preparation and interpretation of standard business forms, such as bills, receipts, checks, notes, time and sight drafts, acceptances, endorsements, invoices, accounts sales, deposit tickets, warehouse receipts, express receipts, bills of lading, statements of account, balance sheets, etc.

Explanation of business symbols and abbreviations.

Bill book, invoice book, special books, loose leaf and voucher systems of bookkeeping.

Each student is to carry on a business of his own, manufacturing, banking, wholesale, retail, jobbing or commission: at first as an individual, then as a partnership, finally as a corporation, thus involving the use of several forms of accounts.

Credit on this course should mean that the school is ready to vouch for the student as one thoroughly versed in the principles and practice of bookkeeping, who lacks only actual business experience to become a competent bookkeeper.

Business Law (½ unit).

The object of this study is not to make "every man his own lawyer," but rather to enable him to keep out of legal complications. For ignorance of the law excuses no one.

To this end, it is necessary to study the legal principles governing business relations, especially contracts, their nature, essentials, and effects; further sales, interest and usury, bills and notes, agency, partnership, corporations, real property and mortgages, liens, attachments, surety and guarantyship, bailments, common carrier, banking, fire insurance, landlord and tenant.

Text book, supplemented by some study of cases (by way of illustration), discussions, and practice in drawing legal papers such as a contract, note, bill of exchange, bill of sale, bill of lading, power of attorney, deed, mortgage, lease, notice of protest, etc.

Stenography and Typewriting (2 units).

This work is expected to occupy not less than two periods daily for two years. No credit should be given for either shorthand or typewriting if taken alone.

The "touch" method is strongly recommended in typewriting.

The object is first, accuracy, and second, speed in taking dictation and transcribing notes. Equally essential are correct spelling, capitalization, punctuation and paragraphing.

No credit should be given unless the following speed is attained: at end of first year, 75 words per minute in dictation and 25 words per minute on the machine; at end of second year, 500 words in 5 minutes in dictation, and 35 words per minute in the transcription of notes.

Thorough training should also be given in care of the machine, and in methods of copying, manifolding and filing papers.

Business Spelling and Correspondence (½ unit).

Preliminary review of 500 common business words. Thorough drill on business correspondence including:

(1) Form of business letters, beginnings and endings, etc.

(2) Choice of words and structure of sentences with reference to clearness and brevity.

(3) Capitalization, punctuation and paragraphing.

(4) Writing and answering telegrams and advertisements.

If the pupil does not write a clear and neat business hand, he should be required to make good his deficiency, or no credit should be granted for the course.

Text book, supplemented by letters relating to the most prominent industries of the locality.

History of Commerce (½ unit).

Knowledge of the past is indispensable to an understanding of the present. The History of Commerce thus forms the natural introduction to the study of present economic conditions. It should, however, follow the usual courses in Ancient, Medieval and Modern History.

The principal commodities, centers and routes of commerce in successive ages. Relation to stage of economic development, division of labor, means of transportation and communication, markets and fairs, their functions in commerce. Special attention to England and the United States; and to the growth of modern colonial empires.

Text book, supplemented by map work and assigned readings.

Economic History of England (½ unit).

A study of English history with special reference to the

causes and effects of her economic development. It should be based on some of the smaller economic histories such as Cheyney, Price, or Cunningham and McArthur.

This course, where given, will naturally follow the courses in general European history, and may take the place of the usual political English history.

Economic History of the United States (½ unit).

A study of American history with special attention to the economic factor. It should be based on some text book such as Wright, Coman or Bogart and supplemented by collateral reading, especially in books such as Semple and Brigham on geographic influences.

This course will naturally follow the one on English history and may take the place of the usual political American history.

Materials of Commerce (½ unit).

A study of the most important food stuffs and raw materials which enter extensively into commerce, with special reference to their source, mode of preparation and principal uses.

A course introductory to commercial geography. Text book, study of specimens and pictures, collateral reading, visits of inspection. The introduction of this subject is not recommended unless samples can be provided of at least two dozen of the chief commercial staples in various stages of preparation.

Commercial Geography (½ unit).

As the history of commerce is concerned with the past of commerce, so commercial geography describes and seeks to explain the industry and commerce of nations to-day. It is "a comparative study of the nations of the world, their commercial prominence and their contest for the trade of the world."

The introductory work should cover: (1) the effect of surface, soil, climate, etc., that is, the physical factor in commerce; (2) the influence of race, religion, education, commercial policies, etc., that is, the human factor in commerce; (3) the effect of economic forces on production and commerce; (4) means of transportation and communication.

Following this should come a detailed study of the United States by sections and then as a whole, with reference to physical features, and climate, natural resources, population, leading industries, transportation facilities and commerce, especially foreign commerce; then a study of the outlying possessions of the United States; and finally, a survey of the other important commercial countries from the same viewpoint.

Text book, supplemented by map work and assigned readings. For purposes of illustration, samples of commercial staples, lantern slides, stereopticon pictures, etc., should be freely employed; and wherever possible, visits of inspection made and informal lectures secured by experts in various industries. Should be preceded by physical geography.

Elementary Economics (½ unit).

The study of Economics is indispensable if the business man is to understand the process in which he has a part, and the tendencies which are at work in the business world of to-day.

In the high school, it is necessary to avoid two extremes: the one, abstract theory; the other, controversial questions. While not omitting theory, emphasis should therefore be placed on historical and descriptive matter.

Text book, with collateral readings, especially on the economic history of England and the United States. In the selection of texts it is well to avoid large and difficult books intended for college classes.

MANUAL TRAINING.

COMMITTEE.

C. M. Woodward (Chairman), Dean of School of Engineering and Architecture, Washington University, St. Louis.

T. K. Lewis, Assistant Professor of Engineering Drawing, Ohio State University.

J. W. Carr, Superintendent of Instruction, Dayton, Ohio.

G. N. Carman, Director, Lewis Institute, Chicago, Illinois.

C. A. Bennett, Professor of Manual Arts, Bradley Polytechnic Institute, Peoria, Illinois.

J. D. Phillips, Professor of Drawing, University of Wisconsin.

J. J. Flather, Professor of Mechanical Engineering, University of Minnesota.

G. F. Weitbrecht, Principal, Mechanic Arts High School, St. Paul, Minnesota

A. C. Newell, Supervisor of Manual Training, West Des Moines, Iowa.

C. H. Bailey, Director of Manual Training, Iowa State Normal School, Cedar Falls, Iowa.

C. R. Richards, Professor of Mechanical Engineering, University of Nebraska.

W. M. Davidson, Superintendent of Instruction, Omaha, Nebraska.

A. A. McDonald, High School, Sioux Falls, South Dakota.

V. C. Alderson, President, State School of Mines, Golden, Colorado.

C. A. Bradley, Principal, Manual Training High School, Denver, Colorado.

Definitions (10 units).

MANUAL TRAINING COMPRISES A SYSTEMATIC STUDY OF THE MANUAL ARTS, EMBRACING (1) THE MECHANIC ARTS, (SHOPWORK, DRAWING); (2) HOUSEHOLD ARTS, (SEWING, COOKING).

The minimum time given per year in order to count as a unit should not be less than the equivalent of 240 hours of 60 minutes. No superior limit is given, but additional hours should not receive additional credit.

Shopwork (4 units).

Every exercise which is involved in what follows should be planned and executed to illustrate an important mechanical principle or process, or a combination of such principles and processes.

The exposition of a tool and the demonstration of a process should be before the entire section of pupils conveniently seated so as to see all that the teacher does, and hear all that he says.

The shop-period of first-year boys ought not to exceed 100 minutes in length; but third and fourth-year pupils can profitably have longer, but less frequent shop-periods; however, those periods should never exceed 180 minutes.

Pupils should never be left to find out for themselves the proper ways of using a tool. The correct ways should be clearly and fully shown and explained. The use of a wrong tool, and the adoption of an illogical or unscientific procedure should at once be checked, and the error should be plainly pointed out.

Bench Work (1 unit).

(a) Fundamental tool processes: Measuring, squaring, gauging, sawing, boring, chiseling; rules for planing.

(b) Constructions involving groove joints and halving; laying out and cutting joints; use of nails, screws and glue; carving and finishing.

(c) Making a glue joint; planing joints, gluing, clamping, surfacing, sandpapering.

(d) Construction by means of mortise-and-tenon joint; laying out duplicate parts, cutting mortise, sawing tenon, gluing and clamping, scraping, finishing.

(e) Construction involving the miter joint; planing parallel edges and sides in the construction of a miter box; rebating, laying out and cutting a brace.

(f) Dovetailing: laying out and cutting dovetails, planing corners, inlaying.

(g) Construction involving the use of the panel: plowing, fitting, gluing, clamping, putting on hinges, finishing.

2. *Wood-Turning and Elementary Metal-Working* (1 unit).

(1) Wood-turning. Use of different kinds of wood. Care of lathe.

(a) Turning spindle, cylinder, taper, convex curve, concave curve, compound curve; turning to given dimensions, finishing and polishing in the lathe.

(b) Faceplate turning.

(c) Chuck turning; built-up stock, fitting.

(2) Metalworking. Working in a variety of metals, including cast-iron, steel, brass, tin, zinc, and copper.

(a) Chipping and Filing; chipping with cold chisel and hammer; filing, testing, tool dressing.

(b) Making small tools. Drilling, filing, fitting, riveting, finishing.

(c) Construction in sheet metal; pattern cutting, bending, folding, wiring, soldering.

(d) Copper work: sawing, beating, hard soldering, repoussé, annealing, coloring with heat and chemicals, etching.

(e) Turning: Hand-tool turning, filing in lathe, polishing in lathe, thread cutting with top and die, hardening, tempering, annealing.

(f) Spinning: cutting templet, turning form in wood to fit templet, spinning zinc or Britannia metal and copper, polishing, lacquering.

3. *Pattern Making, Molding and Forging* (1 unit).

The theory and use of patterns, how built, how divided and why; pattern-making, bench-molding of simple and complex patterns; theory and use of cores, construction of cores and core-prints; casting with lead and alloys.

Construction and management of the forge—fundamental processes; drawing, up-setting, bending, punching, splitting, welding, hardening; shaping steel under the hammer; tempering of different grades; the construction of chains, hooks and forge tools, and wrought-iron articles from original or selected designs; finally the manufacture of a set of standard steel lathe tools. The design and actual construction of a piece of ornamental wrought-iron or steel work.

4. *Bench and Machine Metal Fitting* (1 unit).

Theory of metal-turning, centering; forms of cutting tools and tool-grinding; turning cast-iron, wrought-iron, steel, and brass; use of oil, relation of speed to heat developed; use of taps and dies; screw cutting, chuck-work, mandril and face-plate work; drilling, slotting, planing, gear-cutting, and special work on the milling machine. Having mastered the elements, each student should combine more or less of such elements in a construction, made in accordance with original or selected drawings.

Drawing (2 units).

1. (a) Straight lines; use of T-square, triangles, pencil, ruling pen, dividers, and scale. Conventional lines. Freehand working sketches.

(b) Circles. Use of compasses, center lines, cross-hatching.

(c) Tangents. Location of centers and points of tangency.

(d) Planes of projection; elementary principles of projection; revolution of the planes of projection. Projections of simple geometric figures.

(e) Revolution of objects. "Views" of objects in simple and inclined positions.

(f) Developments: prism, cylinder, pyramid, cone.

(g) Intersections. Axes in the same plane, axes in different planes.

(h) Isometric and cabinet drawing.

(i) Freehand and mechanical lettering; placing, form, slant, spacing, stroke.

(j) Working drawings; furniture.

(k) Working drawings; machine parts.

(l) Building plans; floor plans, elevations.

2. (a) Mechanical perspective.

(b) Freehand drawing in perspective.

(c) Construction of conic sections and helix.

(d) Line shading.

(e) Wash drawing.

(f) Designing for metal work.

(g) Either machine or architectural drawing.

Household Arts and Science (4 units).

1. *Plain Sewing* (1 unit).

Every exercise in sewing should illustrate an important principle or process, or a simple combination of such principles and processes. Hand sewing and sewing machine work must be equally insisted upon.

(a) The various stitches and their special uses.

(b) Hand sewing, fundamental processes.

(c) The use and care of sewing machines and their attachments.

(d) The nature and special uses of cotton, linen, and woolen goods.

(e) The use of patterns; cutting out.
(f) Taking measurements; making of simple garments.

2. *Sewing and Millinery* (1 unit).

(a) Making of shirt waists, wash-dresses, and similar garments.

(b) Millinery: Study of materials for hats; making, altering, and covering hat frames. The planning, making, and trimming of seasonable hats of appropriate materials.

Throughout the course economy and good taste in dress.

Cooking (2 units).

1. Food classified and tested for food principles.

A study of the effect of heat upon foods alone and in combination; experiments with leavening agents, and their uses shown in actual cooking. Bread making. The theory and practice of canning and preserving fruits, vegetables, and meats. Planning, cooking, and serving meals. Waiting on table.

2. The cost of food; market prices; the cost of meals. Household accounts. The family dietary: The planning, weighing, and cooking of apportioned meals. Diets for infants, invalids, and convalescents.

Sanitation: Selection of site, house planning; heating, lighting, and ventilating; water supply; disposal of waste; furnishing and decorating; cleaning processes, including laundry work.

BOARD OF INSPECTORS.

Whitney, A. S. (Chairman), University of Michigan.
Aiton, G. B., State of Minnesota.
Ballou, F. W., University of Cincinnati.
Boyd, W. W., University of Ohio.
Butler, Nathaniel, University of Chicago.
Elliff, J. D., University of Missouri.
Ensign, F. C., University of Iowa.
Heyward, Richard, State of North Dakota.
Holland, E. O., University of Illinois.
Hollister, H. A., University of Illinois.
Johnson, W. H., University of Kansas.
Libby, Walter, Northwestern University.
Reed, A. A., University of Nebraska.
Swanson, C. E., State of South Dakota.
Terry, H. L., State of Wisconsin.
Thompson, Frank E., University of Colorado.
Tressler, A. W., University of Wisconsin.

STANDARDS OF ADMISSION

The aim of the North Central Association of Colleges and Secondary Schools is, first, to bring about a better acquaintance, a keener sympathy and a heartier coöperation between the Colleges and Secondary Schools of this territory; secondly, to consider common educational problems and to devise best ways and means of solving them; and thirdly, to promote the physical, intellectual and moral well being of students by urging proper sanitary conditions of school buildings, adequate library and laboratory facilities, and higher standards of scholarship and of remuneration of teachers. The Association is voluntary, organized and devoted solely to the highest welfare of the boys and girls of this territory, and it bespeaks the cordial and sympathetic support of all school men.

The following constitute the standards of admission to this Association for the present year:

1. No school shall be accredited which does not require fifteen units, as defined by the Association, for graduation.

2. The minimum scholastic attainment of all high school teachers shall be equivalent to graduation from a college belonging to the North Central Association of Colleges and Secondary Schools, including special training in the subjects they teach, although such requirements shall not be construed as retroactive.

3. The number of daily periods of class-room instruction given by any one teacher should not exceed five, each to extend over at least forty minutes

in the clear. (While the Association advises five periods, the Board of In
spectors will reject all schools having more than six recitation periods pe
day for any teacher.)

4. The laboratory and library facilities shall be adequate to the needs o
instruction in the subjects taught as outlined by the Association.

5. The location and construction of the buildings, the lighting, h
and ventilation of the rooms, the nature of the lavatories, corridors, close
water supply, school furniture, apparatus, and methods of cleaning shall
such as to insure hygienic conditions for both pupils and teachers.

6. The efficiency of instruction, the acquired habits of thought an
study, the general intellectual and moral tone of a school are paramount fac
tors, and therefore only schools which rank well in these particulars, as evi
denced by rigid, thorough-going, sympathetic inspection, shall be considere
eligible for the list.

7. Wherever there is reasonable doubt concerning the efficiency of
school, the Association will accept that doubt as ground sufficient to justi
rejection.

8. The Association will decline to consider any school whose teachin
force consists of fewer than four teachers exclusive of the Superintendent.

9. No school shall be considered unless the regular annual blank fur
nished for the purpose shall have been filled out and placed on file with th
inspector.

10. All schools whose records show an abnormal number of pupils pe
teacher, as based on average number belonging, even though they may tech
nically meet all other requirements, are rejected. The Association recogn
thirty as maximum.

11. The time for which schools are accredited shall be limited to one year
dating from the time of the adoption of the list by the Association.

12. The organ of communication between the accredited schools and th
Secretary of the Commission for the purpose of distributing, collecting, an
filing the annual reports of such schools and for such other purposes as th
Association may direct, is as follows:

a. In states having such an official, the Inspector of Schools appointed b
the state university. b. In other states the Inspector of Schools appointed b
state authority, or, if there be no such official, such person or persons as th
Secretary of the Commission may select.

The Association is very conservative, believing that such action will event
ually work to the highest interests of the schools and the Association. I
aims to accredit only those schools which possess organization, teaching force
standards of scholarship, equipment, esprit de corps, etc., of such characte
as will unhesitatingly commend them to any educator, college or universit
in the North Central territory.

ACCREDITED SCHOOLS.
Adopted March 27th, 1908.

Colorado

Aspen
Canon City
Colorado Springs
Colorado State
    Preparatory
Cripple Creek
Denver:
  East Side
  West Side
  North Side
  South Side
  Manual Training
Durango
Florence
Fort Collins
Golden
Grand Junction
Greeley
Idaho Springs
La Junta
Leadville
Longmont
Loveland
Monte Vista
Pueblo:
  Centennial
  Central
Salida
Trinidad
Victor

Illinois

Alton
Augustana Coll. Academy (Rock Island)
Aurora:
  East
  West
Beardstown
Belleville
Belvidere:
  North
  South
Bloomington
Blue Island
Bradley Polytechnic Institute (Peoria)
Cairo
Carthage Coll. Academy
Champaign
Chicago:
  Austin
  Calumet
  Crane (Man. Tr.)
  Curtis
  Englewood
  Hyde Park
  Jefferson
  Lake View
  Marshall
  McKinley
  Medill
  Phillips
  South Chicago
  Tuley
  Waller
Chicago Heights (Bloom Tp.)
Danville
Decatur
DeKalb Tp.
Desplaines (Maine Tp.)
Dixon
DuQuoin Tp.
Elgin
Elgin Academy
Evanston Tp.
Evanston Academy
F. W. Parker (Chicago)
Freeport
Galva
Grand Prairie Seminary (Onarga)
Harrisburg Tp.
Harvey (Thornton Tp.)
Highland Park (Deerfield Tp.)
Hinsdale
Hoopeston
Ill. Woman's Coll. Prep. Dept. (Jacksonville)
Joliet Tp.
J. Sterling Morton Tp.
Kankakee
New Trier Tp.
Kenwood Institute (Chicago)
Kewanee
Lake Forest Academ
La Salle-Peru Tp.
Lyons Tp. (La Gran
Macomb
Mattoon
Maywood and Melr Park Tp.
Moline
Morgan Park Tp.
Normal
N. W. Military Acad
Oak Park Tp.
Ottawa Tp.
Pekin
Peoria
Polo
Pontiac Tp.
Princeton Tp.
Quincy
Rochelle
Rockford
Rock Island
Savanna Tp.
Springfield
Sterling Tp.
Streator Tp.
Sycamore
Tuscola
Waukegan Tp.
Western Mil. Acad. (Upper Alton)
Wheaton

Indiana

Alexandria
Anderson
Attica
Bedford
Bluffton
Connersville
Crawfordsville
Elkhart
Elwood
Evansville

Indiana (Continued)
Fort Wayne
Franklin
Greenfield
Hammond
Indianapolis:
　Manual Training
　Shortridge
Kokomo
Lafayette
Logansport
Michigan City
Muncie
Plymouth
Rensselaer
Rochester
Shelbyville
South Bend
Terre Haute
Valparaiso
Vincennes
Winona Park (Young Women)

Iowa
Algona
Ames
Boone
Burlington
Cedar Rapids
Cherokee
Clarinda
Clinton
Corning
Corydon
Council Bluffs
Creston
Davenport
Decorah
Denison
Des Moines:
　East
　North
　West
Dubuque
Eagle Grove
Fort Dodge
Grinnell
Ida Grove
Iowa City
Keokuk
La Mars
Marengo
Marion
Marshalltown
Mason City
Missouri Valley
Newton
Osage
Onawa
Oskaloosa
Ottumwa
Red Oak
Sheldon
Sioux City
Vinton
Washington
Waterloo:
　East
　West

Kansas
Abilene
Emporia
Fort Scott
Hiawatha
Iola
Kansas City
Lawrence
Leavenworth
Paola
Junction City
Sumner Co.
Wichita
Winfield

Michigan
Adrian
Albion
Alpena
Ann Arbor
Battle Creek
Bay City, E. S.
Bay City, W. S.
Benton Harbor
Benton Harbor Col. Inst.
Bessemer
Cadillac
Calumet
Coldwater
Crystal Falls
Detroit:
　Central
　Delray
　Eastern
　Western
　Higgins
　University
Dowagiac
Evart
Flint
Grand Rapids
Hancock
Houghton
Howell
Ionia
Iron Mountain
Jackson
Kalamazoo
Lansing
Manistee
Manistique
Marshall
Marquette
Menominee
Michigan Military
Monroe
Muskegon
Mt. Clemens
Mt. Pleasant
Niles
Norway
Otsego
Owosso
Petoskey
Port Huron
Portland
Saginaw, E. S.
Saginaw, W. S.
South Haven
St. Johns
St. Joseph
Three Rivers
Union City
Wyandotte

Minnesota
Albert Lea
Anoka
Austin
Blue Earth

Minnesota (Continued)

Crookston
Duluth Central
Ely
Eveleth
Fairmont
Faribault
Fergus Falls
Grand Rapids
Hastings
Hibbing
Hutchinson
Little Falls
Mankato
Marshall
Minneapolis:
  Central
  East
  North
  South
Montevideo
Moorhead
Morris
New Ulm
Northfield
Owatonna
Red Wing
Rochester
St. Cloud
St. James
St. Paul:
  Central
  Cleveland
  Humboldt
St. Peter
Sleepy Eye
Stillwater
Virginia
Waseca
Willmar
Winona

Missouri

Blees Military Academy
Boonesville
Carrollton
Carthage
Chillicothe
Kansas City:
  Central

Nebraska

Manual Training
  Westport
Kemper Military Acad.
Kirkwood
Maryville
Mexico (McMillan
  High)
Nevada
Poplar Bluff
St. Joseph
St. Louis:
  Central
  Manual Training
  McKinley
  Smith Academy
  Yeatman
Stephen's College
Trenton
Webster Grove
Westminster Col. Acad.
William Woods College
Auburn
Beatrice
Blair
Brownell Hall
Falls City
Fairbury
Fremont
Grand Island
Hastings
Lincoln
Lincoln Academy
McCook
Nebraska City
Nebraska Wesleyan
  Academy
Norfolk
Omaha
South Omaha
Superior
York

North Dakota

Devils Lake
Fargo
Grafton
Grand Forks
Jamestown

Ohio

Akron
Ashtabula
Bellefontaine
Bryan
Cambridge
Canton
Chillicothe
Cincinnati:
  Franklin
  Hughes
  Walnut Hill
  Woodward
Circleville
Cleveland:
  Central
  East
  Glenville
  Lincoln
  South
  West
Cleveland Heights
Columbus:
  Central
  East
  North
  South
  School for Girls
Conneaut
Coshocton
Dayton
Delaware
East Cleveland
East Liverpool
Elyria
Findlay
Fostoria
Fremont
Gallipolis
Geneva
Glendale
Greenfield
Greenville
Hamilton
Hillsboro
Ironton
Kenton
Lakewood
Lima
London

Ohio (Continued)
Lorain
Madisonville
Mansfield
Marietta
Marion
Martins Ferry
Marysville
Massillon
Middletown
Mt. Vernon
Nelsonville
Newark
New Philadelphia
Norwood
Oberlin
Oberlin Academy
Oxford College for Women (Academy)
Painesville
Portsmouth
Ravenna
Salem
Sandusky
Steubenville
Toledo
Troy
Van Wert
Wapakoneta
Warren
Washington C. H.
Wellsville
Willoughby
Wooster
Wyoming
Xenia
Youngstown
Zanesville

South Dakota
Aberdeen
All Saints, Sioux Falls
Brookings
Deadwood
Lead
Madison
Mitchell
Sioux Falls
Vermilion
Watertown
Webster
Yankton

Wisconsin
Antigo
Appleton
Ashland
Baraboo
Beaver Dam: Wayland Academy
Beloit
Berlin
Black River Falls
Chippewa Falls
Columbus
Eau Claire
Elkhorn
Evansville
Fond du Lac
Grand Rapids
Hartford
Janesville
Kaukauna
Kenosha
La Crosse
Lancaster
Lodi
Madison
Madison: Wisconsin Academy
Manitowoc: North
Marinette
Marshfield
Medford
Menasha
Menomonie
Merrill
Milwaukee:
 East
 North
 South
 West
Milwaukee-Downer Seminary
Monroe
Neenah
Neillsville
Oconomowoc
Oconto
Oshkosh
Plymouth
Portage
Racine
Racine College Gmar School
Reedsburg
Rhinelander
Ripon
River Falls
Sheboygan
Sinsinawa: St. Clara Academy
Sparta
Stevens Point
Stoughton
Sturgeon Bay
Superior: Blaine
Superior: Nelson D
Washburn
Waukesha
Waukesha: Carroll lege Academy
Waupaca
Wausau
Wauwatosa
Whitewater

this book should be returned on
he date last stamped below

370.6
N864
1908

Lightning Source UK Ltd.
Milton Keynes UK
UKHW010156221218
334409UK00012B/1177/P